LONELY PLANET'S

GLOBAL
BEER
TOUR

CONTENTS

Introduction	3
Glossary	7
How to Make Beer	8

Africa — 12
Ethiopia	14
Israel & Palestinian Territories	16
Lebanon	18
Namibia	20
South Africa	22

Weird Beers	34

The Americas — 36
Argentina	38
Brazil	40
Canada	42
Ecuador	50
USA	52

Food & Beer	96

Asia — 98
China	100
Japan	106
Nepal	116
North Korea	118
Singapore	120
South Korea	122
Thailand	126
Vietnam	129

Hangover Cures	132

Europe — 134
Belgium	136
Czech Republic	146
Denmark	152
France	154
Germany	166
Hungary	178
Iceland	181
Ireland	184

Italy	188
Netherlands	200
Portugal	204
Slovakia	208
United Kingdom	210

Great Ale Trails	234

Oceania — 236
Australia	238
New Zealand	258

Index	268
Acknowledgements	272

INTRODUCTION

There's one thing that all beer fans agree on. If you enjoy drinking good beer, there has been no better time to be alive than right now. Over the last ten years in countries across world – not just the USA, New Zealand and Australia but also in beer's traditional homelands of Britain, Belgium and Germany, and new frontiers in Asia and Africa – there has been a revolution in the range and quality of beers produced by small, independent and creative brewers. For want of a better label, it has been called the craft beer movement.

WHAT IS CRAFT BEER?

'Craft' is a term that is increasingly (and occasionally misleadingly) applied to beers. What does it mean? The US organisation, the Brewer's Association, defines a craft brewer as being small, independent and traditional. By 'small', they mean a brewery that produces less than six million barrels of beer per year. By 'independent' they mean a brewer that is less than 25% owned by anything other than a craft brewer. And by 'traditional' they mean a brewer that uses traditional brewing fermentation techniques and ingredients for flavour. 'Flavored malt beverages', they say, are not beer. See www.craftbeer.com for more details.

Within those parameters, the variety of beers currently being made is nothing short of astounding. The Brewer's Association of the US recognises 150 separate styles of beer. There are classics that have been brewed for centuries, such as pale ales and porters, long-forgotten regional specialities that have been recently discovered by the rest of the world, and also delicious new concoctions, fermented in a brewer's brain somewhere.

Of the 4600 craft brewers in America, notes the Brewer's Association, 95% make fewer than than 15,000 barrels of beer annually. The same is true of other countries: the vast majority of craft brewers are small, local businesses. In the US, 78% of adults of drinking age live within 10 miles of their local brewery. Consequently, local support is vital to their success. What's notable about the new wave of craft beer is that it has raised the standards of breweries across a country, not just those in or near big cities.

Not all the breweries in this book can be classified as 'craft'. Some have been bought out by bigger companies.

INTRODUCTION

Others may already be mainstream brands. But, generally, most the breweries profiled in this book will have been started by a small group of passionate people and it is the dedication and determination of these beer-loving people that has driven this revolution. And in the same way that these people have increased the quality of beer available to us, so they have also pioneered the other key development of the craft beer movement: breweries that we can visit. Many breweries now have taprooms or tasting rooms to welcome beer fans and visiting these venues has become a very enjoyable way to spend an afternoon or evening.

WHY GO BEER TOURING?

This book features a vast range of breweries, from the massive (the Stone empire in San Diego) to the minuscule (Partizan, hunkered under a railway archway in London). We've preferred the independent to the corporate but with so many craft brewers being bought by multinationals we've not been too prescriptive. What matters to us is the quality of the beer and the visitor experience.

So why go to visit these breweries, taprooms and brew pubs when you can usually buy an ever-increasing range of interesting beers in your local supermarket or bottle shop? There are three main reasons. The first is that craft beer doesn't tend to travel well, at least over long distances. It doesn't like getting too hot or too cold and it doesn't like being shaken around. Beer often tastes better the closer it is to home, especially if that's straight from a tap in a tank in the actual brewery.

The next reason is that with the rapid increase in numbers of small-scale craft brewers in recent years, a lot of great beers are never distributed beyond their home state or city. The chances of finding one of Maine's distinctive micro-brewed ales in another country are small. And many traditional beer varieties – for example smoky Rauchbier in Germany– rarely leave their region. To experience them properly you need to go to the source. Contemporary craft breweries are often started by people passionate about beer and if you want to taste what they've been brewing you need to go to them because they won't be able to reach you. In some cases (see Westvleteren in Belgium) you'll even need to queue outside just to buy a case of their most sought-after releases.

And finally, if you want to actually meet some of these obsessed individuals, compare tasting notes, and ask them about their beer or exchange recipes then you're going to have to go on a beer tour.

At Lonely Planet, we approached our Global Beer Tour a little differently. Using our travel resources we've provided details of other sights of interest in the vicinity of each brewery so you can make a day (or a weekend) of your visit. These may be local museums or galleries, more adventurous activities such as hikes or bike rides, or even something as simple but memorable as a great viewpoint. Whether you sample some beer first and then see the sights, or vice versa, is up to you (although we'd recommend tackling some of the more physically demanding activities before rewarding yourself with a beer).

What became immediately apparent when researching this book with our worldwide network of beer-loving travel writers (and well-travelled beer journalists) was that the world of craft beer reached far beyond its anglo-centric strongholds of England, Australia and New Zealand, and the USA and Canada. Those regions may have the highest density of craft breweries and may be driving the current vogue for visiting breweries, but venture into Belgium and Germany and you'll find fascinating, historic breweries to explore. Other countries, in particular Italy and Japan, are fast catching up with their local craft beer scenes. And further afield we reveal breweries you can visit in countries such as Nepal, Vietnam, China and Ethiopia.

HOW TO USE THIS BOOK

Within each of the 32 countries in this book, we've organised the best breweries to visit by city, which are listed alphabetically. In the entry for each brewery we've suggested the must-try beer, and also recommended local sights so beer tourers can explore the local area and the beer. There's a world of great beer to taste, now go and discover it!

GLOSSARY

Types of Beer

Ale Catch-all term for top-fermented beer, after the type of yeast used (now there are many more varieties of yeast), see also Lager

Altbier A dark beer from Dusseldorf, Germany

Biere de Garde A traditional style of beer from northern France that is stored (*garde*)

Bitter A British style of brown beer, mildly flavoured and varying in strength from ordinary to 'best' to extra special

Blonde / Golden Ale A light, gold-hued beer, often a summery choice

Bock A type of German-made lager

Bok A dark beer from the Netherlands

Dubbel A type of Belgian ale using double the usual quantity of malt, making a strong, dark beer

Dunkel A dark lager from Munich

Gose A German sour wheat beer

Gueuze A Belgian beer made with wild yeasts (see Lambic)

Helles A type of lager originally from Munich

India Pale Ale An extra-strong, highly hopped type of pale ale (IPA) from Britain but now thrillingly interpreted by other nations

Kölsch A type of light beer from Cologne, Germany

Kriek A cherry-flavoured beer from Belgium

Lager A bottom-fermeted beer, after the type of yeast used; often stored in cold tanks before sale

Lambic Beers fermented with wild yeasts, often Belgian

Marzen A German lager typically brewed in spring (March)

Pale ale A pale, hoppy ale from Britain, now a craft beer standard

Pilsner A lager from the Czech Republic

Porter A dark, bitter ale from Britain, synonymous with Stout

Rauchbier A type of smoky lager from Bamberg, Germany

Rye beer When rye replaces barley

Saison A type of sharp Belgian ale brewed in spring

Sour A style of beer that includes gueuze and lambic

Stout See Porter; often regarded as a stronger style of porter with sweet and/or roasted flavours

Trappist ales Strong beers brewed by monks (typically in Belgium)

Tripel A strong style of Belgian ale using three times the usual quantity of malt

Weissbier A German style wheat beer

Wheat beer An ale that uses a significant amount of wheat in lieu of barley

White beer A Belgian style of beer made with malted barley and wheat, flavoured with coriander and orange peel

Technical Terms

ABV Alcohol by volume, expressed as percentage of total volume of the beverage

Barrel-aged Process of maturing ale in barrels once used for wine or spirits

Bottle-conditioned Beer that continues to ferment in the bottle

Cask-conditioned Beer that continues to ferment in the cask / barrel

Cold-conditioned A practice of maturing lager in cold tanks for up to three months

Craft brewing Small-scale, creative, independent brewers

Double Used to describe a beer of extra strength, such as Double India Pale Ale (DIPA)

Dry-hopped When hops are added to a beer during fermentation or conditioning (makes it extra-hoppy)

Growler A 64 fl oz (US, or 1892.7ml) container for takeout beer; howlers and squealers are smaller

Hops The buds of a plant originally used to protect beer from spoiling now used for flavour

Imperial Most usually applied to an extra-strong style of stout

Malt Grain, typically barley, that has started germination then been halted by heating in a kiln

Pasteurisation Heat-treating beer to kill bacteria

Pint A typical measure of beer in Britain of 568ml, also available in half-pints; a US pint is 473ml

Pot A common Australian measurement of beer, 285ml

Schooner A measurement of beer in Australia of 425ml, or about two-thirds of a pint

THE INGR

You've heard of the holy trinity, well, meet the sacred quartet. Although there is almost no limit on what you can add to a brew (blue cheese, bull testicles and an entire margarita pizza are a few recent examples), beer begins with four core ingredients.

WATER

At least 90 percent of any given beer is water. It is, rather ironically, the driest of ingredients to discuss – it doesn't have the heavenly aroma of hops nor the colour-giving properties of malt. But water has a crucial effect on the final beer and indeed, the mineral make-up of a region's water has historically dictated which styles would be produced where – stouts in Ireland, pale ales in Burton upon Trent, pilsners in Plzen.

MALT

Starting its life as plain old barley, the base grain used in beer goes through an important process to unleash the sugars within. Without sugar, there is no alcohol, but malt (or malted barley) contributes far more to what is poured into your glass. It's also largely responsible for the body, or mouthfeel, of the beer, it contributes flavours and aromas such as coffee, toffee, biscuit, chocolate and toast, and is the ingredient that gives beer its many hues of amber, gold and brown.

9

HOPS

Ah, wonderful hops – the ingredient beer geeks tend to get most excited about. Hops have many uses in the beer world – originally used as a preservative, they add bitterness, flavour and some spectacular aromas, and are often considered to be the 'salt and pepper' of beer. American and Antipodean hops tend to exhibit aromas of tropical fruit, citrus and pine, whereas European examples are earthier and lend a muted spice to the beer.

EDIENTS

YEAST

Brewers make wort, yeast makes beer – it's a phrase you'll hear often in the beer world. Once the brewer has done his bit, the yeast are 'pitched' (a brewing term that basically means 'added') to the fermenter. And then we wait – from a few days to a few weeks, depending on the type of beer. Yeast eat the sugars within the wort and are often said to 'belch out CO2 and fart out ethanol'. Not the most appetising thought perhaps, but it speaks to the unpretentious nature of beer and demonstrates that it is the yeast that will turn the vat of malty tea into delicious beer.

1. MILLING

Malt is the source of sugar in beer – crucial, since without sugar there can be no alcohol. The malted barley is gently crushed to ensure that the starches found within are later converted to sugar.

Once you've gathered your ingredients, the beer-making process is deceptively simple but allows for the fine-tuning of recipes. Here's how the magic happens.

THE BREWIN

6. MATURING

Depending on the style and alcohol content, the beer will be kept in a keg, bottle or barrel for anything from a couple of weeks to several years while the flavours mellow and change.

7. KEGGING AND BOTTLING

The ready-to-drink beer is transferred to kegs, casks or bottles. CO_2 may be added to carbonate it. Some brewers prefer to carbonate naturally by allowing a secondary fermentation in the bottle or cask.

3. BOILING

The liquid – known as wort – is separated from the soggy grain and boiled, usually for 60-90 minutes. During this time, hops are added for bittering, flavour and aroma.

2. MASHING

The crushed grain is steeped in warm water (around 60-70°C) for about an hour – think of it as making a giant cup of malty tea.

G PROCESS

4. COOLING

The wort is cooled as quickly as possible to avoid any bacteria developing in the soon-to-be-beer, and then transferred to a fermenter.

5. FERMENTATION

Once cooled, yeast is added and the wort begins to ferment. Ales are fermented for 7-10 days at around 18-25°C, while lagers are fermented for 2-3 weeks at a temperature of 6-13°C.

AFRI
THE MIDI

TOP 3 BEER TOWNS

13

CA &
OLE EAST

CAPE TOWN

Cape Town carries the craft beer banner in South Africa, with not just a growing number of craft brewers (with taprooms, such as Devil's Peak) but also new craft beer bars and shops. November sees the Cape Town Festival of Beer in Green Point usher in summer; you're bound to find your favourite new sundowner!

ADDIS ABABA

It's not the most obvious location for beer lovers but the Ethiopian capital looks set to offer more than chilled lager to visitors. There's already a German-influenced microbrewery in the city and more will follow. With a nightlife that features a strong live music scene, there's certainly demand for a greater variety of beer.

TEL AVIV

The party capital of the Middle East may still be more about after-dark club hopping than the bitter, green buds but the city has recently welcomed two new craft breweries, Jem's and the Dancing Camel, and its bars are increasingly stocking a wider range of local and imported craft beers.

ETHIOPIA

How to ask for a beer in local language ? I-ba-kih bee-ra
i-fuh-li-ga-luh-hu (I'd like a beer please)
How to say cheers? Leh-tay-nah-chen
Signature beer style? Tella – made with sorghum and tef
Local bar snack? Kolo – mixed, roasted grains
Do: Be prepared for 'gursa', if dining with Ethiopians, when
the host pops a morsel of food into the guest's mouth – it
would be offensive to refuse

Beer is booming in Ethiopia. The country might not
be exploding in a deluge of heavily hopped IPAs or
drowning under a sea of endless craft beer fests, but ever
since the government began to sell off its breweries to
private companies, global beer producers have scrambled
to get a foot in the door. Consumption is up, brewery
numbers are up and of course, variety is on the up – at
least in terms of the brands available. For the most part,
everything in the fridges is a variation on the same theme
– pale lager designed to be drunk in quantity. For visitors
to Ethiopia, sinking more than a couple of local lagers is
an easy feat, not least because this is one of the cheapest

places around to grab a beer.

It's not all lager, lager, lager though, with some of the
major breweries also producing stout and the occasional
specialty lager appearing alongside familiar blonde
versions. Premium brands are launching, such as Habesha
Breweries, with its labels, name and message tapping
heavily into local culture and it seems only a matter of time
before new beer styles edge their way in. When it comes
to craft beer, the pickings are still slim, with Addis-based
Garden Bräu flying the flag for Ethiopian microbreweries.
But with barley grown throughout the country and the
national thirst for beer on the rise, it's likely that more
beer-loving entrepreneurs will follow, and Ethiopia's place
on the African beer map will be secured.

GARDEN BRÄU

Bole 03 St, 670 Block 63-5, Addis Ababa;
www.beergardeninn.com; +251 116 182 591

◆ Food   ◆ Bar
◆ Family

Dusty Addis Ababa is probably not the place you'd expect to find an orderly beer garden with a Bavarian air.

The beers here are brewed to the Reinheitsgebot – the German purity law that states only water, malted barley, hops and yeast can be used in the brewing process. Hops used in the two brews (a light and a dark ale) are imported from Germany, and even the menu has more than a hint of German influence – the injera and *tibs* (sautéed meat and vegetables) seen on most Ethiopian menus are replaced here with sausage platters, piles of fries and a particularly tasty roast chicken. The unfiltered Blonde Ale is the pick of the beers – sip a pint or order a 3L beer tower to share at your table.

THINGS TO DO NEARBY

'Red Terror' Martyrs Memorial Museum
Displays at this heart-rending museum highlight the brutal regime of the Derg, when an estimated 500,000 people were murdered.
www.rtmmm.org

Yod Abyssinia Traditional Food
For a snapshot of Ethiopian culture, try this popular restaurant. Sip tangy tej and munch on injera and its various accompaniments while enjoying traditional music and dance.

DASHEN HOUSE

Gondor, Amhara

◆ Food   ◆ Bar   ◆ Transport
◆ Tour   ◆ Takeout

If you want to take a break from *tej*, Ethiopia's traditional honey wine, Dashen churns out bottles of lager from its industrial-style brewery on the outskirts of Gonder. Tours can be arranged, and branded goodies, such as t-shirts and key-rings, are often brought out as gifts. Most visitors opt out of a tour to get straight to the good bit: sitting in the grassy beer garden – a rare treat in Northern Ethiopia – with a cold pint.

There is only beer here (no other beverages on the menu) and it's cheap, thirst-quenching and, of course, as fresh as it gets. You might even find a flavourful, unfiltered version available on tap – perfect with a plate of spicy *tibs* (sautéed meat and vegetables) and injera, the elastic Ethiopian flatbread.

THINGS TO DO NEARBY

Fasil Ghebbi
Grab a local guide and stroll around the 17th-century fortress city; its numerous castles have earned Gonder the label 'Africa's Camelot'.

Simien Mountains National Park
You'll need a few days (and a compulsory guide) to explore the dramatic scenery of the Simien Mountains. Hikes can be challenging, particularly due to the altitude.

ISRAEL &
THE PALESTINIAN
TERRITORIES

How to order a beer? Ifshar kos bira bevakasha?
How to say cheers? L'Chaim! (meaning 'To life!')
Signature beer style? Amber ales with fruity flavours
Local bar snack? Olives (usually complimentary)
Don't: Be afraid to taste beers first

Not usually known for its beer, Israel and the Palestinian Territories was traditionally a winemaking region, though it's said that the Babylonian Rabbi Papa brewed beer here as early as the 4th-century BC. The first modern brewery, Nesher, was founded in 1940 to quench the thirst of Aussies stationed in British Mandate Palestine. Nesher Malt beer is still sold today by Tempo, brewers of the Maccabee and Goldstar labels that dominated the Israeli market for decades. Then, in the mid-'90s, competition

came from the small Palestinian village of Taybeh in the West Bank. Although alcohol is forbidden in Islam, the 1500 residents of Taybeh were allowed to produce and sell beer due to its all-Christian population. Taybeh quickly grew in popularity among young Israelis and its annual Taybeh Oktoberfest remains a crowd-puller.

But the beer buzz in Israel really began after 2005, when the first microbreweries emerged. Initially led by American immigrants, passionate about brewing quality beer, with establishments such as Dancing Camel (in Tel Aviv) and Jem's (in Petah Tikva), the craft beer trend was later adopted by Israeli brewers. Today, bottles of boutique ales such as Alexander, Malka, Negev, Bazelet and Shapiro can be found in bars and shops across Israel. Locals take time to enjoy a beer with some fresh olives or salted edamame beans; after a long day in the heat of Tel Aviv, that first sip is always welcome.

ALEXANDER BREWERY

19 Tzvi Hanahal St, Emek Hefer;
www.alexander-beer.co.il; +972 74 703 4094

◆ Food   ◆ Tour
◆ Family   ◆ Takeout

One of the first Israeli microbreweries, Alexander was founded in 2008 by Ori Sagy, a former Israeli Air Force pilot, who travelled the world learning about beer for more than 25 years. Located in the Hefer Valley – a green belt of kibbutzim inland from Netanya and south of Haifa – the brewhouse is named after a nearby stream. During a 45-minute tour, visitors can 'scientifically' examine the brewery equipment, imported from Braukon, Germany and enjoy some tastings. Alexander makes two main beers: Blonde, a Belgian-style fruity beer; and Ambrée, made

from roasted malts. If you're lucky, you can also sample its seasonal beers – Green, has a twist of grapefruit, guava and mango, but it's Black, with dark chocolate and espresso, that satisfies the indulgent.

THINGS TO DO NEARBY

Mikhmoret Beach
One of the best beaches in Israel, with broad sand dunes, plenty of space to chill by the Mediterranean or go for a bicycle ride.

Utopia Park
This 'rainforest paradise' conservation park, part of Kibbutz Bahan, has a botanical garden housing tropical birds, fish ponds, a maze and more than 20,000 orchids. *www.utopiapark.co.il/english*

DANCING CAMEL BREWERY

Hata'asiya 12, Tel Aviv;
www.dancingcamel.com; +972 3 624 2783

◆ Food   ◆ Bar   ◆ Transport
◆ Tour   ◆ Takeout

'Born in the USA' but 'Made in the Middle East' this microbrewery has a transatlantic flavour. Founded by New Jersey-native and ex-Wall St trader David Cohen in 2005, it's set in a renovated 1930s warehouse in the Yad Harutzim industrial area of Tel Aviv. From the outside, it looks like a regular bar. Yet inside, it houses a US-style pub and a spacious events hall. Their brewing equipment was imported from the old Flying Pig brewery in Everett, Washington but is now used to make kosher brews.

All the eight beers have an American feel, ranging from

'patriotic' orange pale ales to black stouts. Its classic is a strong but sweet ale: The Olde Papa combines hops, malts and local date honey, supposedly an ancient recipe from Rabbi Papa.

THINGS TO DO NEARBY

Sarona Market
Opened in 2015, Sarona is an upmarket indoor food market; the largest in Israel. It hosts big-name Israeli chefs, and both local and international produce. *www.saronamarket.co.il/en*

Porter & Sons
This restaurant for beer lovers has a hearty menu, and also more than 50 draft beers, including local crafts, such as Shapiro, Bazelet and Malka. *www.porterandsons.rest.co.il*

LEBANON

How to order a beer? Baddé bira
How to say cheers? Keessak for a man,
Keessik for a woman
Signature beer style? Pilsner, light and ice cold
Local bar snack? Bowl of mixed Lebanese nuts -
pistachios, cashews, peanuts roasted corn; or the
healthy alternative - raw carrots with salt and lemon
Don't: Be put off if everyone is drinking Alwa Pils as
most bars also stock craft beers

Up until recently, Lebanon has been a one pils
nation – Almaza, family-brewed since 1933, ten
years before independence from the French, who tended
to prefer the local wine. Enjoying an ice cold Almaza,
just 4º proof, symbolises the Lebanese love of having
fun, sunbathing on the beach, sitting out on the terrace
of a fashionable Beirut cafe - the perfect solution to
forget all the troubles that have rained down on their
country during long decades of conflict.

But the king of Middle Eastern beers is now owned by
Heineken, and although Almaza has diversified with a

Pure Malt brew and a host of non-alcoholic fruit flavours
to appeal to the local Muslim population, there is some
serious competition today from new innovative local
microbreweries. In the typical Lebanese spirit to carry on
as if all is normal, 961 Beer was founded by Mazen Hajjar
in July 2006 when Beirut was under siege by Israel. He
started experimenting by brewing in his kitchen but
today, this brewmaster produces some two million litres
of authentic craft ales ranging from witbier and porter to
Lebanese pale ale.

An hour's drive out of Beirut, at the seaside resort of
Batroun, there is the more low key Colonel Brewery, who
specialises more in hoppy, bitter lagers and alcoholic
fruit beers, and the latest brewery on the scene has
chosen the iconic name Beirut for its eminently quaffable
light pils that they hope will take the place of Almaza.

19

COLONEL BREWERY

Bayadir St, Batroun;
www.colonelbeer.com; +961 3 743 543

◆ Food ◆ Tour ◆ Takeout
◆ Family ◆ Bar ◆ Transport

Going on a Beirut pub crawl, we noticed that every-where stocks Colonel Beer. It's from Lebanon's very own microbrewery, located in the historic seaside resort of Batroun, 50km (31 miles) further north. Founded by local boy, Jamil Iladdad, the Colonel is housed in a stunning eco-friendly building made entirely from recycled wooden pallets, with vegetal walls and a green roof. Inside there is a state-of-the-art microbrewery, a restaurant and a pub, all surrounded by a lush beer garden with retro furniture.

Speciality brews include Czech-style lager and Pils, ranging from classic Light German, made with Bavarian malt, to bitter, hoppy American lager. Colonel's master brewer likes exotic ingredients too, concocting ales with passion fruit, lychee and even pumpkin. For a full tasting,

THINGS TO DO NEARBY

Phoenician Wall
Batroun is one of the world's oldest cities, founded by the Phoenicians. Stroll beside their 225m-long maritime wall, built 2000 years ago, miraculously preserved today.

Chez Maguy
Follow wobbly signs to this foodie institution, its tumbledown shacks surrounded by the sea. A favourite of Anthony Bourdain, Maguy's speciality are wild scallops harvested by divers.

St Stephen's Church
Batroun's fishing port is dominated by this quietly imposing stone Maronite church, with its square crenellated towers, arched entrance and decorated facade. Packed with worshippers on Sundays.

Ixsir Winery
Drive 10km (6 miles) inland from Batroun and you're in rolling hills surrounded by vineyards. Visit Ixsir's cellar, taste surprising wines and have lunch beneath a shady cedar tree.
www.ixsir.com.lb

order its beer flight, with five glasses of your choice. Sit at the bar and the huge fermentation tanks of the microbrewery are right in front of you behind a glass wall. Picking up brewing skills in UK and European breweries, Jamil opened the Colonel in 2014 and it is already a runaway success, illustrating that despite Lebanon's instability, anything is possible here. Don't miss the Red Irish, a rich, silky amber beer brewed with caramel malt.

NAMIBIA

How to ask for a beer? 'N bier, asseblief
How to say cheers? Prost!
Signature beer style? Lager brewed to the Reinheitsgebot
Local bar snack? Kapana – slices of beef, spiced and barbecued
Do: Keep an eye out for oshikundu, a traditional opaque beer made with millet

It's no great surprise that a country with a strong German heritage – and a dry, desert climate – has a sizeable thirst for beer. Some lists even place Namibia towards the top of the global beer consumption table alongside heavyweights like Germany and the Czech Republic. Beer production here began at the start of the 20th century and there were soon a quartet of breweries operating across the country. By 1920, the breweries had all been bought by German businessmen Hermann Ohlthaver and Carl List, and so Namibia Breweries Ltd was born.

NBL, as it is known, dominates the local beer landscape

with its range of lagers, Pilsners and the occasional speciality brew. Namibia's first microbrewery was Camelthorn, launching in 2009 with a range that included Weissbier and a brew containing South African rooibos (a plant used as a herbal tea). Ahead of its time, Camelthorn closed its doors and the brand was absorbed by NBL while the brewery – and its brewer – can now be found serving in South Africa's craft beer revolution.

Today there are once more the first rumblings of a craft beer culture in Namibia, with nanobreweries emerging in Windhoek and on the Skeleton Coast. Meanwhile, down in Swakopmund, NBL have launched their own microbrewery, serving beers that introduce locals to styles far beyond pale lager without ever straying from the company's diligent adherence to the 1516 German *Reinheitsgebot*.

SWAKOPMUND BREWING CO.

Molen Weg, Swakopmund; +264 64 411 4410

◆ Food   ◆ Tour
◆ Family   ◆ Bar

 Part of Namibia Breweries, this small-batch micro-brewery sticks to the company's Reinheitsgebot roots, using only water, malted barley, hops and yeast in its German-style brews. Based at the Brewer & Butcher, a pub within the seaside Strand Hotel, this is the first time a brewery has operated in Swakopmund since 2005, when the Hansa Brewery closed its kettles. With floor-to-ceiling windows and a patio decked out with comfy couches, the brewery makes the most of its oceanside location. Inside, the vibe is German beer hall, with high ceilings and long tables filled with people sampling the regular beers and seasonal offerings. While the Märzen pairs well with the sticky ribs and chargrilled steaks, it's the crisp Kölsch that makes the best summer sipper.

THINGS TO DO NEARBY

Sandboarding
Swakopmund is known for its outdoor adventures, and what better way to acquaint yourself with the surrounding desert than to slide down the dunes on a board.

Swakopmund Brauhaus
Although this place doesn't brew its own beer, there's a good selection of local and imported brews on offer. Drinking from a boot-shaped glass is optional.
www.swakopmund brauhaus.com

NAMIBIA BREWERIES LIMITED

Iscor St, Northern Industrial Area, Windhoek; www.nambrew.com; +264 61 320 4999

◆ Food
◆ Transport

 Dating back to start of the 20th century, Namibia Breweries is the country's largest brewing company by far, producing Namibia's favourite beer, Tafel Lager. Its other big seller is Windhoek, which comes in lager and light variations. But it's not all about the blondes. Namibia Breweries also produce small batches of Weissbier as well as the hotly anticipated Urbock, a German-style bock that is brewed just once a year and released as a winter warmer beer each May. Tours of the brewery begin at the water plant, explaining how the brewery manages to source enough H2O in the desert. Sustainability is a buzzword here, with solar power and water-recycling playing key roles. Afterwards, sample all of the company's Reinheitsgebot compliant brews in the underground pub.

THINGS TO DO NEARBY

Joe's Beerhouse
This Windhoek institution serves a selection of game meat, giant eisbein (pickled ham hock), sausage platters, and a range of beers from Namibia, South Africa and Germany.
www.joesbeerhouse.com

Katu Tours
Explore Windhoek's township on a bicycle, guided by a friendly local, Anna Mafwila. Stops include local restaurants, the market and perhaps a township tavern.
www.katutours.com

SOUTH AFRICA

How to order a beer? Kan ek n bier kry asseblief
(Afrikaans); Ngicela ubhiya (Zulu)
How to say cheers? There are 11 official languages,
but plain old cheers works across the board
Signature beer style? Pale lager... perhaps with some
indigenous herbs
Local bar snack? A packet of biltong (spiced, dried meat)
Do: Ask if any craft beers are available – the movement
is young, but growing and there are some superb beers
to be found, though they're not always on the menu

It all began with a lager. It doesn't matter which
starting point you take for the South African beer
renaissance – it still started with a pint of cold, sparkling, golden lager. The country's oldest microbrewery is
Mitchell's, launching in the super-scenic Garden Route
town of Knysna way back in 1983. Its first beer – a lager of
course – was soon joined by an English bitter and, later,
a stout, a Scotch ale and its somewhat sweet Milk and
Honey, but it would be years before Mitchell's would be
joined by another microbrewery.

As the decades passed, other breweries came and
went, though a few from the mid 1990s and early 2000s
remain. But the revolution proper would not begin until
around 2010, and again it was lager that got people moving
away from, well, their other lagers. Jack Black's Brewing
Company launched in 2007 and was followed a few years
later by Darling Brew. Both would launch their brands with a
premium lager and both would receive a bolster from Cape
Town's flourishing farmers market scene, where hipsters,
hippies and foodies shopped for artisanal bread, meat,
cheese and, of course, beer. Suddenly, beer was everywhere.
Brands popped up overnight, people were swapping their
customary glass of Sauvignon Blanc for a pint of craft lager,
and anyone with a spare patch of land was hosting a small-

scale beer festival on the weekend.

Things really began to boom in 2014 and since then,
brewery numbers have increased by 50% each year. Today
there are close to 200 microbreweries scattered across all
nine of South Africa's provinces, and these days it's not all
about lager. While many brands still launch with the beer
style closest to the average South African heart, most offer
a core range that features anything from traditional German
Weissbier to a California Common, a Belgian Pale Ale or
an English IPA spiced with endemic South African herbs.
In fact, there is a definite trend towards the proudly South
African pint, with brewers substituting locally grown barley
for more traditional grains, such as sorghum or flavouring

BAR TALK – JC STEYN

Our beer scene has shown tremendous growth – consumers have fallen in love with exploratory and way-out beers

TOP 5 BEERS

- **Blockhouse IPA** Devil's Peak Brewing
- **Loxton Lager**
- **Pilsner** Cape Brewing Company
- **Lager** Jack Black's Brewing
- **Mjolnir IPA** Anvil Brewery

their beers with minty *buchu* or earthy rooibos, both of which grow only in a small slice of the Western Cape.

But it's not all about creating new styles and keeping it local. Some of South Africa's best-loved beers are American-style IPAs, heavily dosed with imported hops, while the global trend towards barrel-aged and sour styles is just beginning to take hold, particularly in Cape Town. Just a few years ago it was unthinkable to find anything but mass-produced lager on tap in your average South African bar, but these days you'd be hard-pushed to find a city restaurant that doesn't serve at least one local craft brew. And yes, more often than not, that will likely be a beer that's well suited to the country's climate – a cool, crisp, refreshing lager.

JACK BLACK'S BREWING COMPANY

10 Brigid Rd, Diep River, Cape Town;
www.jackblackbeer.com, +27 21 286 1220

◆ Food   ◆ Tour   ◆ Takeout
◆ Family ◆ Bar   ◆ Transport

THINGS TO DO NEARBY

Muizenberg Beach
Perfect for beginners, Muizenberg is one of Cape Town's top surfing beaches. Join a lesson or just grab a beer in a restaurant on the revamped beachfront strip.

Constantia Wine Valley
Swap grain for grape in South Africa's oldest wine region. Groot Constantia, Buitenverwachting and Eagle's Nest all have plenty to offer the visitor. **www. constantiawineroute.com**

Tokai Forest
Gentle walks wind through this forest in the Table Mountain National Park, or for something more challenging, take the 6km (3½ mile) path up to Elephant's Eye Cave.

La Colombe
The tasting menu at this fine dining restaurant at Constantia Nek offers delectable cuisine and comes accompanied by an encyclopaedic wine list. **www.lacolombe.co.za**

Although microbreweries existed in South Africa before Jack Black, it was its lager that helped get Capetonians hooked on craft beer. Launched in 2007, the brand existed as a contract brewery for almost a decade but finally opened its own premises in 2016. The hip, warehouse-like space in Cape Town's suburbs is the pinnacle of industrial chic – the long tables were created from the packaging materials the German-built brewery was delivered in, while the decor features polished motorbikes, along with murals painted by local street artists.

Jack Black's young brewer is also a German import, something that seems evident when you sip his well-balanced Weissbier. Food is simple and tasty – burgers, platters and the best fries in Cape Town. Weekends see local chefs participating in kitchen takeovers, or food trucks parking in the beer garden to feed hungry hipsters and local families, while live bands perform soft rock covers on stage. On tap you'll find Cape Pale Ale, brewed using only local ingredients, Skeleton Coast IPA, Atlantic Weiss plus a range of limited edition R&D brews. But kick off your visit with a pint of Jack Black Brewers Lager and raise your glass to the beer that helped launch South Africa's craft beer revolution.

NEWLANDS BREWERY

3 Main Rd, Newlands, Cape Town;
www.newlandsbrewery.co.za, +27 21 658 7440

◆ Tour   ◆ Transport
◆ Bar

South Africa's oldest brewery stands in one of Cape Town's most affluent suburbs. Dating back to 1820, the brewery has long been a part of South African Breweries (SAB), the country's megabrewery. Book ahead for the excellent tour, which touches on the country's brewing history and takes a peek into the old oast house, where hops were once dried. After a walk through the modern-day brewery and past the mesmerising bottling line, you reach the most recent addition – the Newlands Spring Brewery, a brewhouse producing easy-drinking ales and Weissbier. Tours end in the Jacob Letterstedt Pub, named for the brewery's Swedish founder. Grab a tasting tray of the Newlands Spring and finish with a pint of Castle, Africa's earliest lager, first brewed in 1895.

THINGS TO DO NEARBY

Newlands Cricket Stadium
With spectacular views of Table Mountain, plus draught beer straight from the brewery, Newlands has to be one of the best places to watch a cricket match.
www.newlandscricket.com

Vineyard Hotel
Whether you sip cocktails on the verandah, take high tea on the lawn or wander the rambling gardens, this is a fine place for Table Mountain views.
www.vineyard.co.za

DEVIL'S PEAK BREWING COMPANY

95 Durham Ave, Salt River, Cape Town;
www.devilspeakbrewing.co.za, +27 21 200 5818

◆ Food ◆ Transport
◆ Bar

With its eclectic decor, American-inspired food, shiny copper kettles and world-class beers, Devil's Peak has turned the industrial suburb of Salt River into a must-visit spot for beer geeks, foodies, hipsters and tourists. Once a workshop in an area to be avoided, the space now houses one of South Africa's most popular breweries, with vast windows offering views of the mountain that lends the brewpub its name.

The menu features dishes such as pulled pork, truffle fries, chicken and waffles, and an award-winning cheeseburger, but it's the beers that keep this place firmly on every South African beer bucket list. The core range includes a light lager, an Amber Ale, and a superlative American IPA, while speciality beers on tap rotate and include a Black IPA, an English Pale Ale and a Double IPA.

But the Devil's Peak team are all about experimentation, the head brewer – a former winemaker – being particularly fond of barrel-aged brews, beer-wine hybrids and sour styles. Devil's Peak leads the way in cutting-edge beers in South Africa, though it is the King's Blockhouse IPA – possibly South Africa's most highly awarded and most-respected beer – that you should place right at the top of your 'to-taste' list when you visit the taproom.

THINGS TO DO NEARBY

Test Kitchen
You'll need to book months ahead to score a table at Luke Dale-Roberts' flagship restaurant, generally considered to be the best eatery in South Africa.
www.thetestkitchen.co.za

Woodstock Brew Route
Woodstock, a gritty suburb adjoining Salt River, is home to Cape Town's highest concentration of breweries, including Drifter Brewing Co, Riot Beer, the Brewers Co-op and Woodstock Brewery.

Table Mountain
Tackle a challenging trek up Devil's Peak, join the straightforward two-hour Platteklip Gorge Hike or hitch a ride on the cable car atop Cape Town's number one sight.
www.tmnp.co.za

Company's Garden
Just 5km (3 miles) from Devil's Peak's in the city centre, this urban park is lined with museums and galleries: a great place for a pre-beer wander.

ANVIL ALE HOUSE

R540, Dullstroom, Mpumalanga;
www.anvilbrewery.com; +27 13 254 0197

◆ Food   ◆ Bar
◆ Family   ◆ Takeout

Found at the eastern edge of town, Anvil is a tiny pub with a pleasant patio for the summer months and a toasty fire for Dullstroom's chilly winter. It's an unpretentious place frequented by locals and Jo'burg weekenders who come for the region's fly-fishing, but Anvil is also becoming a pilgrimage for beer lovers, here to sample the crisp ales prepared by brewer Theo de Beer. Food is simple – locally made cheese or sausage platters, followed by boozy cake featuring Anvil's Stout. Beer-wise, try White Anvil, a Belgian-style Witbier flavoured with coriander seed and dried peel from locally grown naartjies (similar to a satsuma/mandarin). The star of the show, though, is Mjolnir – an award-winning American IPA with great whiffs of tropical fruit and pine.

THINGS TO DO NEARBY

Dullstroom Bird of Prey & Rehabilitation Centre
Get up close with a range of raptors in one of the regular flying displays and learn about the dangers threatening certain species of bird.
www.birdsofprey.co.za

Wild About Whisky
If you fancy something stronger than beer, this small bar boasts one of the largest whisky collections in the southern hemisphere. Join the owner for a tutored tasting. *www. wildaboutwhisky.com*

S43 – THAT BREWING COMPANY

43 Station Dr, Durban; www.thatbrewingco.co.za,
+27 31 303 2747

◆ Food   ◆ Transport
◆ Bar

Just as breweries are popping up in previously dodgy parts of Cape Town and Johannesburg, so they are beginning to inhabit gentrified sections of Durban. S43 sits in a complex of bespoke clothing stores and artists' studios alongside the train tracks. As trains trundle past, sip on ales created by the young team at That Brewing Company. The most experimental brewery in the area, it's always worth asking if there's something special on tap. The cavernous space is filled with couch-like seating, much of it on wheels, allowing the space to be rejigged for live music sessions and busy weekend parties. The APA and Weiss are among the most popular pints, but do ask if there's any of the excellent American Stout available.

THINGS TO DO NEARBY

Moses Mabhida Stadium
Built for the 2010 World Cup, the football stadium is one of Durban's top attractions. Take the Skycar to the top or hike up to the iconic arch.
www.mmstadium.com

Hollywood Bets Bunny Bar
Lunch in the back of a betting shop? This is actually one of Durban's best places to sample a classic Bunny Chow – a hollowed-out bread loaf filled with curry.

WORLD OF BEER

15 Helen Joseph St , Newtown, Johannesburg;
www.worldofbeer.co.za, +27 11 836 4900

◆ Food   ◆ Tour   ◆ Transport
◆ Family   ◆ Bar

There's no brewery here, but you will find a highly entertaining tour giving great background into beer production and South Africa's beer history. It is at times weird and more than a little cheesy, but the hour-long tour is certainly a lot of fun. It includes a puppet show discussing beer in ancient Egypt, offers the chance to slurp traditional *umqombothi* (sorghum beer) from a communal clay pot, takes you on a walk through gold-rush era Johannesburg and sees you sipping a cold Castle Lager in a mock-up apartheid-era shebeen.

The second part of the tour covers the ingredients and brewing process, setting you up for the best bit of all – two beers of your choice in the on-site pub.

THINGS TO DO NEARBY

Museum Africa
The centrepiece of this rambling museum is an exhibit on the 1956–61 Treason Trials, while other rooms offer insight into Jo'burg's social, economic and cultural history.

Sci-Bono Discovery Centre
Kids large and small will enjoy all the interactive exhibits at this hands-on, well-organised science museum, housed in a former power station.
www.sci-bono.co.za

AFRO CARIBBEAN BREWING COMPANY

157 2nd Ave, Kenilworth;
www.bananajamcafe.co.za, +27 21 674 0186

◆ Food   ◆ Bar   ◆ Transport
◆ Family   ◆ Takeout

Afro Caribbean is one of Cape Town's must-visit beer spots, not just for the cool, California-style brewpub on the 1st floor but also for Banana Jam, the Caribbean restaurant downstairs.

Both under the same beer-mad ownership, Banana Jam has long been considered *the* craft beer bar, with its 30 taps offering local, national and international beers. Design your own taster tray to sip in the always-busy garden or grab a pint to go with the restaurant's cuisine. Upstairs it's all unfinished wood, surf decor and

high stools, with a bar that opens for mini festivals and big-screen rugby. There's always something new on tap, but the flagship Coconut IPA is a must, ideally paired with Banana Jam's goat curry.

THINGS TO DO NEARBY

Kirstenbosch National Botanical Garden
Work up a thirst on this 52,800 sq-km garden's many trails. Take the Tree Canopy Walkway for amazing views from the treetops. ***www.sanbi.org/ gardens/kirstenbosch***

Wynberg Village
Browse the artsy shops, check out Victorian architecture, grab lunch and stroll in the park in this quiet suburb not far from Wynberg's busy main road.

CAPE BREWING COMPANY

Suid-Agter Paarl Rd, Paarl;
www.capebrewing.co.za, +27 21 863 2270

◆ Food ◆ Bar
◆ Family ◆ Takeout

Cape Brewing Company is a destination brewery par excellence. Sitting on the picturesque Spice Route winery, CBC, as it is better known, is part of an artisanal village concept. Before visiting the brewery, you can stop off for a tasting at the chocolatier, sample a cappuccino from the roastery, nibble on salami at the charcuterie and taste spicy Shiraz in the tasting room. For lunch choose from one of three restaurants – a pizzeria, fine dining or burgers and biltong (a spiced dried meat snack and a great accompaniment to beer).

The brewery itself is one of South Africa's finest. The state-of-the-art German system is headed by Bavarian brewmaster Wolfgang Koedel, whose lager, Pilsner, Weiss and IPA have all been awarded medals in local and international competitions. Although tours aren't offered, you can view the entire brewery from the tasting room, and

THINGS TO DO NEARBY

Fairview
Next door to Spice Route and under the same ownership, Fairview is one of the Cape's most popular wineries, noted for its cheese tasting.
www.fairview.co.za

Giraffe House
If you're travelling with kids, this animal park is a worthy stop. You get a bucket of food on arrival to feed the giraffe, eland, farm animals and birds.
www.giraffehouse.co.za

Babylonstoren
The highlight of this wine and fruit farm is not the booze but the marvellous 2.5-sq-km gardens – book a tour in advance.
www.babylonstoren.com

Paarl Mountain Nature Reserve
High above the vineyards, this hilltop reserve is a fine place for a picnic and a wander. It's also home to the Afrikaans Language Monument.

informative wall panels give the lowdown on the brewing process. Join a tutored tasting, then grab a pint of your favourite to enjoy with views stretching all the way to Cape Town. Picking just one pint is tricky – for something light and moreish take a Pilsner, while hopheads will do well to grab a Cape of Good Hops – CBC's fragrant Imperial IPA.

UBUNTU KRAAL BREWERY

11846 Senokoanyana St, Soweto;
www.sowetogold.co.za, +27 76 706 98 23

◆ Family   ◆ Takeout
◆ Bar

The first brewery in Soweto has received plenty of press attention from around the world. A short walk from the restaurants and museums of Vilakazi St, Ubuntu Kraal is a conference and wedding venue with a brewery tucked away in the back. The covered patio pays homage to the region's heritage, with framed photos of Sowetan sporting stars, singers and struggle heroes. Generally frequented more by visitors than locals, the beer garden is a chilled place to sip a beer while taking in the reams of information you've ingested in Soweto's superb museums. Speciality beers include ales flavoured with cherry, apple and ginger, but it is the Soweto Gold Superior Lager that goes down a treat after some time spent exploring the city.

THINGS TO DO NEARBY

Apartheid Museum
Located halfway between Johannesburg and Soweto, this excellently presented museum depicts the rise and fall of the segregation and oppression era in South Africa. *www.apartheidmuseum.org*

Orlando Towers
The former cooling towers are now adrenaline sports central in Gauteng. If you don't fancy abseiling or bungeeing, you could just watch the action from the braai restaurant. *www.orlandotowers.co.za*

KRIEK (Brouwerij Lindemans, Belgium)

Take your Lambic beers up a notch with the addition of fruit. This classic cherry version is another entrant that has history rather than contemporary styling on its side. It's an acquired taste for some, tart and sour, but try it on a hot summer day – you'll come around.

MARRICKVILLE PORK ROLL (Batch Brewing Co, Australia)

In a suburb of Sydney known for a strong Vietnamese community comes a beer that wears its local heart on its weird sleeve. A Vietnamese Pork Roll complete with processed pork meats, coriander, carrot and chilli has donated its ingredients to this beer – and it does just what it says on the tin!

ROCKY MOUNTAIN OYSTER STOUT (Wynkoop Brewing Company, USA)

The oysters in question here are actually bull's testicles. Let that sink in for a minute... just as the testicles did into the mash for this beer. No longer available, this heavy-duty stout deserves a mention, if only for the cojones required to tell your marketing department that you're brewing with genitals.

WEIRD

There's the German purity law, and then there's the complete anarchy of modern beer making – no ingredient is safe, no palate will be spared. If, like your travel, you like to go off the beaten beer track, here are a few out-there options.

CHICHA (South America, or Dogfish Head, USA)

This traditional alcoholic beverage hails from South America, made from maize that's chewed, spat and collected to form a fermentable mash. Dogfish Head brewery tried its hand at this, staff contributing to the masticated corn base. A limited release, but you just know someone, somewhere, will try again...

SRIRACHA STOUT (Rogue USA)

Some beer makers seem intent on inventing a concoction that no one has ever asked for. Stout plus garlic-chilli sauce? Um ... sure, love to. Said no-one. But you're not anyone and you're going to put this on the bucket list. Dark, rich and genuinely spicy, it is a good chance to take your breath away.

CHOCOLATE LOBSTER

(Dogfish Head, USA)

Dogfish Head is a big small brewery, and they ... 'go there'! Their commitment to beer is uncompromising, with a number of classic beers available all over the world. But this beer, which comes with a shellfish allergy warning, is not a traveller. Head to their home to experience the rich, velvety, oceanic pour.

BEERS

HVALUR 2

(Brugghús Steðja, Iceland)

There might be a theme developing, but let's cut to the chase. This is a beer brewed with sheep dung smoked whale's testicles. There's no other way to say it. It is apparently smoky and it's unquestionably weird – but let's leave the whales alone already!

SNAKE VENOM

(Brewmeister, Scotland)

Most beer comes in at around 5% alcohol. A big Belgian might come in at 9%, maybe 10% ... the weirdness here doesn't come from a bodily fluid or seafood item – it comes from having 67% alcohol. No session ale, a single shot of the spirit-like brew should be enough.

AECHT SCHLENKERLA RAUCHBIER MÄRZEN

(Schlenkerla, Germany)

Despite the call-out to the German Purity Laws (ie beer must contain water, malt, yeast and hops), don't think it's just modern ales that can take you to the weird side. Try this German smoked wheat beer for size. You'll swear a smoked pig was liquefied – big, chewy and kind of challenging.

BLACK TRUFFLE BEER

(Moody Tongue, USA)

For the beer drinker with deep pockets comes this funky, truffle-infused Pilsner that was designed to accompany, you guessed it, truffle dishes. Difficult to justify maybe, but if you've got it, flaunt it.

THE AM

AMERICA'S

SAN DIEGO

Sun, surf and great beer: of all California's famed cities, San Diego, in the south of the state, rules for beer tourists. It's home to world-class breweries (Ballast Point and Stone Brewing), and has a number of appealing neighborhoods and sightseeing highlights to explore.

ASHEVILLE

The community of North Carolina's Asheville is bonded together by beer. In this out-of-the-way gateway to the Great Smoky Mountains National Park, the 40 or so breweries (including Burial, see p57) and regular beer festivals are a key (and often family-friendly) part of local life.

PORTLAND, ME

There's a distinctive identity to the hazy, extra-juicy IPAs and pale ales from the northeast USA and Portland, Maine, is the place to go to experience it – they don't let a lot out of the region! With breweries such as Allagash and Bissell Brothers, plus lots to see and do, Portland is a great beer city.

PORTLAND, OR

Portland, Oregon, is fastidious about the finer things in life: bicycles, coffee, granola, food trucks, the great outdoors – and, of course, beer. It has long produced some of the best brews in the US, from the likes of The Commons, but its beer scene keeps evolving. It's a seriously fun place.

DENVER

In clean, green Colorado, it would take you many weeks to exhaust Denver's supply of outstanding breweries. Many are highly inventive (salted caramel porter? Only in Colorado!). And every fall hundreds more brewers arrive for the Great American Beer Festival.

ARGENTINA

How to ask for a beer in local language?
Una cerveza por favor
How to say cheers? Salud!
Signature beer style? Golden ale
Local bar snack? Picadas (tasting boards of cured meats and cheeses)
Do: Order IPA (Indian Pale Ale) by asking for 'eepah'

It's long been known as a wine-lover's paradise, but now there's good news for hopheads venturing to the land of football and meat: Argentina is in the midst of a craft beer revolution. Tired of the poor quality lager produced by the industrial breweries, pioneering breweries such as Antares in Mar del Plata started to produce their own quality artisan beers. And since 2012, craft beer has really taken off. Across the country, garages are being transformed into mini beer factories, while in Buenos Aires it's hard to keep up with the number of new craft beer pubs opening every month. Meanwhile, brewers get

together to exchange tips at regular craft beer festivals.

But although quality craft beer is suddenly easy to find in Argentina, it's by no means new. Like the country's wine industry, beer-making was connected to European immigration. A German named Otto Tipp is said to have brought the first hops bulbs to El Bolsón in Patagonia, now the country's biggest producer of hops. Santa Fe also has a strong beer making tradition; when beer maestro Otto Schneider arrived from Germany in 1906 he declared it to be the best location in Argentina for a beer factory because the properties of the river Parana were similar to the Czech area of Plzeň.

These days, the current crop of brewers like to experiment. Look out for beers with local inflections, such as amber ale with *dulce de leche*, and *yerba mate* infused lager.

ON TAP

Costa Rica 5527, Buenos Aires;
www.ontap.com.ar; +54 11 4771 5424

◆ Food   ◆ Takeout
◆ Bar   ◆ Transport

With up to 20 different draft beers on sale from across Argentina, this popular hipster haunt is the best place in Buenos Aires to tap into the city's exploding craft beer scene. Here you're likely to bump into Marcelo Terren of Bröeders, who started brewing in his mother's kitchen a few years ago after tasting craft beer on his travels; Bröeders now produces 7000L a month and Terren runs monthly courses for home-brewers at Bröeders' original premises in Palermo. Check On Tap's giant blackboard for beers by Quarryman, Chevere, and Juguetes Perdidos, which also runs weekly tours and tastings at its brewery in greater Buenos Aires. Coffee lovers should sample Bröeders Imperial Coffee Stout if it's available (it sells out fast).

THINGS TO DO NEARBY

Cementerio de la Recoleta
Peek into crypts and admire elaborate tombs, as you wander around the city of the dead, where some of Argentina's most illustrious characters are buried.

Parque 3 de Febrero
Join the local fitness fanatics power-walking, jogging, rollerblading and cycling around the city's biggest park – or sit under a shady tree and watch them.

LA URIBEÑA

Valeria de Crotto 901, Uribelarrea,
Partido de Cañuelas, Provincia de Buenos Aires;
www.cervezalauribenia.com.ar; +54 222 640 3001

◆ Food   ◆ Tour   ◆ Takeout
◆ Family   ◆ Bar

Decades before the craft beer revolution swept across Argentina, Enrique Rey started brewing in his garage after being inspired by a German neighbor who was a hobbyist home-brewer. After 10 years honing his skills, Rey moved to the sleepy village of Uribelarrea, 80km (50 miles) southwest of Buenos Aires, where he painstakingly renovated a crumbling 19th century *pulpería* (general store) and opened an atmospheric brewpub, La Uribeña, in 2006. Inside, a cascade of salamis hangs from the ceiling and a window looks into the room where the pilsner, red ale and stout are now brewed by Rey's sons. Try to visit during Uribelarrea's annual craft beer festival in early October. The red ale alone justifies the journey.

THINGS TO DO NEARBY

Museo Historico '17 de Octubre'
Take a detour to the town of San Vicente to visit the former country retreat of Juan and Evita Perón, now a little-known but fascinating museum. ***www.gba.gob.ar/cultura/museos***

Estancia La Figura
Work up a thirst by joining the gauchos on horseback, taking a swim or playing tennis at this traditional estancia on the outskirts of Uribelarrea. ***www.estancialafigura.com.ar***

BRAZIL

How to ask for a beer in local language?
Um chope, por favor!
How to say cheers? Saude!
Signature beer style? Pilsner
Local bar snack? Coxinhas (batter-fried shredded chicken thigh served with hot sauce)
Do: Ask for little or no head, known locally as colarinho ('Little Collar') or you will get half a glass of foam

Brazil is a beer country. Ordering a *chope* (draft beer) at a *boteco* (neighborhood bar) or a stone-cold, super-sized bottle of classic Pilsner at the beach are as an integral part of the tropical South American giant's culture as *futebol* and samba. But until very recently, few Brazilians were drinking the good stuff. To ward off the sweltering tropical heat, any beer will do.

But then there's Bohemia. This Petrópolis-brewed classic dates to 1853, when German immigrants fired up the fermenters and began brewing for the Portuguese royal family. Today, Bohemia remains the best of Brazil's everyday choices, along with brands such as Original and Serramalte.

But you'll need to travel to the colder confines of the southern Brazilian state of Santa Catarina to find the most hop-spoiled Brazilians. In the German-settled cities of Blumenau, Joinville and Pomerode, a rich culture of *Reinheitsgebot* has thrived in artisan breweries for the last century. But due to small production and lack of nationwide transport infrastructure, the German-Brazilians were content to keep their local *cerveja* to themselves. To this day, Eisenbahn, the area's most well-known brew, is still the only one readily available throughout the whole of Brazil, thanks to the industrial might of Japanese-owned Brasil Kirin. Otherwise, you'll need to attend Blumenau's massive Oktoberfest (the world's third biggest) to sample the best of the area. Today, thankfully, the craft beer revolution is in full-swing, with countless craft breweries cropping up in such beer-savvy cities as Porto Alegre, Curitiba, Belo Horizonte, São Paulo and Rio.

CERVEJARIA BOHEMIA

Petrópolis, Brazil; www.bohemia.com.br,
+55-24-2020-9050

◆ Food ◆ Tour ◆ Takeout
◆ Family ◆ Bar ◆ Transport

THINGS TO DO NEARBY

Museu Imperial
This striking 19th Century palace was once the summer stomping grounds of Portuguese royalty. Don't miss the 1.95kg imperial crown, peppered with 639 diamonds. *www.museuimperial.gov.br*

Museu Casa de Santos Dumont
The charming summer home and museum of Brazil's father of aviation is a must-stop for flight enthusiasts (and fans of Cartier wristwatches!).

Pousada da Alcobaça
The refurbished mansion and glass-walled dining room at this mountain *pousada* makes for a one of Brazil's most impressive Saturday *feijoadas* (stews). *www.pousadadaalcobaca.com.br*

Parque Nacional da Serra dos Orgãos
This mountainous national park between Petrópolis and Teresópolis is Brazil's trekking and climbing hotspot, with several peaks above 2200m. *www.parnaso.tur.br*

Brazil's oldest brewery was founded by German immigrants in the mountainous summer getaway of Petrópolis in 1853, where it was once the tipple of choice of the Portuguese royal family. Though mass production of its traditional pale lager moved to São Paulo in 1998, Bohemia re-opened its original location as a specialty brewery, museum and bar/restaurant in 2012. The interactive guided tour traces the history of beer in general as well as from Bohemia's perspective, and includes samplings and a visit to the barrel-aging beer cave.

While the brand's bread and butter has always been its Pilsner, the country's best beat-the-tropical-heat *cerveja*, in recent years it has delved into the craft scene with artisanal pale ales, lagers, Weiss beers and barley wines, a series of brews made with native ingredients like rose pepper, yerba-mate and *jabuticaba* (an intense, grape-like fruit) and

an award-winning session stout made with chocolate, mint and orange peel. The industrial-chic restaurant and taproom features nine choices, all brewed on premises, including exclusive one-off, draft-only offerings every October; and there's an impressive emporium with additional craft-ish choices, both local (Buda Beer, Cazzera, Da Côrte, Duzé) and national (Wäls, Colorado etc). Try the classic Pilsner - it's the only location in Brazil that serves it on draft.

CANADA

How to ask for a beer in local language?
Can I have a beer, please
How to say cheers? Cheers!
Signature beer style? Pilsner
Local bar snack? Poutine – not so much a snack but
a post-beer calorific feast of French fries, gravy and
cheese curds
Do: Ask for a taste of a beer before buying a pint

Immigration has blessed Canada's brewing scene
with some mighty fine genes: British, French, German
and Belgian settlers brought tastes and techniques from
home and as a result there are distinctive beer styles across
the vast breadth of Canada.

From the east, Québec is home to a Francophone
community of *bon viveurs*. Montréal is the epicentre of
bold brewing in Canada, perhaps thanks to the European
influence. Numerous breweries in the downtown area
alone, such as Le Saint-Bock, make strong Belgian ales and
experiment with barrel-aging and interesting yeasts, much
as the original Trappist monasteries did. In Nova Scotia's
youthful capital, Halifax, there's more of a pub-going,
Anglophone angle, thanks to British, Irish and Scottish
descendents, hence one of Nova Scotia's oldest brewing
names, Alexander Keith, being best known for a (distinctly
disappointing) IPA. A new breed of breweries with buzzing
taprooms, such as Good Robot, is moving things forward.

Heading west, as the settlers did, Ontario has the largest
number of breweries in Canada and in recent years Toronto's
beer bars, such as Bar Volo, have led the way in introducing
great new beers. These bars are increasingly stocked by
local breweries, such as Steam Whistle (see overleaf).

But it's not until you arrive out west, in British Columbia,
that the Canadian craft brewing scene comes of age.

Vancouver is the venue for much of the best beer being
made in Canada today and in part this may be because
of its proximity to the American Northwest, as influences
and punchy Pacific hops seep over the border. It's been
a recent development because it wasn't until 2013 that
breweries were permitted to host taprooms. That has
been the catalyst for an explosion of microbreweries in
Vancouver – add to that a local population of young, active,
outdoorsy types who love finishing off a mountain bike
ride or an afternoon of kayaking or skiing with a couple of
cold beers and the future is bright for British Columbia's
beer drinkers. Signature styles are much more influenced
by North American tastes so expect big IPAs and pale ales.
In Vancouver's new tasting rooms it's all about the brews:
expect sociable trestle tables, tasting paddles, chilled-out
sounds and no televisions.

MEANDER RIVER BREWERY

906 Woodville Rd, Ashdale, Nova Scotia;
www.meanderriverfarm.ca; +1 902 757 3484

◆ Family   ◆ Takeout
◆ Tour

At this idyllic rural cottage brewery, visitors can walk among the trailing hop plants and even help tend to them on its farm, which cultivates its very own hop yard, as well as lavender. The brewery works in harmony with its environment and beers are produced keeping one eye on what can be grown on-site or bought locally from other Nova Scotian farms; if you're looking for a sustainable beer, this is it. The brewery's spent grain becomes compost and helps feed the livestock, while excess water from the brewing process is channelled into irrigating the hops used to make the beer, and the chickens, pigs and turkeys help fertilize the crops. Honey cultivated on the farm is harvested for Meander River's Honey Brown Ale, and its Homegrown golden beer is wet-hopped with hops

THINGS TO DO NEARBY

Annapolis Valley
A slice of bucolic life, Annapolis Valley is bursting with boutique wineries and farmers markets. Wolfville and Annapolis Royal are particularly lovely historic boltholes.

Hall's Harbour Lobster Pound
The dot-on-the-map fishing community of Hall's Harbour makes the perfect setting for a plain yet princely meal of boiled lobster with butter. *www. hallsharbourlobster.com*

Tidal Bore Rafting
The Bay of Fundy has the highest tides in the world, which can make for one hell of a rafting adventure during the 'tidal bore' natural phenomenon. *www.tidalborerafting.com*

Halifax
Nova Scotia's capital has a salty seadog heart. Join a tour of the historic Alexander Keith's brewery, then head to hip North End for quirky cafes and craft beers.

exclusively plucked fresh from the hop yard and brewed within 24 hours. The whole operation is an understated, family affair, aided by a Community Supported Brewery scheme that offers fans the chance to invest in the business. Meander River's most astounding brew is the smoky, salt-tinged Surf & Turf Scotch – an award-winning seasonal dark ale that flaunts the flavours of Nova Scotia with seaweed and peated malt.

CLOCKTOWER BREWPUB

89 Clarence St, Ottawa, Ontario;
www.clocktower.ca; +1 613 241 8783

◆ Food ◆ Takeout
◆ Bar ◆ Transport

Now with five outlets scattered throughout Canada's capital in Ontario, Clocktower is the city's longest-running microbrewery. The original brewpub is in Glebe St, but the Byward Market branch is right in the thick of Ottawa's dining and drinking district. Grab a table overlooking Clarence St and order that most Canadian of bar snacks: a plate of hot wings. To douse the heat, try the Kölsch or Raspberry Wheat, or if you prefer to accentuate spice, wash the wings down with a pint of the seasonal IPA, if it's on tap.

Best of all, you can fill up a growler and continue sipping at home. In winter, the Whalesbone oyster stout, with its roasted coffee aroma, is as good a way as any to try and keep Ottawa's biting cold at bay.

THINGS TO DO NEARBY

Parliament Hill
The best free activity in Ottawa is a guided tour of the neo-Gothic parliament buildings, finishing off with an elevator ride to the top of the Peace Tower.
www.parl.gc.ca/vis

Canadian Museum of History
Across the river in Hull, Québec, this superb museum documents 20,000 years of human history in Canada through colourful and interactive exhibits.
www.historymuseum.ca

MILL STREET BREWERY

21 Tank House Ln, Toronto, Ontario;
www.millstreetbrewery.com; +1 416 681 0338

◆ Food ◆ Bar ◆ Transport
◆ Family ◆ Takeout

At the start of the 21st century, developers began to revamp a cluster of industrial Victorian buildings just east of Toronto's downtown area. The result is The Distillery Historic District, one of the city's prime places to shop, dine and sip. The hip area is filled with artisanal bakeries, chocolatiers, bespoke clothing stores and, of course, a popular craft brewery.

Although now owned by megabrewer AB InBev, Mill Street's beers have remained the same, with a core range of six, plus rotating seasonal and special brews. The interior is all dark wood and bare brick walls, or on warm days grab a table on the patio for some people-watching. The hop-forward Tankhouse Canadian Pale Ale is a fine accompaniment for a plate of poutine.

THINGS TO DO NEARBY

Toronto Islands
Ferries and water taxis shuttle people to some of Lake Ontario's islands – great places to wander, cycle or treat the kids to some family-friendly fun.
www.city.toronto.on.ca

St Lawrence Market
With more than 120 vendors, this is a prime spot to pick up a picnic of artisanal bread, meat and cheese to accompany your latest beer purchase. *www.stlawrencemarket.com*

STEAM WHISTLE BREWING

255 Bremner Blvd, Toronto, Ontario;
www.steamwhistle.ca; +1 416 362 2337

◆ Food   ◆ Bar   ◆ Transport
◆ Tour   ◆ Takeout

THINGS TO DO NEARBY

CN Tower
Zoom up the CN Tower
for views of the city and
beyond. If you eat at the
restaurant, your trip to the
top is free.
www.cntower.ca

Hockey Hall of Fame
Try your hand against
history's hockey greats
with the interactive
exhibits and brush up
on everything to do with
Canada's best-loved sport.
www.hhof.com

**Ripley's Aquarium of
Canada**
Set aside a morning to
explore Canada's largest
(and well laid-out)
aquarium; arrive early to
avoid the crowds. *www.
ripleyaquariums.com/
canada*

Rogers Centre
If there are no baseball
or football games taking
place, join a behind-the-
scenes tour of Toronto's
technically awe-inspiring
premier stadium, with its
fully retractable roof.
www.rogerscentre.com

While other breweries may dabble in stouts
containing roasted bull testicles, lagers featuring
moondust, dark beers flavoured with coffee beans that
have passed through a mammal's digestive tract or ales
recreated from ancient Egyptian recipes, Steam Whistle
stick to its simple motto: do one thing really, really well.

It has been brewing its sole beer, a crisp, thirst-quenching Pilsner, since the brewery first opened its doors in
2000. The hugely popular brewery tour is one of Toronto's
top activities, so booking ahead is recommended (though
on weekends it's first-come, first-served). The half-hour
tours kick off with a sample of the Pilsner to keep you
suitably watered while you shuffle past the mash tun,
kettle, fermenters and bottling line. Afterwards you can
continue tasting and soak up the German- and Czech-

hopped brew with simple bar food – pretzels, sandwiches
and potato chips.

If you fancy a little art with your brew, a gallery features
rotating exhibitions from local artists. For the rest, the
convivial bar is a great place to hang out and sip on one
superbly executed Pilsner. And if you're really lucky, you
might get to sample the unfiltered version of its signature
brew – full-flavoured, bready and extremely more-ish.

BRASSNECK BREWERY

2184 Main St, Vancouver, British Columbia;
www.brassneck.ca; +1 604 259 7686

◆ Food   ◆ Takeout
◆ Bar   ◆ Transport

THINGS TO DO NEARBY

Cartems Donuterie
Main St's favourite hipster doughnut shop serves its top-selling triple chocolate and Canadian whiskey bacon treats to a growing band of sugar-dusted fans.
www.cartems.com

Hot Art Wet City
Vancouver's best pop culture gallery combines affordable, often surrealist works from mostly local artists, with comedy nights, lively art workshops and party-like show openings.
www.hotartwetcity.com

Fox Cabaret
Colonizing (and fully transforming) a grubby old porn cinema, this slender-roomed Mt Pleasant club lures local cool kids with its dance floor and live bands.
www.foxcabaret.com

Pulpfiction Books
This used bookstore, a local legend, is lined with shelves crammed with tomes on everything from string theory to home-brewing. *www.pulpfiction booksvancouver.com*

When UK expat Nigel Springthorpe moved to Vancouver a few years back, the local beer selection was dominated by fizzy factory lagers. But after taking over Gastown bar Alibi Room, he created a 50-line taphouse dedicated to sourcing and serving the region's most flavorsome microbrews. Vancouverites were hooked – and the next step was to build his own brewery. Opened in 2013, Brassneck was an instant hit. With veteran brewmaster Conrad Gmoser on board, the two concocted 50 new beers in their first six months, enticing local ale nuts to keep dropping by for the latest releases. The brewery's tasting room is a big part of this success: lined with wood planks punched with gaps that reveal the beer tanks beyond, it's one of Vancouver's warmest watering holes. Adding a cured sausage from the counter jars is recommended here – go for the bison – while food trucks also often park out front (you can bring your grub inside). But liquid sustenance is Brassneck's main appeal: its growler-filling station is always busy and its gold-lettered takeout containers are the perfect souvenir for visiting beer fans. Just be sure to fill yours with some crisply delicious Passive Aggressive Dry-Hopped Pale Ale.

CALLISTER BREWING COMPANY

1338 Franklin St, Vancouver, British Columbia;
www.callisterbrewing.com; +1 604 569 2739

◆ Bar ◆ Transport
◆ Takeout

The city's most unusual microbrewery is actually a four-pack of tiny nano-breweries sharing the same shiny-tanked East Vancouver site. For lazy drinkers, that means launching a taste-tripping local beer crawl without ever having to leave your lacquered barrel table in the facility's art-lined, concrete-floored tasting room. Ideal for exploring British Columbia's love affair with hoppy IPAs, this is also the home of what claims to be Canada's only cask-exclusive brewery. Adopting the traditional UK approach to beer making, Real Cask Brewing ages its smooth, subtle ales straight in the cask. It typically offering several enticing options: don't miss the beautifully balanced old-style Best Bitter – the kind of beer your tipsy granddad used to sip after work.

THINGS TO DO NEARBY

Tiny Finery
Highlight of a nearby stretch of cool indie stores and eateries on Hastings St, this little shop showcases locally produced arts, crafts, clothing and jewelry.
www.tinyfinery.ca

Dayton Boots
A link to East Van's gritty past, the hardworking footwear made on-site by this 1946-founded company has been reclaimed by the younger generation in recent years.
www.daytonboots.com

OFF THE RAIL BREWING

1351 Adanac St, Vancouver, British Columbia;
www.offtherailbrewing.com; +1 604 563 5767

◆ Bar   ◆ Transport
◆ Takeout

Named in reference to the legendary Railway Club pub that brewer–owner Steve Forsyth used to run downtown, this sociable 2nd-floor East Vancouver microbrewery pours a surprisingly diverse array of tipples for such a small tasting room.

But looks are deceptive: the bar may be barely big enough to swing a brewery cat but the tanks across the hallway are always busy. The result is a large menu of eight or so regular libations, plus a smaller chalkboard of intriguing limited-run brews: this is where the locals look first when they roll through the door. The trick here is to order a flight of tiny sample glasses to discover your favorite – just be sure to include the award-winning Raj Mahal India Ale.

THINGS TO DO NEARBY

Commercial Drive
Vancouver's most bohemian street, this stroll-able smorgasbord of indie shops and restaurants – aka The Drive – is worth a laid-back afternoon of anyone's time. *www.thedrive.ca*

Crème de la Crumb
Fuel-up before your East Van brewery crawl at this bakeshop, a local favorite that uses all-natural ingredients – miss the chocolate pear crumb cake at your peril. *www. cremedelacrumb.com*

POWELL STREET CRAFT BREWERY

1357 Powell St, Vancouver, British Columbia;
www.powellbeer.com; +1 604 558 2537

◆ Bar　　◆ Transport
◆ Takeout

Much of the credit for Vancouver's status as a pilgrimage-worthy craft beer capital is due to its grassroots home-brewing scene. Many of the city's top ale-makers jumped from crafting beer for enthusiastic friends to opening small production facilities at the nano-brewing level. The best of the bunch? Powell Street Craft Brewery.

But soon after David Bowkett and wife Nicole opened their little storefront facility a few years back, they encountered a serious problem. Their beers were so popular – especially after their Old Jalopy Pale Ale surprised all by winning a Canadian Brewing Award's Beer of the Year accolade – that their tanks routinely ran dry. The solution? An early relocation along the street (the brewery's name presumably limits where they can go) and an upgrade to a larger microbrewery operation. The change delivered a

THINGS TO DO NEARBY

Odd Society Spirits
Reflecting one of Canada's other craft booze scenes, Vancouver has several distillery tasting rooms, including this delicious gin, vodka and white whiskey maker. *www. oddsocietyspirits.com*

Bistro Wagon Rouge
Combining a laid-back diner vibe (no bookings!) with a menu of French bistro classics, this small local-secret spot is the area's best restaurant – cassoulet recommended. *www. bistrowagonrouge.com*

Princeton Pub
A blast-from-the-past pub that still lures workers from the nearby docks, this is the Vancouver bar that gentrification forgot. Don't miss Sunday's karaoke night. *www. theprincetonpub.ca*

New Brighton Park
A short drive east delivers this shoreline green oasis alongside Burrard Inlet. Expect to spot herons, hawks and bald eagles hungrily eyeing the marine life below.

capacity boost, a larger tasting room and the opportunity for Bowkett to experiment with a wider range of libations. Along with Old Jalopy and some superbly hopped IPAs, that means an innovative sour beer program plus some ever-intriguing seasonals on the tasting room's behind-the-bar chalkboard menu. Fans of darker brews, though, should ready their taste buds for some Dive Bomb Porter, a rich, velvet-smooth charmer.

© John Lee

ECUADOR

How to ask for a beer in local language?
Una cerveza, por favor
How to say cheers? Salud!
Signature beer style? APAs and IPAs in craft terms
Local bar snack? Canchas (toasted, salted nut kernels), often with spicy salsa
Don't: Expect craft beer to be available in too many other restaurants or bars away from the brewpubs: red tape still makes this challenging

Ecuador's craft beer movement is so nascent it has yet to become fully definable. For decades, asking for a beer here meant asking for a Pilsner or a Club Premium. These two beers, produced by the same company, Guayaquil-based Cervecería Nacional Ecuador, monopolised the industry, sating thirsts but not offering much in terms of complexity. This ensured Ecuador remained – until relatively recently – unadventurous for beer lovers.

But this diminutive nation is a popular place for foreigners to relocate and, parched by the paucity of choice, a

handful of entrepreneurial expats set out to build a craft beer culture from scratch. Unsurprisingly, given that most foreigners are from the US, it was Americans that influenced the beer movement the most. The founders of Bandido Brewery in Quito hail from the Western US, Montañita Brewery is run by a Californian couple, and a Texan heads up Zarza Brewing Co in Loja. German-owned craft breweries and, hearteningly, a handful of Ecuadorian-owned breweries are at the helm of the movement too.

The beer scene is in its infancy, and local legislation has yet to embrace the essential experimental element of craft brewing: currently, the process of introducing new beer styles is a protracted one. But now is an exciting time to tap into Ecuadorian microbrewing. Ecuador boasts some of the highest biodiversity on the planet, and its unique plants lend flamboyance to new brews, highlighting that the future of craft brewing here could be as colorful and varied as nature.

ZARZA BREWING COMPANY

Cnr Puerto Bolívar & Esmeraldas, Loja;
www.zarzabrewing.com; +593 7 257 1413

◆ Food   ◆ Bar
◆ Tour   ◆ Takeout

Set up by a Texan who moved to Ecuador and then developed a hankering for quality craft beer (before Zarza, the Ecuadorian mountains had very little), this brewpub showcases up to 20 brews throughout the year. It retains the personal feel of a new start-up, and you'll still find the owner–brewer serving behind the bar. A US–Latin American food menu punctuated by some feisty salsas (the BBQ salsa is concocted with the brewery's stout) helps soak up the booze. Zarza makes its own yeast and draws on the globe's best grains to create a distinctive IPA; a Belgian-style ale; an American blonde ale; and a coppery, smoky ESA (English Special Ale), but it's the stout imbued with mocha undertones that's most popular.

THINGS TO DO NEARBY

Puerta de la Ciudad
Loja's castellated city gate is a multi-tiered museum-cum-gallery-cum-viewpoint, with informative displays on Loja and pretty panoramas from the upper balconies.

Parque Nacional Podocarpus
Located 10km south of Loja, Podocarpus National Park has swathes of cloud forest and lowland forest, more than 1000 endemic plant species and hiking trails.

BANDIDO BREWING

Cnr Olmedo E1-136 & Fermín Cevallos, Quito;
www.bandidobrewing.com; +593 2 228 6504

◆ Food   ◆ Takeout
◆ Bar   ◆ Transport

'Adventurers and alchemists' are how the folks at Bandidos bill themselves, and as craft brewers in Ecuador they're certainly setting Andean-high standards. Brightening up a colonial abode in Quito's Old Town, the brewpub's bar even boasts its own chapel. The friends who set up Bandidos are most proud of their IPAs and it's here you'll taste the playful, pioneering use of eclectic Ecuadorian ingredients alongside percipient hop selections that typify the Bandidos approach. Try the Rio Negro stout, flavoured with the cacao the country is famous for, or the Honey Ginger Saison, a pale ale sweetened and spiced by honey and ginger. But it's the *La Gua.p.a*, a play on the Spanish word for gorgeous, which takes you into uncharted territory. this floral yet earthy American pale ale is a medley of Willamette hops, which flourish in the founders' homeland of Oregon and *guayusa*, a caffeine-packed leaf from the Amazon Basin.

THINGS TO DO NEARBY

Museo del Banco Central
Near Parque El Ejido to the northeast of the Old Town is perhaps the nation's most important museum. Its Ecuadorian art collection is unrivalled.

TeleferiQo
A must-do in Ecuador's capital: take this cable car ride up the volcanic slopes of Volcán Pichincha to 4100m and some seriously breathtaking vistas.

USA

How to ask for a beer in local language? A beer, please
How to say cheers? Cheers!
Signature beer style? Double IPA (among many others)
Local bar snack? The three Ps: peanuts, pretzels
and potato chips
Do: Plan on adding 15% or more to your bill:
bartenders usually depend on tips to make a living

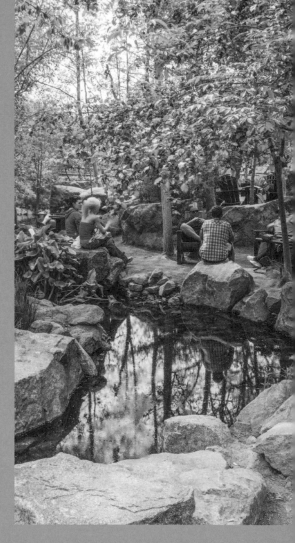

What happens when things get so bad, they just can't get any worse? They get better. And in the case of beer in the United States, after that things get absolutely incredible. According to the Brewers' Association, the 50 states got down to 80 functioning breweries by 1983, with 92% of the market held by just six massive beer makers. (To put that into context, those 80 US breweries in 1983 were serving a total population over 226.5 million. In 1873, when the country's population was only 39 million, America had a much more diverse beer scene, with its former high point of 4131 active breweries.) Not only were there very few breweries by the 1980s, but the beer they produced was bland and flavorless by international standards. American beer culture appeared dead.

But then came homebrewing – which blossomed after it was legalized by the federal government in 1978 – and the first microbreweries and brewpubs. The trickle of new beer producers that started to appear in the '80s and '90s became a full-on deluge in the 2000s and onwards. In 2016, the US finally surpassed its 1873-high in terms of total breweries. What's even better: the brews they're producing are world leaders in terms of variety, interest – and deliciousness.

The global craft beer phenomenon was arguably invented in the US, and in terms of coming up with new brewing styles and techniques, the US remains the leader. If there is one country global craft beer lovers should visit, this is it. And if you're lucky enough to be from here, you've plenty of craft beer destinations within easy

reach. But where? The US is a continent-size country, and where you should travel depends on what you want to try: while you can find outstanding examples of every style just about everywhere, certain regions have their own specializations. In the northeast, you'll find the extremely fruity and often cloudy beers known as New England IPAs, like the revered Heady Topper from The Alchemist or Sip of Sunshine from Lawson's Finest Liquids. In Oregon, you'll find a number of rich and intense Black IPAs, aka Cascadian Dark Ales, such as Hop in the Dark CDA from Deschutes or Dad's Little Helper from Rogue. Perhaps due to the heat, Florida developed a native sour fruit beer

BAR TALK - GREG KOCH

With aromatic hop bitterness, the West Coast IPA has become one of the leading craft beer styles around the world today

TOP 5 BEERS

- **Lord Sorachi** Brooklyn Brewery
- **Kentucky Breakfast Stout** Founders Brewing Company
- **Go to IPA** Green Flash Brewing Company
- **Zombie Dust** 3 Floyds Brewing Company
- **La Roja** Jolly Pumpkin Artisan Ales

culture, led by breweries Cigar City, Funky Buddha and Cycle Brewing. In Southern California, you'll find the beer culture that made aggressively bitter brews such as West Coast IPA from Green Flash and Arrogant Bastard from Stone Brewing household names.

The American craft scene is so dynamic nowadays that just about every city or town has great beer options, from brewpubs and micros to specialty beer bars and beer-themed restaurants. And if you think things are good in the US today, with its all-time-high in terms of total breweries, just wait a while: thousands of new craft breweries are expected to open here in the next few years.

MARBLE BREWERY

111 Marble Ave NW, Albuquerque, New Mexico;
www.marblebrewery.com; +1 505 243 2739

◆ Food   ◆ Tour   ◆ Transport
◆ Family   ◆ Bar

THINGS TO DO NEARBY

Old Town
Albuquerque's historic plaza, home to shops, galleries and the San Felipe de Neri church, has anchored the square since the city was founded in the early 1700s.

Breaking Bad Cycling Tour
Cycle past Jesse Pinkman's house and Tuco's hideout on this tour of TV show *Breaking Bad* sites led by locals Heather and Josh Arnold. ***www. routesrentals.com***

Sandia Peak Tramway
Ride the longest aerial tram in the USA up to the top of Sandia Peak (3163m) for riveting views of Albuquerque and plenty of mountain-hiking opportunities. ***www. sandiapeak.com***

Duran's Central Pharmacy
Don't miss this local institution that serves New Mexican fare (burritos, enchiladas and sopaipillas) in a secret dining room at the back of a pharmacy. ***www.durancentral pharmacy.com***

In what must be one of the world's most centrally located breweries, Marble's original brewery and bar is situated in a converted HVAC warehouse right in downtown Albuquerque. Founded in 2008, Marble's beers are among the most widely distributed in New Mexico, and it was one of the first microbreweries to bring big-hopped, high-Alcohol-By-Volume (ABV) craft beer to the state. The downtown drinking space is comfy and welcoming. You can view the brewing vats from the taphouse bar or come on a Thursday afternoon for a free guided tour. Outside, there is a patio drinking area and an open-air stage where it hosts bluegrass and roots bands during the summer.

In recent years, Marble has expanded its operations to incorporate more bars, including an additional taproom on Albuquerque's West Side and one in the Northeast Heights. When the TV show *Breaking Bad* was filming in Albuquerque, Marble's downtown bar was a favorite hangout of the cast and crew – actor Bryan Cranston could be spotted here many nights. It's always got a special brew or two on, but don't miss the Wildflower Wheat, brewed with New Mexico wildflower honey, and the caramel, dry-hopped Red Ale.

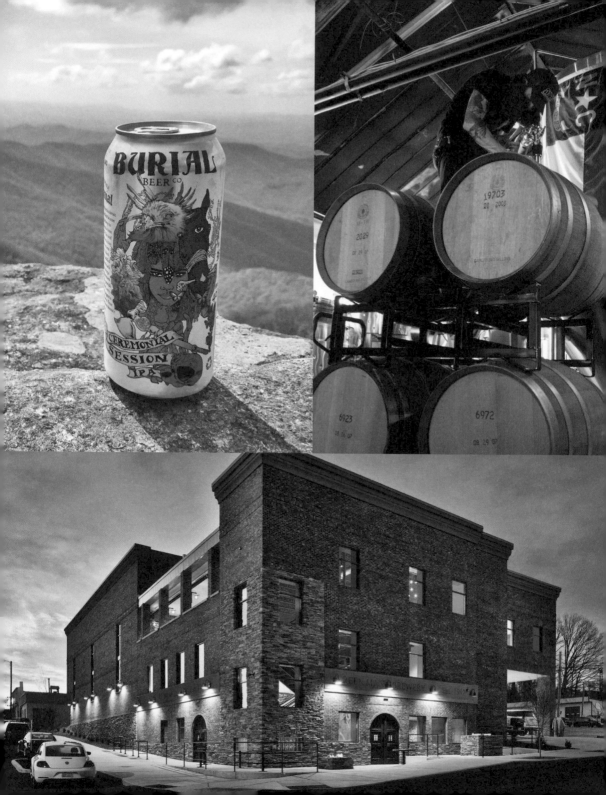

BURIAL BEER CO

40 Collier Ave, Asheville, North Carolina;
www.burialbeer.com; +1 828 475 2739

◆ Food ◆ Tour ◆ Takeout
◆ Family ◆ Bar ◆ Transport

You won't find any flagship beers at Burial Beer Co's rustic South Slope taproom, just a changing line-up of seasonal, specialty and Belgian brews. A revivalist brewery, Burial recreates forgotten beer styles and brewing methods. Modern techniques are used as needed to create phenomenal beer. The founders? Three friends from Seattle who moved here in 2014 to implement this vision. Their efforts quickly paid off, and their second brewery is opening near the Biltmore Estate in 2017, in facilities that were barracks for 1930s Civilian Conservation Corps (CCC)

workers building the Blue Ridge Parkway. Dubbed Forestry Camp, the revitalized complex will feature a craft beer bar, a cocktail bar and a restaurant. Try the Skillet Donut South, an amazing stout that is beloved by many.

THINGS TO DO NEARBY

Biltmore Estate
Embrace the excess at George and Edith Vanderbilt's grand home, completed in 1895. The Banquet Hall, with its 70ft-high ceiling, is a showstopper.
www.biltmore.com

Blue Ridge Parkway
This leafy byway twists through the Blue Ridge Mountains, connecting Shenandoah National Park in Virginia with Great Smoky Mountains National Park, west of Asheville.
www.nps.gov/blri

GREEN MAN BREWERY

27 Buxton Ave, Asheville, North Carolina;
www.greenmanbrewery.com; +1 828-252-5502

◆ Tour ◆ Takeout
◆ Bar ◆ Transport

A beloved community watering-hole, Green Man Brewery jump-started Asheville's craft beer scene when it opened in 1997. Soccer fans have gathered at its South Slope tasting room, Dirty Jack's, for years to watch matches and quaff English-style ales. As for the Green Man, he's a leafy pagan deity associated with merriment and drinking.
   Today, Dirty Jack's relaxes in the shadows of the new Greenmansion: home to a packaging hall, retail 'brewtique' and indoor/outdoor tasting room, this three-story behe-

moth opened on St Patrick's Day in 2016. Views of Mt Pisgah from the top-floor tasting room are best enjoyed with a pint of Green Man ESB, infused with British malts and hops, and hints of caramel, toffee and chocolate.

THINGS TO DO NEARBY

Cúrate
Settle in for a Spanish dinner party at Chef Katie Button's stylish downtown tapas restaurant, Cúrate. Unless it's late at night, reservations are essential.
www.heirloomhg.com/ curate

Lazoom Tours
Comedy. Ghosts. Or bands and beer. Take your pick of tours then climb aboard the big purple bus for a wacky roll through the city.
www.lazoomtours.com

WICKED WEED BREWING

91 Biltmore Ave, Asheville, North Carolina;
https://wickedweedbrewing.com; +1 828 575 9599

◆ Food ◆ Tour ◆ Takeout
◆ Family ◆ Bar ◆ Transport

THINGS TO DO NEARBY

Brewery Tours
Focus on craft and taste at a few select breweries with Asheville Brewery Tours or South Slope Brewery Tours. For self-guided tours, visit *www.ashevillealetrail.com*.

French Broad Chocolate Lounge
Step inside this downtown emporium for chocolate morsels, from dark chocolate salted caramel honey truffles to mint chocolate chunk brownies. *www.frenchbroad chocolates.com*

Drum Circle
In warmer months, walk to the weekly Friday night drum circle at Pritchard Park downtown. About a dozen drummers start gathering around 5pm.

Omni Grove Park Inn
Rest up for drinking at this striking resort, a 100-year-old classic famous for its rock walls, mountain views and subterranean spa. The grand lobby? Breathtaking. *www.omnihotels.com/ hotels/asheville-grove-park*

A wall-sized portrait of Henry VIII surveys the scene at Wicked Weed Brewing, a convivial brewpub anchoring the South Slope Brewery District. Why Henry VIII? According to lore, the temperamental British monarch once called hops a 'wicked and pernicious weed' that ruined the taste of beer. The hoppy ales at Wicked Weed prove the king wrong – just ask the folks knocking back pints upstairs, downstairs and on the patios at this welcoming place. Who's here? Thirsty backpackers fresh (or not so fresh) from hiking trails in the nearby Blue Ridge Mountains. A handful of hipsters might slip in from the Aloft hotel a few doors down, while families grab tables for the gourmet pub fare. Our favorite spot? The front patio, a prime space for down-town people-watching. On weekends, bachelor parties, girlfriends on getaways, and youthful revelers imbibe elbow-to-elbow in the downstairs beer bar. Buy a t-shirt and beers to-go in the bottle shop. A few blocks away at the Funkatorium (147 Coxe Ave.), a Wicked Weed spin-off, the helpful brew team offers tours and serve up flavor-packed sour and farmhouse ales. Don't leave Wicked Weed without trying the flagship Pernicious IPA: a bold, West Coast-style IPA, which shows Henry VIII who's boss.

JESTER KING

13005 Fitzhugh Rd, Austin, Texas;
www.jesterkingbrewery.com; +1 512 537 5100

◆ Food ◆ Tour ◆ Takeout
◆ Family ◆ Bar

This rustic farmhouse brewery lies on a working ranch in the beautiful Hill Country just outside of Austin, with cattle occasionally wandering through its sprawling grounds. Much of its production is fermented in barrels, and the brewery employs its own mix of yeast and local bacteria, sourcing its critters from a nearby cider press or by leaving unfermented wort outside overnight, which results in wild-tasting, often sour and almost always highly charismatic beers, like the extremely refreshing Le Petit Prince Farmhouse Table Beer. Collaborations with area producers include Snörkel, a Gose-style sour ale made with oyster mushrooms from Logro Farms, which uses Jester Kings' spent grain. Pints are served in the brewery's barrel room and beer garden, with artisanal wood-fired pizzas and vegan cupcakes available at Stanley's next door. Free tours are available, though opening hours are limited to

THINGS TO DO NEARBY

Alamo Drafthouse
The original location of this cult cinema chain offers outrageous B-movie marathons, quote-alongs, cap-gun-shoot-alongs and more, along with great beer and snacks.
www.drafthouse.com

Contemporary Austin
This avant garde art museum has two locations, one at the urbane Jones Center downtown, the other at the Laguna Gloria sculpture park and villa.
www.thecontemporary austin.org

Congress Bridge Bats
Every night at dusk, crowds watch the largest urban bat colony in North America – some 1.5 million Mexican free-tail bats – leave their home under Congress Avenue Bridge.
www.batcon.org/congress

Continental Club
Rocking the trendy South Congress strip since 1955, this legendary music club has hosted shows by Stevie Ray Vaughn, the Replacements and Led Zep legend Robert Plant.
www.continentalclub.com

Fridays, Saturdays and Sundays. Guest bottles come from some of the best new breweries in the country, including Funkwerks and Jolly Pumpkin, while brewery-only releases, such as Buddha's Brew, a Farmhouse Ale re-fermented with kombucha, make Jester King an absolute must-see if you're anywhere near central Texas. Make one of these own-releases, Atrial Rubicite, a barrel-aged raspberry sour ale, your must-try beer.

DESCHUTES BREWERY & PUBLIC HOUSE

1044 NW Bond St, Bend, Oregon;
www.deschutesbrewery.com; +1 541 382 9242

◆ Food   ◆ Tour   ◆ Takeout
◆ Family   ◆ Bar   ◆ Transport

Yes, there are lots of breweries in Bend (22 and counting), but none have the prowess of Deschutes. The brewery launched as a small brewpub back in 1988, the early days of American craft brewing.

Since then, it's become one of the largest craft breweries in the US, something you can feel when you walk through the doors. It's a noisy and bustling space filled with the mountain town's locals and visitors, people who've worked up a thirst on the trails, slopes, rivers, and rock walls nearby. Sit at the bar to ogle the tanks where brewers make experimental brews, a small part of the brewing setup that helped some of Oregon's finest professional brewers, who got their start working at Deschutes, learn the ropes.

Most of the beers are named after nearby natural wonders, including the Deschutes River; the brewery

THINGS TO DO NEARBY

McMenamins Old St Francis School Soaking Pool
Slip into the steaming waters of this turquoise-tiled, heated soaking pool, which can be transcendent when light streams through the stained-glass windows.
www.mcmenamins.com

Phil's Trail
Mountain bike some of Bend's most accessible and diverse cross-country singletrack, which winds and climbs through arid forest, just minutes from town.

Water Sports on Deschutes River
Rent a stand-up paddleboard, a tube, a kayak, or a canoe, then launch your craft at Riverbend Park beach and enjoy a water tour through town.

Chow
Dig into one of the best brunches in town, which is defined by friendly service and seasonal ingredients in everything from eggs Benedict to pumpkin ginger-spiced pancakes.
www.chowbend.com

is located on its banks less than 2 miles (3km) from the downtown brewpub: to get a behind-the-scenes peek there, book a free tour.

Classic Deschutes beers include Black Butte Porter, Mirror Pond Pale Ale and Fresh Squeezed IPA. If you're lucky, you can try The Abyss (which debuted in 2006), a rich and boozy imperial stout aged in bourbon and pinot noir barrels.

FIELDWORK BREWING CO.

1160 Sixth Street, Berkeley, California;
www.fieldworkbrewing.com; +1 510 898 1203

◆ Food ◆ Bar ◆ Takeout
◆ Family ◆ Transport

Follow your nose to this Berkeley-based brewery and taproom in a quiet northwest corner of town near the freeway. Head brewer and co-founder Alex Tweet (formerly of Ballast Point and Modern Times in San Diego, see p89) brews with an emphasis on aroma and can sometimes be found crushing and sniffing hops before deciding on a purchase. The results of his high olfactory standards are evident in the glass. Try the beer flight (with the excellent tasting notes to hand) to explore the range, which is weighted towards sours and saisons but also features a number of IPAs and usually a dark beer or two. There's an ever-changing selection on tap (and growler refills), including plenty of quirky brews. A refreshing favorite is the citrusy Farmhouse Wheat saison, and the Galaxy Juice, which surfs in on a wave of pineapple from the Galaxy hops.

THINGS TO DO NEARBY

Torpedo Room
Sierra Nevada's (see p69) Fourth Street bar is where the brewery's rare and exotic species are displayed, such as the monstrously good barrel-aged Narwhal Imperial Stout.
www.sierranevada.com

Farmers' Markets
Browse stalls of local producers at Downtown Berkeley's Saturday Farmers' Markets. You'll find baked goods, preserves, organic fruits, cheeses, oils and more. Held on Tuesday, Thursday and Saturday.

University of California, Berkeley
Sample campus life at this famous university: climb the Campanile bell tower for views over the Bay, explore the parks and gardens, get a coffee at the Free Speech Movement cafe.

Westbrae Biergarten
Local brews and revolving choice of food truck (make a date for the BBQ) draw families to this small, open-air beer garden in a quiet corner of north Berkeley. ***www.westbraebiergarten.com***

The cool and minimalist interior, suffused in natural light, is packed at weekends but outdoor seating lessens the pressure. Thankfully there's no TV (though a projector was screening an important Golden State Warriors basketball game on our visit – this is the East Bay after all). Some of the behind-the-scenes brewery action is on view if you look out the back and Alex might be behind the bar. Since 2016, Fieldwork has operated a sister taproom in Sacramento.

AVERY BREWERY

4910 Nautilus Ct, Boulder, Colorado;
www.averybrewing.com; +1 303 440 4324

◆ Food   ◆ Tour   ◆ Takeout
◆ Family ◆ Bar   ◆ Transport

THINGS TO DO NEARBY

Chautauqua Park
No trip to Boulder is complete without climbing through Chautauqua's open meadows and ponderosa pine forests to the massive sandstone slabs known as the Flatirons.
www.chautauqua.com

Pearl Street
Downtown Boulder's pedestrian promenade comes alive with street performers, farm-to-table restaurants, oodles of local boutiques, sculptures to climb on and fountains to run through.

Rocky Mountain National Park
Top-of-the-world majesty: the Continental Divide, imposing granite peaks, glacial lakes, one of the country's highest paved roads, and much fauna and flora. ***www.nps.gov/romo***

Boulder Creek
Tubing through town is a favorite summer activity; alternatively, follow the riverside path on foot or by bike beneath the granite domes of Boulder Canyon.

Avery's beers are much like their hometown: idiosyncratic, idealistic and distinctly compelling. Established in Boulder in 1993, the brewery was founded by Adam Avery, who was originally a disgruntled law student before deciding to switch gears to accommodate his passions: home-brewing and spending more time outdoors. A fondness for going off-piste resulted in beers that weren't always marketed for the mainstream and, indeed, the company got off to a slow start. The brewery's first big hit, a barley wine called Hog Heaven, was named after Avery's initial belief that the public would only enjoy the brew when pigs fly. He may have been wrong on that account, but hard-won success wound up solidifying a penchant for the uncommon.

At the company's new facilities (opened in 2015), you'll find a whopping 30 beers on tap, including a range of pucker-up sours and potent rum- and whiskey-barrel-aged creations. Two dining areas – the sun-drenched taproom/patio (with a smoker for the BBQ) and the upstairs restaurant – serve up everything from soft pretzels to pozole, with an emphasis on products straight from Colorado farms. Celebrate a hard day's play with a pint of unfiltered White Rascal: a zesty Belgian *witbier* with notes of coriander and orange.

SIERRA NEVADA BREWING CO.

1075 East 20th Street, Chico, California;
www.sierranevada.com; +1 530 893 3520

◆ Food   ◆ Tour   ◆ Takeout
◆ Family ◆ Bar

THINGS TO DO NEARBY

Mountain biking
Guess what, Sierra Nevada brewery is in the Sierra Nevada range. That means great mountain biking. Top spot is Downieville, two hours' drive away. *www.yubaexpeditions.com*

The Big Room
The brewery has its own music venue in Chico, the Big Room, which hosts Americana and roots acts. Jazz, blues, folk or country, there's a varied events calendar. And good beer.

Farmers' Market
Saturdays and Wednesdays are when Chico's farmers' market is set up for the morning. Check out the seasonal and local produce all year round, plus breads, preserves and snacks. *www.chicofarmersmarket.com*

Gateway Science Museum
Designed to open its visitors' minds to the wonders of science, this California State University museum has exhibitions that cover topics from asteroids to bugs. *www.csuchico.edu*

Sierra Nevada's star on the beer walk of fame is assured. The brewery popularised the modern American Pale Ale, now the world's dominant craft beer style. Its first batch was brewed in 1980 and the green-labelled bottles are now sold across the world. So, to visit Sierra Nevada is to attain beervana. What wonders will you find here? Beautifully polished copper stills. A vast solar array of 10,500 panels. The heady scents of the fermentation room. The old, the new and the ever-changing.

The headquarters (there's also an outpost in Mills River, North Carolina) offers a more corporate experience than some craft breweries but it's no less interesting for that. Daily themed tours (some free, others costing $10-30) cover all aspects of the brewery. The Engineering tour takes in the high-tech chilling system; the Hop Head tour covers hop history and biology, and visits the experimental hop fields; meet the composting machine on the Sustainability tour; or simply sup brews straight from the tanks on the Beer Geek tour. Something for everyone. And the beers: well, you may taste the Pale Ale anywhere in the world but Sierra Nevada brews an extraordinary range of special beers – try them at the Taproom. The Torpedo is an IPA with a little extra oomph.

BLACK SHIRT BREWING CO.

3719 Walnut St, Denver, Colorado;
www.blackshirtbrewingco.com; +1 303 993 2799

◆ Food   ◆ Tour   ◆ Takeout

◆ Family   ◆ Bar   ◆ Transport

Brothers Chad and Branden Miller dreamed up Black Shirt Brewing back in 1999, sitting on the porch of their family home in tiny Westcliffe, Colorado, mulling the meaning of life. They had a passion for brewing, especially red ale – to this day that's all they brew, in homage to their home state (Colorado meaning 'red colored' in Spanish). Today, they're master artisans – BSB's handcrafted ales take two months to three years to brew, ranging from IPAs to stouts.

Similar care extends to the taproom – black-shirted staff (a nod to counter culture), lopsided stemware (to showcase the beer's aroma), guitars (their own), and live music (a window into the BSB community). Must try beer: Red Evelyn – a tribute to the brothers' grandmother.

THINGS TO DO NEARBY

The Source
A repurposed iron foundry, this marketplace features artisanal breads and booze, locally sourced produce and meats, and Acorn, one of the best restaurants in town. *www.thesourcedenver.com*

Infinite Monkey Theorum
This urban winery has a laid-back vibe and lots of seating, inside and out. Delicious wines served by the glass, can, even slushy machine. *www.theinfinite monkeytheorem.com*

RENEGADE BREWING CO.

925 W 9th Ave, Denver, Colorado;
www.renegadebrewing.com; +1 720 401 4089

◆ Food   ◆ Bar   ◆ Transport
◆ Tour   ◆ Takeout

THINGS TO DO NEARBY

First Friday
Once a month, galleries along Santa Fe Drive stay open late, so Denverites can gallery-hop and indulge in food truck fare. *www.artdistrictonsantafe. com; www.rivernorthart. com*

Denver Art Museum
Visit DAM for its spectacular range of exhibits including an American Indian Art collection with 20,000 objects dating from prehistoric times. *www. denverartmuseum.org*

United States Mint
Learn how the pennies in your pocket got there by taking a tour of the US Mint. Tours are free and last 45 minutes. Reservations required. *www.usmint.gov*

Cherry Creek Regional Trail
Bike or walk along Cherry Creek Trail, a 40-mile (64km) paved path that starts in downtown Denver and meanders through urban landscapes and state parks.

When Renegade opened in 2011, it hit Denver's burgeoning brewery market hard, quickly earning several awards for its craft brews and taproom. Five years and 40 new competitors later, Renegade continues to rock the town. Its creative, layered beers integrate such flavors as lemongrass, curry, and beets without leaving behind Coloradan faves like rye ale and smack-you-in-the-face triple IPAs.

Founded by Brian and Khara O'Connell, the seed that became Renegade was a Christmas gift: a home brewing kit. It was a hobby that quickly turned into a passion and led, years later, to Denver's edgy Arts District on Santa Fe. Here the O'Connells opened their taproom – an airy room with a winding bar and garage doors that open onto a street-front patio. No TVs. No distractions. Just a mix of professionals, artists, and students coming together to enjoy good beer. The taproom is busy most weekdays, bustling on weekends. And come First Friday, it's a house party – tables pushed to the sides, lines at the bar, even plastic cups sometimes. But still, it retains an essential sense of community. Must try beer: Redacted, a well-balanced rye IPA that has been on tap (and a top seller) since day one.

HOODOO BREWING CO

1951 Fox Ave, Fairbanks, Alaska;
www.hoodoobrew.com; +1 907 459 2337

◆ Food   ◆ Tour   ◆ Takeout
◆ Family   ◆ Bar

Hidden away in Alaska's gateway-to-the-Arctic city of Fairbanks, Hoodoo counts itself as the second most northerly brewery in North America. But, just as Alaska can be mildly eccentric, so can Hoodoo. Aside from its industrial chic taproom and *biergarten*, the brewery maintains a running club, hosts pre-opening yoga classes on selective Saturdays and limits drinkers to a healthy (or inhibitive) two-pint maximum. Fortunately, there's no restriction on what you can take away. Hoodoo's best beers are loaded with heavy Teutonic overtones (the taproom enthusiastically celebrates Oktoberfest); the crisp, smooth German Kölsch and Bavarian Weissbier varietals are popular. To remind yourself you're still technically in the US, try the harder-hitting Northwest IPA, which measures in at a gutsy 7.2% ABV.

THINGS TO DO NEARBY

University of Alaska Museum of the North
Artefact-rich exhibits on the geology, history, culture and trivia of Alaska adorn the interconnecting rooms of one of the state's best museums. *www.uaf. edu/museum*

Morris Thompson Cultural & Visitors Center
This ingenious mix of Alaskan history museum, info point and cultural center is in a modern building in Fairbanks' low-key downtown. *www. morristhompson center.org*

NEW BELGIUM BREWERY

500 Linden St, Fort Collins, Colorado;
www.newbelgium.com; +1 970 221 0524

- ◆ Food
- ◆ Family
- ◆ Tour
- ◆ Bar
- ◆ Takeout
- ◆ Transport

In 1988, a Fort Collins engineer named Jeff Lebesch lugged a mountain bike and a beer lover's pocket guide over to Belgium, cycled across the country, jotted down some Belgian beer-making tips and piqued Flemish curiosity with his bike's 'fat tires'. Three years later, Jeff and Kim Jordan co-founded New Belgium with a brewing operation set up in their basement and a label designed by their next-door neighbor. The beers born from the seminal bike tour? The Trappist Dubbel Abbey and, of course, the iconic Fat Tire.

Today, the sustainably driven, employee-owned mother-ship is top of tourists' to-do lists, with a perpetually packed-out taproom and quirky tours that fill up weeks in advance. And no wonder – they start with a beer, they pause halfway through for a beer, and they finish with a beer. Yes, you'll be pleasantly buzzed by the end, but still sober enough to take in the highlights, in particular the head-spinning sour room, where wild ales are aged in former wine barrels, and the pilot brewery, where the experimental Lips of Faith batches are created. Don't leave without sampling a malty amber Fat Tire, fresh from the tap. And if Fort Collins is too far for you, New Belgium's traveling carnival of beer, bikes and music, the Tour de Fat, might come to you.

THINGS TO DO NEARBY

Fort Collins Bike Share
Cruising town on two wheels with Fort Collins' bike share, you can explore downtown and riverside trails and, of course, bike to the brew. *bike.zagster.com/fortcollins*

Horsetooth Mountain & Reservoir
Get ready for action: stand-up paddleboarding, hiking, rock climbing and 30 miles (40km) of singletrack for mountain bikers. Cool off post-fun in the reservoir. *www.co.larimer.co.us*

Cache la Poudre River
The most scenic stretch of Rocky Mountain paradise nearby, the Poudre beckons with whitewater adventure, fly fishing, hiking and outdoor shows at the Mishawaka. *www.poudreheritage.org*

Colorado Room
A good pit stop on your Fort Collins bike tour, this casual eatery serves delectable sliders (try the bison), Rocky Mountain oysters and gravy-smothered poutine. *www.thecoloradoroom.com*

ODELL BREWING CO.

800 E Lincoln Ave, Fort Collins, Colorado;
www.odellbrewing.com; +1 970 498 9070

◆ Food   ◆ Tour   ◆ Takeout
◆ Family   ◆ Bar   ◆ Transport

If you love the smell of hops crushed between your fingertips, you'll love this small-batch Western brewer. Fort Collins' first craft start-up, Odell began in 1989, with keg deliveries made to local bars from the back of co-founders Doug and Wynne's yellow pickup. Over 25 years later, the focus is still on hoppy aromas (it boasts one of the USA's largest hop backs) and damn good unpasteurized ales.

The kick-back taproom and outdoor patio here – food truck included – will certainly hold your attention for as long as it takes you to get through the 21 beers on tap, divided into pilot projects, classics and local faves. Having trouble deciding? Hop on Odell's flavor wagon with its big, balanced 7% IPA.

THINGS TO DO NEARBY

Soapstone Prairie
Mountain-bike or hoof it through Colorado's rolling prairie, where the bison and antelope roam, and the Rockies cap a spectacular big-sky backdrop. *www. fcgov.com/naturalareas/ finder/soapstone*

Phantom Canyon Preserve
Spot bald eagles and red-tailed hawks in this little-known roadless sanctuary northwest of Fort Collins. There are only two ways into the canyon: on a guided tour or as a volunteer.

STUMPTOWN BREWERY

15045 River Rd, Guerneville, California;
www.stumptown.com; +1 707 869 0705

◆ Food   ◆ Bar
◆ Family ◆ Transport

THINGS TO DO NEARBY

Nimble & Finn's
Swanky sweets are served up at this ice cream shop. Flavors change seasonally, but expect innovative options, such as lavender honeycomb and strawberry buttermilk. *www. nimbleandfinns.com*

Armstrong Redwoods State Natural Reserve
While Guerneville used to be known as Stumptown due to logging, Armstrong Reserve was mercifully spared the ax. Impressive redwoods provide shade for strolls. *www.parks.ca.gov*

Johnson's Beach
Beach revelers delight in this small stretch of sand along the river, where you can rent kayaks, paddleboats, canoes and umbrellas. It's also ideal for camping. *www. johnsonsbeach.com*

Rainbow Cattle Company
Guerneville has been welcoming the Bay Area's LGBT population since the '70s. Embrace history and play some pinball and shuffleboard at this well-loved and friendly gay bar. *www.queersteer.com*

The folks at Stumptown Brewery have a cheeky attitude that permeates the small brewpub, where bathrooms are designated 'Chicks' or 'Dicks', and some of the brews come with some fairly racy names. If you're easily offended, this may not be your scene. But for the open-minded beer adventurer, this is the place to be, with the deck being Stumptown's biggest draw – the sun-drenched beer garden is the largest in Guerneville. It overlooks a grassy stretch of shoreline along the Russian River, where it hosts casual kickball games as well as bigger fetes, such as the annual Russian River Beer Revival and BBQ Cook Off. Back inside, the dimly lit establishment boasts a full bar, featuring four of its own drafts as well as a handful of other beers from local breweries. The kitchen turns out hearty cuisine, such as smoked brisket sandwiches, garlic Asiago fries, and heaps of crispy bacon to garnish the Bloody Marys. Such offerings keep the clamoring brunch crowd happy, as do the well-balanced brews. Rat Bastard is the local favorite, an English-style Pale Ale. At 5.8% ABV, the Bastard isn't quite a session beer, but it's smooth enough to sip all day while lazing by the river.

DOUBLE MOUNTAIN BREWERY

8 Fourth St, Hood River, Oregon;
www.doublemountainbrewery.com; +1 541 387 0042

◆ Food ◆ Bar ◆ Transport
◆ Family ◆ Takeout

Double Mountain, a Hood River institution, continues to pump out super-hoppy beers both here and in its new Portland location. The Hood River brewpub taproom can be packed with outdoor recreationists, especially on the weekends when there's also live music, but despite the wait times and bustle, the pub feels friendly and laid-back. There's also the possibility of perfectly charred pizzas from the brick oven; try the Truffle Shuffle for a well-deserved carb boost after skiing or hiking in Columbia River Gorge. The beers hit the spot –

The Vaporizer, a dry-hopped pale ale, being one of Oregon's best. If you're lucky, you can try the Killer Green, a fresh hop IPA that you'll only find on tap for a few precious weeks during the fall.

THINGS TO DO NEARBY

Columbia River Gorge
Hike the many steep and lovely trails that lead through canyons in this spectacular gorge, carved by floods and glaciers some 15,000 years ago.

Cathedral Ridge Winery
Stop by for a wine tasting (with or without cheese) and learn about the vintners in the area. Reservations required for a tour. *www. cathedralridgewinery.com*

PFRIEM

707 Portway Ave, Ste 101, Hood River, Oregon;
www.pfriembeer.com; +1 541 321 0490

◆ Food ◆ Bar
◆ Family ◆ Takeout

THINGS TO DO NEARBY

Hood River Fruit Loop
Take a self-guided driving tour of this cluster of farms and fruit stands, which sell everything from cherries and lavender to pumpkins and wine. *www.hoodriverfruitloop.com*

Cooper Spur Trail
Hike the flanks of glacier-covered Mt Hood during a steady, steep ascent that takes you to the edge of Eliot Glacier for some spectacular views.

Big Winds
Rent a stand-up paddleboard, a kiteboard, or a windsurf board, then head to the Columbia River and meet the gales of this world class, adrenaline-junkie destination. *www.bigwinds.com*

Mt Hood Meadows Ski Resort
Just 35 miles (56km) from town, this lift-served winter wonderland is open November to May. Keep an eye on upcoming events, including seasonal brew festivals. *www.skihood.com*

Ever since Pfriem opened its doors in 2012, the brewery has set a new bechmark for Oregon beers, inspired by some of the most revered Belgian styles. You can sense the dedication to beer and the culture of beer drinking when you step into the tasting room, which feels warm, homey and communal, despite the close proximity to the huge, gleaming fermenter tanks filled with beers in varying degrees of progress.

Josh Pfriem, the co-owner/brewer, says his beers are also Northwest – as well as Belgian – inspired, which leaves plenty of room for interpretation and experimentation. And yet, Josh excels at brewing the most classic styles, such as Pfriem's crisp and floral Pilsner. Enjoy a pint outdoors on the patio, which has a firepit, and order from a small Belgian-influenced menu, which shouldn't be underestimated: the food is well accomplished.

Tuck into a Mt Shadow pork chop with Yukon potato, winter squash, kale and apple hash, and a chanterelle demi-glace while enjoying the view across the street to Tom McCall Waterfront Park, which borders the mighty Columbia River, playground for windsurfers, kiteboarders, salmon, and seals. End your delightful meal with the Belgian-style Strong Blonde Ale, clovey and warm, with a smooth body and a slightly sweet finish.

LANIKAI

175 Hamakua Dr, Kailua, Hawaii;
www.facebook.com/lanikaibrewing

◆ Bar   ◆ Transport
◆ Takeout

THINGS TO DO NEARBY

Cruise the East Coast in a Mustang
Drop the top down, crank the tunes and hit the road north from Waikiki. Wind your way along O'ahu's eastern coastline for a spectacular drive. *www.mustang-hire.com/Waikiki.aspx*

Mokulua Islands Kayak Tour
Get the blood pumping and explore these small islands off the Kailua coast on a five-hour paddle. Definitely something to do *before* your brewery visit! *www.twogoodkayaks.com/guided-tour.html*

Kailua Beach Park
This wide arc of white sand drapes the turquoise waters of Kailua Bay, bookended by volcanic headlands and lined with swaying palm trees: the ultimate place to chill.

Diamond Head
This sacred peak and dramatic backdrop for Waikiki Beach is ideal to climb for catching the sunrise, sunset, or just the best view of this stunning coastline.

When you try to conjure up what a small craft brewery in Hawaii should look like, then you're probably picturing something pretty close to this cool set-up. Lanikai is located in a little side alley in the town of Kailua on the island of O'ahu. There's no telephone number and the front of the brewery is fairly basic, with a small sign that justifies the delicious beery smell that wafts out onto the street.

The back of the brewery overlooks a lush green valley, and you'll most likely find owner Steve fussing over his shiny new brew tanks, his hair still dripping wet from his morning surf. There isn't much space to hang out, but there is a small tasting room where you can try the Lanikai range, which is all crafted using unique Hawaiian herbs and botanicals. The Moku Imperial IPA (infused with the native *pikake*, a white flower usually associated with Hawaiian leis) is a local hibiscus and honey saison that sits at a dangerous 8.1% but goes down like fine nectar. But the don't-miss beer is the smooth-as-silk Pillbox Porter, brewed with two different types of vanilla strains (from The Big Island and Tahiti).

MAUI BREWING COMPANY

605 Lipoa Parkway, Kihei, Hawaii;
www.mauibrewingco.com; +1 808 213 3002

◆ Food   ◆ Bar
◆ Tour   ◆ Takeout

THINGS TO DO NEARBY

Snorkeling
Turtles and tropical fish thrive in the Maui surf. Rent a mask and fins then kick off from shore. Top spots include Ulua Beach and Maluaka Beach.

Da Kitchen Express
For a filling Hawaiian lunch that tastes great and won't break the bank, head to Da Kitchen Express. The Kalua pork is always a good idea. *www.dakitchen.com*

Hawaiian Islands Humpback Whale National Marine Sanctuary
Humpback whales breed off the coast from late November through April. Learn about the leviathians and see what you can spot from the oceanfront deck.

Keawakapu Beach
Extending from south Kihei to Wailea's Mokapu Beach, this is a less crowded spot to take a stroll, practice yoga in the soft sand atch the sunset.

Visitors wear beer goggles – literally – while touring Maui Brewing Co in Kihei. They're a fun and protective touch for groups heading into the 42,000 sq-ft production facility, which opened its big garage doors in 2015. Perched on 5 acres in a technology park in the shadows of Haleakalā volcano, this glossy facility doesn't look very Hawaiian. But step inside. Flip-flops (called *slip-pahs*) are the footwear of choice, and 'alohas' are warm. And the beers? From the Pineapple Mana Wheat to the Coconut Hiwa Porter, they embrace local ingredients. And with two-dozen or so different beers on tap, you won't go thirsty. Food trucks are parked nearby, and after a day of tropical adventuring, it's the perfect spot to kick back and toast the island life.

Maui Brewing is a celebration of all things Hawaiian, a primary goal of founder Garrett Marrero. A San Diego native, Marrero decided during a Maui vacation in the mid-2000s that the Valley Isle needed a brewery. After closing his financial consulting business, Marrero crafted a brewery business plan: to produce quality beer, operate sustainably, respect the local community and encourage the enjoyment of life. Start your enjoyment with the popular Bikini Blonde, an easy-sipping lager.

DOGFISH HEAD BREWERY

6 Cannery Village Center, Milton, Delaware;
www.dogfish.com; +1 302 684 1000

◆ Food   ◆ Bar
◆ Tour   ◆ Takeout

Dogfish Head dominates Milton. That's largely down to the success of founder Sam Calagione, who is known for two things. One, starring in the *Brew Masters* TV series from 2010. And two, spinning out never-ending weird and wonderfully inventive concoctions like a beer-crazed pinball wizard. Take, for example, the Beer for Breakfast stout, brewed with Guatemalan cold press coffee (OK), Massachusetts maple syrup (right...) and Delaware's own pork based product, 'scrapple' (seriously?). But it works. Today, the brewery collaborates with partners in Italy and chefs such as Mario Batali, and is uniquely influential. A visit to the Milton taproom and a free tour shows exactly what Sam Calagione has achieved in the past 20 years. His 90 Minute IPA is one of the best, with pine-y hop and fruit flavours.

THINGS TO DO NEARBY

Edward H McCabe Nature Reserve
Canoe along the Broadkill River from Milton, wielding binoculars to spot the migratory songbirds that flock to the native trees in this watery sanctuary. *www.nature.org*

Milton Farmers' Market
Farmers' Markets are a great way of taking the pulse of a place. At Milton's, you can find anything from oysters to mushrooms, plus some great gelato. *www.miltondefarmersmarket.org*

BIG SKY BREWING CO.

5417 Trumpeter Way, Missoula, Montana;
www.bigskybrew.com; +1 406 549 2777

◆ Tour   ◆ Takeout
◆ Bar

Missoula is a university city with a historic downtown in the mountainous American west. Surrounded by forest, plains and the Rockies, this is frontier country. Indeed, explorers Meriwether Lewis and William Clark passed by present-day Missoula in 1805. Neal Leathers, Bjorn Nabozney and Brad Robinson were similarly pioneering when they founded Big Sky Brewing and produced their first batch of beer, Whistle Pig Red Ale, almost two centuries later in 1995. Now based conveniently close to Missoula's airport, Big Sky is best known for its malty Moose Drool brown ale. The taproom offers four free samples of the beers plus a view into the facility. Don't miss the benchmark-setting Ivan the Terrible, a 10% ABV Russian Imperial stout made with English hops and American malt then aged for four months in bourbon barrels.

THINGS TO DO NEARBY

Smokejumper Visitor Center
America's largest smokejumper base – those brave souls who parachute into the wilderness to fight fires all summer long – is here. Take a free tour to learn about their exploits.

Draught Works
Drop into this downtown brewpub for a beer or two. Due to lots of indoor and outdoor space, good beers and a very welcoming buzz, it's the pick of the city's pubs. *www.draughtworksbrewery.com*

SURLY BREWING CO.

520 Malcolm Ave SE, Minneapolis, Minnesota;
www.surlybrewing.com, +1 763 999 4040

◆ Food ◆ Tour ◆ Transport
◆ Family ◆ Bar

THINGS TO DO NEARBY

Weisman Art Museum
Set in a swooping silver building by architect Frank Gehry, the galleries hold cool, hodgepodge collections of 20th-century American art, ceramics and Korean furniture.
www.wam.umn.edu

Stone Arch Bridge
This vintage bridge spans the Mississippi River and offers great views. It's part of a biking-hiking path that loops by small waterfalls, mill ruins and parks.
www.stonearchbridge.com

Guthrie Theater
See a play in Minneapolis' top theater, or simply walk in the cobalt blue building to admire its stunning architecture, especially the cantilevered Endless Bridge. *www. guthrietheater.org*

Glam Doll Donuts
Visit this punk pink shop for some of the most popular and unique donuts in town. Kudos to the salted caramel and chocolate Calendar Girl.
www.glamdolldonuts.com

Sprawling beside train yards and steel grain silos, the enormity of Surly's mod-industrial complex will astound. Beyond the 300-seat beer hall striped with long communal tables, and the deck that spills outside through sliding glass doors, and the expansive fire pit-dotted patio, there is an enormous grassy lawn where dogs and kids romp, and a disc golf league takes place weekly. It's so big that half the building is in Minneapolis, while the other half is in its twin city St Paul. And the place still fills to capacity. The brewery launched in 2005, and expanded to this site in 2014. 'Anger fueled by the inability to find good beer' sparked the company's name, so the story goes. Surly's brews are always intense and aggressively hopped. Around 20 are on tap, including CynicAle, a Belgian-style saison; and Todd The Axe Man, a West Coast-style IPA named after the head brewer who plays guitar in a local metal band. Surly has already earned a place in history: it spurred Minnesota to change the law so that breweries could add taprooms – legislation known as the Surly Bill. Don't leave without trying Furious, the flagship American IPA–British ESB hybrid.

3 FLOYDS BREWING CO.

9750 Indiana Parkway, Munster, Indiana;
www.3floyds.com, +1 219 922 4425

◆ Food   ◆ Bar
◆ Tour   ◆ Takeout

THINGS TO DO NEARBY

18th Street Brewery
It's another industrial and graffitied brewery that's a favorite with beer aficionados, 7 miles (11km) north of 3 Floyds. The house-smoked sausages and double IPAs rock. *www.18thstreetbrewery.com*

Carmelite Shrines
Displaced Polish monks fleeing WWII built a series of fluorescent, sponge-rock shrines at Munster's Carmelite Monastery. Open on Sundays April through October, or by appointment. *www.carmelitefathers.com*

Pullman National Monument
See a railroad capitalist's fallen utopia. The community's design and architecture make for a fascinating walkabout. Tours take in the historic sights. *www.nps.gov/pull*

Burnham Prairie Nature Preserve
The short trails on this 80-acre nature preserve are ideal for hiking and bird-watching. Herons, egrets and warblers don't seem to mind the surrounding industrial sites.

Arriving at the drab gray brew-house, in a middle-of-nowhere industrial park under a Podunk water tower, it's hard to believe some of the world's most sought-after beers flow from here.

But 3 Floyds is 'not normal,' as the motto goes. Heavy metal music blares. Neon-hued, *Dungeons & Dragons*-type art hangs on the walls. There are no rustic barn wood tables or cozy beer bottle chandeliers. Instead there are burly beards and tattoo sleeves all around. And hoppy suds.

3 Floyds has earned its cult following by brewing with tons of weird hops. Beer geeks drive for miles for pints of Zombie Dust, a flowery pale ale, or Gumballhead, an orangey wheat ale. Brothers Nick and Simon and their father Mike Floyd opened the brewery in 1996. They're expanding the site to produce 100,000 barrels annually

and to distill spirits, including a Dark Lord whiskey.

Which brings us to the most important date on 3 Floyds' calendar: Dark Lord Day (the last Saturday in April). Try to time your pilgrimage for this bacchanalian festival celebrating the release of Dark Lord: a Russian Imperial Stout made with coffee, Mexican vanilla and Indian sugar; available just one day a year, it sells out in mere minutes.

LAGUNITAS BREWING COMPANY

1280 North McDowell Blvd, Petaluma, California;
www.lagunitas.com; +1 707 778 8776

◆ Food   ◆ Tour   ◆ Takeout
◆ Family   ◆ Bar

THINGS TO DO NEARBY

Marin French Cheese Company

Lean into Petaluma's farm-friendly vibe with a stop at this cute cheese shop. Nothing experimenta – just creamy Brie, Camembert and petit breakfast blends. *marinfrenchcheese.com*

Helen Putnam Regional Park

Walk off the beer and burger with an easy stroll through the green hills of Helen Putnam Regional Park. Like Lagunitas, this park is dog-friendly. *parks. sonomacounty.ca.gov*

Historic Downtown Petaluma

Neighboring towns saw historic buildings destroyed by the 1906 earthquake but Petaluma survived, making this shopping district a unique example of Victorian architecture.

Central Market

Farm-to-table fare is served in the rustic-meets-upscale dining room of Central Market, where ingredients come from the owners' farm and everything is made in-house. *www.centralmarket petaluma.com*

You wouldn't expect to find a world-class taproom in a glorified suburban parking lot, but Lagunitas defies expectations. From its humble beginnings in 1993, Lagunitas has grown into a brewing giant, while managing to keep its generous and fun spirit intact. At the lively Petaluma taproom, friendly staff serve up hoppy brews and good food, with beef and lamb sourced from 'Lagu-meat-as', the Lagunitas-owned neighboring farm. In the dog-friendly beer garden, bands play, while scores of people and pooches lounge in the sun. The taproom is closed Monday and Tuesday, with the space donated to local nonprofit organizations, but tours of the brewery are still offered every day. Plan a weekday tour if possible to enjoy a stop into the brewery's original taproom, a charm-ingly slap-dash loft space where clocks are perpetually set to 4:20. After touring the facilities, where massive speakers blast rock & roll at vats of malting barley, head back to the main attraction – the bar. With dozens of options on tap, there's a beer here for every palate. Lagunitas was among the first microbreweries to produce an IPA as its flagship brew, and the hop-heavy blend is still a fan favorite and a great place to start.

ALLAGASH BREWING CO

50 Industrial Way, Portland, Maine;
www.allagash.com; +1 207 878 5385

◆ Tour
◆ Takeout

THINGS TO DO NEARBY

Novare Res Bier Cafe
Enjoy some 'fermented beverages' at Portland's venerable beer bar in the Old Port District. With 30 taps there's always something interesting to try. *www. novareresbiercafe.com*

Bikes and Brews Tour
Befitting one of the most cycle-friendly cities in the USA, Summer Feet Cycling offers a pedal-powered tour of Portland's breweries and distilleries including history and tastings. *www. summerfeet.net*

Portland Head Lighthouse
Encompassing Civil War history, a museum of navigation and an invigorating location at the mouth of the harbour, Maine's oldest lighthouse is a beacon. *www. portlandheadlight.com*

Casco Bay
Several operators offer sea kayaking trips around Casco Bay's pine-covered islands (weather permitting). It's a great way to tune into the local marine love (and try to spot a lobster).

How many breweries have their own house-strain of Brettanomyces yeast? Allagash, which specializes in Belgian-style beers, often using wild yeasts, does. What sets Portland, Maine, apart from its West Coast namesake is the fact that you'll only find the city's best brews here. That in itself merits a trip to the sea-sprayed northeast, especially when the tasting options include wonderful one-offs such as the dry-hopped, oak barrel-aged Golden Brett ale. The city also has the highest number of craft breweries per capita in the USA (beating Asheville and Portland, Oregon). The most famous of these is Allagash, which has long been ahead of the trend for sours and other Belgian-style brews. Inside its unprepossessing industrial unit in Portland's northern suburbs is a wild barrel room containing a vast array of beers, some flavoured with local fruits such as raspberries and cherries. But there's none of the monastic secrecy of an actual abbey here: free daily tours, seven days per week (book online) include tastings of four samples. You can buy (but not drink) more beers in the shop. They're all interesting, but look out especially for the funky Cuvee d'Industrial, aged in French and American oak barrels.

BISSELL BROTHERS BREWING CO.

4 Thompsons Point, Portland, Maine;
www.bissellbrothers.com; +1 207 808 8258

◆ Bar   ◆ Takeout
◆ Transport

THINGS TO DO NEARBY

International Cryptozoology Museum
Fascinated by the Loch Ness Monster, Bigfoot and other elusive creatures? Then this Thompsons Point museum – like Nessie, the only one of its kind in the world – is for you!

Arts District
Downtown Portland's arts quarter is being revitalised by new restaurants, galleries, museums (including the excellent Portland Museum of Art) and housing for a growing and vibrant community.

LL Bean
Need new (warmer) footwear at 3am? Maine-based LL Bean's flagship Outlet Store is in Freeport, 20 minutes' drive north. And yes, it's open 24hrs a day. *www.llbean.com*

OTTO
For some excellent, crispy-based pizza after your beer tasting, OTTO has multiple locations in downtown Portland and some deliciously original toppings. *www. ottoportland.com*

In their new home on Thompsons Point, the Bissell Brothers have space for a vast, airy taproom (complete with a mezzanine that overlooks the business end of the brewery) decorated with street art murals and wood beams, plus an outdoor area and space for food trucks. It's about three miles across town from downtown Portland, or join the Fore River Parkway trail if cycling. The venue cements the Brothers' reputation as running one of Maine's must-visit breweries.

Head brewer Noah Bissell seems to understand that it is better to do a few things very well than be a jack of all trades. So, the range of Bissell Brothers beers is relatively small but perfectly formed. Its hit hop-forward IPA, The

Substance, is a mainstay of the local beer scene. The alternative IPA, The Reciprocal, is a great example of a hazy, northeastern IPA - powerfully dry, and heady with tropical fruits (pineapple, mango, grapefruit), thanks to hops from the southern hemisphere. The Swish is a punchy double IPA available from October to April and eagerly awaited by its fans. They're all great – so good in fact that it is hard to find them outside the state of Maine.

BREAKSIDE BREWERY

820 NE Dekum St, Portland, Oregon;
www.breakside.com; +1 503 719 6475

◆ Food ◆ Bar ◆ Transport
◆ Family ◆ Takeout

Breakside's head brewer, Ben Edmunds, doesn't shy away from experimentation. There was that year he freeze dried fresh hops to make an outstanding fresh hop ale; he collaborates with chefs to make one-off beers with ingredients such as peppers and tomatoes; and he tries to mimic ice creams through beer.

He also makes some of Oregon's juiciest and most balanced IPAs, including the Breakside and Wanderlust. The Dekum pub is the place to taste his latest creations. It's a small wedge of a space with long communal wooden picnic tables on the sidewalk: the perfect spot for cyclists after their rides, and for families with lemonades and crayons. Don't leave without trying Edmunds' dessert-like Salted Caramel Stout.

THINGS TO DO NEARBY

Bushwacker Cider
Across the street from Breakside, this cider lover's mecca has 200 ciders in bottles and 12 on tap. Order your pint then play a round of pool. *www.bushwhacker cider.com*

Tamale Boy
Expertly wrapped in corn husks or banana leaves, these tamales are a delicious Portland interpretation of the Mexican staple. Don't miss the outdoor firepit. *www. tamaleboy.com*

COMMONS BREWERY

630 SE Belmont St, Portland, Oregon;
www.commonsbrewery.com; +1 503 343 5501

◆ Food ◆ Takeout
◆ Bar ◆ Transport

The Commons is renowned as one of Portland's best breweries and the 13 taps in this tasting room will make you want to return for another round. Even though the beers are mostly low-alcohol ales brewed with European yeasts (sorry, no IPAs), you still won't make it through the list in one visit. And you'll want to. The tasting room oozes sophistication, with its exposed brick walls and high ceilings, and cheesemonger Steve Jones helps curate the cheese pairings, so foodies won't be disappointed. Because of the brewery's proximity to downtown (just across the river), it can get crowded, especially on the weekends. But it's worth the visit for the famed Urban Farmhouse Ale, with its hint of flowers and grass, and a crisp finish.

THINGS TO DO NEARBY

Nong's Khao Man Gai
What started out as food trucks has become a famous brick-and-mortar restaurant that makes one special dish – Thai chicken and rice. And that's all you need. *www.khaomangai. com*

Eastbank Esplanade
Stroll along the Willamette River, which slices Portland into east and west. This riverside walkway offers great views of the city's glittering waterfront, prettiest at nightfall.

ECLIPTIC BREWING

825 North Cook St, Portland, Oregon;
www.eclipticbrewing.com; +1 503 265 8002

◆ Food ◆ Tour ◆ Takeout
◆ Family ◆ Bar ◆ Transport

Step inside this celestial- and interstellar-inspired brewery in North Portland, and you'll immediately notice orbs and constellations built into the sparse and modern architecture.

Oregon brewing legend John Harris (who got his start at Deschutes and also brewed for McMenamins and Full Sail) is the owner–brewer here, and he has a thing for astronomy. Order a pint (or a spiral-shaped taster tray) of beers named after stars and constellations, which usually equates to a taplist filled out with a stout, a sour, something barrel aged, and of course, an IPA. In chilly months, try the rich and chocolatey Capella Porter or during sunnier days, look for the Zenith Grapefruit Gose, a refreshing beer with a punch of citrus.

THINGS TO DO NEARBY

Por Que No
Come for the crave-worthy *carnitas* tacos, creamy *horchata*, punchy margaritas, and thick guacamole. The Bryan's Bowl brings it all together in a perfect medley. *www.porquenotacos.com*

Biketown
Portland's bike-share system has been operating since 2015 and this fleet of bright orange bikes are the perfect way to get around town. Bring your own helmet. *www.biketownpdx.com*

Widmer Brothers Brewing
One of Portland's founding breweries is just down the hill. Try the beer it's famous for: the American-style Hefeweizen; brewed across the street, it doesn't get any fresher. *www.widmerbrothers.com*

Loyly
Relax in this gorgeous communal sauna and steam room, inspired by Scandinavia. Add a spa treatment, such as a Swedish massage, to enhance your visit. *www.loyly.net*

From the outdoor patio, you can watch cars whiz across the arch of the Fremont Bridge with the sparkling lights of the west side as a backdrop. You'll find yourself among a varied crowd: Portland Trailblazer fans on the way to a game, coworkers happy at happy hour, and families having early dinners in the dining room. Don't miss the barrel-aged Orange Giant Barleywine, a potent belly-warmer that's perfect on the darkest, wettest days of Portland's winter.

BALLAST POINT TASTING ROOM AND KITCHEN

2215 India Street, San Diego, California;
www.ballastpoint.com; +1 619 255 7213

◆ Food   ◆ Tour   ◆ Takeout
◆ Family ◆ Bar   ◆ Transport

The Little Italy neighbourhood on the north side of San Diego is a long-established gourmet quarter but there's more to it than Italian delis and pizza joints. Ballast Point brewery celebrated its 20th anniversary in 2016, though its founding owner, Jack White (no, not that one), had sold and left the company by then to start a distillery. With this central and lively location (one of six), Ballast Point has become one of the most popular, family-friendly beer destinations in San Diego, with a large line-up of beverages to taste and a menu of burgers, tacos and snacks.

The brewery's signature Sculpin is a deliciously fruity IPA with mango and peach flavours – arguably one of the best in the US. The sculpin is a fish with a strong sting; beware the beer's 7% ABV.

THINGS TO DO NEARBY

Farmers' Markets
Enjoy artisan foods and local produce at San Diego's weekly Farmers' Market in Little Italy on Saturday mornings (and is in North Park on Thursday afternoons). *www. sdweeklymarkets.com*

USS Midway Museum
You can't miss it: the colossal aircraft carrier moored downtown. Now a museum, complete with airplanes, the Midway is San Diego's number one sight: this is a Navy town, after all. *www.midway.org*

MODERN TIMES

3000 Upas St, San Diego, California;
www.moderntimesbeer.com; +1 619 269 5222

◆ Family   ◆ Takeout
◆ Bar   ◆ Transport

THINGS TO DO NEARBY

San Diego Zoo
Regarded as one of the best zoos in the world, San Diego Zoo pioneered open-air, cageless enclosures, though that didn't stop Mundu the koala escaping in 2014.
zoo.sandiegozoo.org

San Diego Natural History Museum
Learn about the local ecosystems and southern California wildlife at this excellent museum in Balboa Park. It also hosts camps, hikes and whale-watching tours. ***www.sdnhm.org***

North Park Beer Co
Handsome Arts & Crafts-inspired style with a selection of house-brewed beers, including a red ale, pale ale and a stout. Mastiff Sausage Co provides the pork-based sustenance.
www.northparkbeerco.com

San Diego Velodrome
Into beer? Then you might also like bikes (the type you pedal). Check out some track racing in Balboa Park at one of three velodromes in southwest USA.
www.sdvelodrome.com

Modern Times may be a relatively recent addition to San Diego's enviable beer scene but it won a 'best new brewery' accolade from RateBeer in its first year. Founder Jacob McKean's self-proclaimed mission is to run one of the best breweries in the world – and having started his beer career at Stone (see over), he's seen one in action. But McKean, although a keen home brewer, doesn't get involved in the process at Modern Times, leaving it to his experts, who include beer guru Michael Tonsmeire, aka the Mad Fermentationist (check his blog for the low-down on home brewing). They've developed a highly regarded range of four year-round brews, supplemented by a seasonal rotation that includes a pale ale for summer and an autumnal rye IPA.

Modern Times' original taproom, the Point Loma Fermentorium has a funky interior but is in an out-of-the-way part of town. The latest tasting room, the Flavordome, is in smart North Park, where there's a bit more going on in the neighbourhood. Its must-try beer? The Black House oatmeal coffee stout, made with beans from Modern Times in-house roastery (one pound of coffee is enough for 46 gallons of beer if you want to try it at home).

© Modern Times

STONE BREWING

1999 Citracado Parkway, Escondido, San Diego, California;
www.stonebrewing.com; +1 760 294-7899

◆ Food ◆ Bar ◆ Transport
◆ Tour ◆ Takeout

THINGS TO DO NEARBY

California Center for the Arts
This concert hall, theatre and museum in Escondido hosts a ton of entertaining events including regular jazz jams and a Day of the Dead Festival.
www.artcenter.org

Cruisin' Grand
On warm Friday nights from April to September, Escondido's Grand Avenue is filled with a parade of pre-1970s automobiles, from hot rods to classic cars.
www.cruisingrand.com

Surf Encinitas
Enticing Encinitas, 20 miles from Escondido, is a classic Californian surf town, with boards in every garage. Famous waves include Cardiff Reef, Swamis and D Street but there are breaks all along the coast.

Legoland California
For families and grown-up fans of making cool stuff out of little plastic blocks, Lego has its California theme park 20 miles away in Carlsbad.
www.legoland.com

Stone's story starts with founders Greg Koch and Steve Wagner's homebrews in the early 1990s. The pair set up their first microbrewery in 1996 and were early advocates of the bigger, hoppier IPA styles that are now hugely popular. 'It was a passion project,' says Greg Koch. However, back then these beers were a tougher sell. Persistence has paid off, however, and Stone is the 10th largest craft producer in the USA and one of the pioneers of the classic West Coast IPA. The Stone empire includes the World Bistro and Gardens here (known as much for its exceptional food as its beer), an outpost in Berlin (see p171) and, in 2018 Stone's 99-room hotel will open in Escondido – room service includes growler delivery.

Greg Koch describes Stone as a seminal band that continuously reinvents itself. If it's a band, then its hits include the Ruination Double IPA with its off-the-chart hops. 'We have often pushed the boundaries when it comes to aromatic and flavorful hop bitterness,' says Koch. Stone also uses local ingredients, such as parsley, sage, rosemary and thyme in their Dogfish Head/Victory/Stone Saison du BUFF. Recently, the famed Arrogant Bastard Ale on was sent on tour, sharing the recipe with small craft breweries (such as Bootleg, p247) around the world.

RUSSIAN RIVER BREWING COMPANY

725 4th St, Santa Rosa, California;
www.russianriverbrewing.com; +1 707 545 2337

◆ Food   ◆ Bar   ◆ Transport
◆ Family   ◆ Takeout

THINGS TO DO NEARBY

Kunde Family Winery
Pack a picnic and check
out Kunde Family Winery,
where you can take a
'hike and taste' four-hour
tour across its 1850-acre
estate. ***www.kunde.com***

Charles M Schulz Museum
Snoopy, Charlie Brown and
the gang are celebrated
in this sweet museum,
home to the world's largest
collection of original
Peanuts artwork.
schulzmuseum.org

**Luther Burbank
Home & Gardens**
Get back to nature with a
stroll around the stunning
gardens of Luther Burbank,
a famed horticulturist who
created more than 800
new plant varieties. ***www.
lutherburbank.org***

Spinster Sisters
Fresh, locally sourced food
is served up in this quaint
eatery, where the work of
local artists adorns the
walls, and a lending library
is prominently featured.
thespinstersisters.com

In Sonoma County, beer and wine exist alongside each other in fermented harmony. Nowhere is this more apparent than at Russian River Brewing Company. Established by Korbel, makers of ubiquitous sparkling wines, RRBC was sold to brewmaster Vinnie Cilurzo and his wife Natalie in 2003. Since then, the Cilurzos have been brewing an impressive selection of stouts, Belgian-inspired ales, barrel-aged sours and, of course, IPAs.

These are served up at the hopping taproom in charming downtown Santa Rosa, alongside pizzas, sandwiches and other suds-soaking fare. While the menu caters to meat-lovers and vegetarians alike, let's be honest – we're all here for the beer. Indecisive imbibers can relax and enjoy a massive sampler, featuring all 18 draft beers. The most infamous of its offerings is Pliny the Younger,

a triple IPA; its annual February release incites unprecedented levels of excitement, as people line up around the block to get a taste. While the younger Pliny enjoys an extremely limited release, the flagship double IPA can be enjoyed year-round. Notes of citrus and pine and a clean finish make it clear why Pliny the Elder, named for an ancient Roman philosopher, has such a thoughtful following; see what you think of it.

PIKE PUB & BREWERY

1415 1st Ave, Seattle, Washington;
www.pikebrewing.com; +1 206 622 6044

◆ Food ◆ Tour ◆ Takeout
◆ Family ◆ Bar ◆ Transport

THINGS TO DO NEARBY

Pike Place Market
The hive of Seattle sits just outside the Pike Pub's doors from where it buzzes daily with fish throwers, buskers, flower-sellers, artisan cheese-makers and thick crowds.
www.pikeplacemarket.org

Gum Wall
One of Seattle's most disgusting yet alluring sights, the gum wall is an ever-changing communal art exhibit that invites passing gum-chewers to furnish it with well-masticated morsels.

Seattle Art Museum
Seattle's underrated art museum is a three-site affair, with a downtown HQ known for its strong representation of abstract, Native American and Pacific Northwest art. ***www. seattleartmuseum.org***

Seattle Great Wheel
For good rotating views of Seattle's spruced up waterfront and its background islands and mountains, grab a pod in this giant Ferris wheel. ***www.seattlegreatwheel. com***

Standing at the vanguard of the North American microbrewery revolution, the family-owned Pike Pub opened in Seattle's famous Pike Place Market in the late 1980s, when 'mullet' hairstyles were still high fashion and drinkers were more interested in pairing their beer with cigarettes than sustainable grass-fed hamburgers in gluten-free buns. Representing the market's simple but religiously expounded philosophy of 'meet the producer' (free brewery tours are offered), the Pike has been shaping new tastes ever since. Its handcrafted beer is concocted from local Yakima Valley hops in a busy multilevel space that incorporates beer-making equipment, quirky hanging bicycles and a unique museum that explains, via 9000 years of beer history, how microbrewing has become such a cool international phenomenon. Reflecting the increasing sophistication of craft brewer-

ies, the Pike's expert bar staff act like seasoned oenologists, talking you through the beer's taste notes while helping pair its signature brews with gourmet pub grub. For a step up from the default Pale Ale, try Pike's XXXXX Stout, a heavy Guinness-like drink with an appealing dark chocolate flavor that not only offsets the effects of a slow soaking in Seattle's drizzle, but also acts as a perfect accompaniment to the local Puget Sound oysters.

POPULUXE BREWING

826b NW 49th St, Seattle, Washington;
www.populuxebrewing.com; +1 206 706 3400

◆ Food   ◆ Bar   ◆ Transport
◆ Family   ◆ Takeout

Microbreweries too large for you? Emulating Seattle's innovative coffee bars, the latest trend in beer culture is for downsizing. The city's nano-brewing movement began like a secret club pioneered by beer-geeks and weekend warriors, keen to ferment high quality small-batch beers that emphasized fun and creativity over profits. One of its most enlightened members is Populuxe Brewing, a tiny beer factory with a dedicated following in Ballard. On entering its limited-hours taproom with rotating menu of around 10 pot-luck beers, you'll feel as if you've gate-crashed an after-hours pub party where everyone knows everyone else. Pull up a stool, line your stomach from the local food trucks parked outside and – weather permitting – enjoy an alfresco game of cornhole.

THINGS TO DO NEARBY

Nordic Heritage Museum
Despite its plethora of bars, Ballard wasn't built on beer, but on the backs of hard-working Nordic immigrants. This excellent museum relates their coming-to-America stories.
www.nordicmuseum.org

Hiram M Chittenden Locks
Watch birds, fishing boats, motor yachts, kayaks and salmon negotiating the locks on a sunny evening from the grassy banks of Carl English Jr Botanical Gardens. Bliss.

COPPERTAIL

2601 East 2nd Ave, Tampa, Florida;
www.coppertailbrewing.com; 1 813 247 1500

◆ Food   ◆ Tour   ◆ Takeout
◆ Family   ◆ Bar   ◆ Transport

Coppertail is the name of a sea monster that lives in Tampa Bay. Or at least, that's what this brewery founder's five-year-old daughter thought when the name was conceived in 2013. Her imagination inspired a fantastical set of illustrations emblazoned on its beer bottles and taproom walls. The brewery's raison d'être is to produce flavorful beers for the Florida lifestyle: think thirst-quenchers with bursts of citrus, designed to be paired with seafood, spice and barbecue. Attitude and humor are core traits of the brewery and its beer branding, so when you visit you might find Wheat Stroke, a citrusy American wheat ale, or Dark Swim, a porter that goes down 'like a midnight dip in the warm Gulf waters off St Pete Beach'. Coppertail likes to keep things simple with tried-and-tested old-world brewing techniques, so it only uses natural carbonation, whole leaf hops, and doesn't filter its beers. Its cavernous Ybor City taproom is a hive of activity. Try the Free Dive IPA, packed with citrus flavor and pine aromas.

THINGS TO DO NEARBY

Stand-up Paddleboarding
This is a very zen way to glide across Tampa's harbour, feel the bath-warm water between your toes and perhaps spy local stingrays and dolphins.
www.urbankai.com

Brew Bus
Sign up for a guided tour of three to four local breweries, or the Local Loop hop-on/off option around Ybor City and Seminole Heights on Sundays.
www.brewbususa.com

Beer's not usually the first option when it comes to pairing alcohol with food, but beyond the beer and hotdog, there are some surprising and downright perfect combinations to consider.

LAMBIC FRUIT BEER WITH DARK CHOCOLATE

The tart, dry tang of a Lambic fruit beer (a cherry or raspberry, but avoid the sweeter varieties) cuts through the richness of the chocolate, but is itself softened – the balance is a real hit. Make it a chocolate fondant and you'll have dessert heaven.

VINDALOO & A HOPPY IPA

Vindaloo curries blend spices with a vinegar edge, not a subtle dish by any stretch of the imagination. Fight fire with fire and crack a solid American IPA (a Stone IPA from California would be great). The vivid hoppy bitterness provides a meeting point for the tangy complexity of the curry. Luckily, you're in the middle!

PORTER & BEEF BURGUNDY

Wine and beer, together at last! The rich unctuous French stew carries the moderate roasted maltiness of a porter (how about a Sierra Nevada Porter?) like a charm. It might be the faint edge of the wine that bonds so well to the warmth of the beer. A modern classic!

MARRIAGES M

COOPERS PALE ALE & A PIE FLOATER

Green label, green soup – the partnership begins. It continues; this cloudy pale is a refreshing, mild ale and sits well with the great Australian meat pie floating in a thick pea soup.

HEFEWEIZEN WITH JAMAICAN JERK CHICKEN

The unmistakeable tropical vibrancy of jerk chicken finds a great friend in a Hefeweizen – try a Schöfferhofer and you'll be struck by how well the subtle banana notes of the beer contribute to the theme – you'll be transported to a Caribbean island in a flash.

BELGIAN PALE ALE & STRONG HARD CHEESES

A strong English-style cheddar or perhaps an aged Comté from France meets the dry, intense Belgian pale – a Duvel would do the trick. Its deep flavours aren't overwhelmed by the cheese, and the dry finish leaves your palate fresh. Delicious.

WEIHENSTEPHANER HEFEWEISSBIER DUNKEL & TRUFFLES

Truffle-flavoured anything – scrambled eggs, pasta, a luxury burger ... that funky earthy flavour needs a little brightness, but the depth requires some body too. A dark wheat beer is unbeatable here, warm but not rich with subtle floral notes that elevate the truffle.

DE IN HEAVEN

PLOUGHMAN'S LUNCH & AN ENGLISH ALE

Some things just belong together – they're not mind-blowing, but they work together, avoiding stepping on each other's toes and make you happy. The mix of elements on a ploughman's lunch (cheese, pickles, bread, ham, onions) would challenge some beers, but find perhaps a St Peter's English Ale and marvel at its across-the-board just-rightness.

SALT & PEPPER SQUID WITH ANCHOR STEAM

It's the ultimate Vietnamese beer food: crispy, starch-battered, fried squid with chilli, coriander, five spice, white pepper and salt, and settling the palate with an ice-cold Anchor Steam to slice through the grease is a genuine summertime pleasure.

GUINNESS & OYSTERS NATURAL

It's an unlikely relationship, but the hearty stout heaviness matches the iodine-brininess of the oyster, a savoury-sweet explosion ensues. An absolute must-try

TOP 3 BEER TOWNS

SIA

TOKYO

Japan has embraced craft beer and its capital is packed with tiny bars celebrating the country's best brews. On your trip visit a micro pub strip – not so much for the variety of beers, but for the beery, good-times vibe. Nonbei Yokocho (Drunkard's Alley) in Shibuya is a unique experience.

HO CHI MINH CITY

With an annual craft beer festival, a plethora of micro-breweries (including Pasteur Street, see p130, and newly arrived East West Brewing) and enticing little bars, the quality beer revolution has revitalised Ho Chi Minh's drinking scene. Beer tourists will be spoiled for tasty snacks too.

BĚIJĪNG

China has not been slow to start its own craft beer scene, which is centred on its capital. The thriving array of breweries is led by Great Leap (see p103), which is located down one of the city's historic *hutongs* (alleyways), symbolising the merging of the old and the new.

CHINA

How to ask for a beer in local language?
Qǐng gěi wǒ yìbēi píjiǔ
How to say cheers? Gānbèi!
Signature beer style? Pale lager
Local bar snack? Charcoal-grilled meat skewers
Don't: If drinking in a group, don't fill your own glass up but wait for your companion to fill it, and then fill theirs

Beer, like many things, has a long history in China; some would argue, as long as the history of China itself. In 2016, archaeologists discovered residue from ceramic vessels uncovered in Shaanxi province that proved the Chinese were brewing barley-based beer some 5000 years ago. Oracle bones have shown that beer was used in rituals and funeral rites as early as the Xia dynasty, sometime before 1600 BC. Early modern breweries were set up in China by the Russians, Japanese, Czechs and Germans, and it was the latter who established the most successful brewery in China: Tsingtao Brewery. During China's opening up

to the west in the 1970s and '80s, some of the first and most successful international joint ventures were breweries, and this led to there being a plethora of local breweries producing beer in every corner of China. Though there wasn't much variety as to the style of the beer (almost all were 2-4% pale lagers), the drink became an absolute staple at the Chinese banquet dinner, and every city and region proudly boasted that their local beer was the best.

Over time, Western expats became more and more embedded in China's social fabric, and they brought with them a desire for variety in the beer they were drinking. Some, such as American Carl Setzer of Great Leap, began home brewing or partnered with locals who shared a passion for beer. This movement was felt most strongly in Běijīng, where space is not at a premium and disused *hutong* (alleyway) spaces were available for conversion into

TOP 5 BEERS

- **Yama Sichuan Porter** Moonzen
- **Yunnan Amber** Great Leap
- **First Immortal DIPA** Slow Boat
- **Heroic Water, Imperial River Pale Ale** Master Gao
- **Ringside Red** Boxing Cat

nano-breweries and tasting rooms. The brewing scene has thrived with China's continued economic expansion, with brewers using local ingredients and even branching out into the hop-growing business.

Understandably, the craft beer movement has grown up most easily in cities with high populations of western expats – Běijīng, Shànghǎi, Chéngdū and Shēnzhèn have all been at the fore of the brewing scene. But Chinese tastes for beer variety have grown as the middle class has expanded, and now a contingent of young, in-the-know Chinese can be found drinking alongside expats and even dominating the scene in craft beer bars around the country.

The first types of craft beers to be made in China drew on the country's German brewing heritage, and later, micro-breweries produced beers that were primarily American in style – juicy IPAs and pale ales were an easier sell than darker beers and high-ABV bombshells. But as the brewing scene has developed, brewers have pushed the limits and incorporated Chinese ingredients, such as Sichuan peppercorn, local honey, Osmanthus flower and Chinese tea, to create some truly exciting beers. And now, even in the country's far-flung reaches, Qīnghǎi and Sìchuān on the Tibetan plateau and Gānsù in the Gobi Desert, you'll find locals brewing in small batches, using the fresh mountain water, barley and odd fruits such as wolfberry, to create some of the world's most unusual and exciting brews.

GREAT LEAP BREWING

6 Doujiao Hutong, Di'Anmenwai Ave, Dongcheng, Běijīng;
www.greatleapbrewing.com; +86 010 5717 1399

◆ Food   ◆ Transport
◆ Bar

THINGS TO DO NEARBY

Forbidden City

The world's largest ancient palace and Běijīng's calling card, the Forbidden City housed the emperor and his staff during the Ming and Qing dynasties.
www.dpm.org.cn

Bell Tower & Drum Tower

Built in 1272 when Běijīng was under Mongol rule, these two resplendent towers held the bells and gongs that served as the city's official timekeepers.

Nanluogu Xiang Hutong

Formerly a ramshackle residential alley, this hutong is now packed with cafes, bars and shops. Venture into the quieter side alleys to see traditional Běijīng life.

Hòuhai Lakes

Go paddle-boating, cycling or ice skating in winter at Qiánhai, Hòuhai and Xīhai – three inter-connected lakes that form the centre of Běijīng's outdoor life.

Established by husband-and-wife partners Carl Setzer and Liu Fang in 2010, Great Leap was Běijīng's first craft beer success story. The name Great Leap (Da Yue) is drawn from a Song dynasty poem, which says you should take great leaps (risks) when you are young so that you can bounce back easily if you fail. When the couple decided to quit their high-paying jobs to open a craft brewery (Carl was originally a home-brewer whose beers became famous at local parties), Liu Fang's grandfather insisted they name it 'Da Yue'.

Great Leap's original location, Great Leap #6, is in a 110-year-old residence and former Qing dynasty library, down a hidden Běijīng hutong (alleyway) too narrow for cars. The tiny brewpub has 10 taps selling only Great Leap beer (plus their homemade ginger beer) and there's a courtyard where you can watch the Běijīng neighbourhood. Their most popular beers include the Iron Buddha Blonde, an ale infused with oolong tea; and the Little General IPA and Hop God 120 Imperial IPA, both made entirely with Chinese ingredients, including Qīngdao flower hops from Gānsù province. Try the Honey Ma Gold, which is brewed with Sìchuān peppercorn and Mùtiányù Great Wall honey.

MOONZEN BREWERY

2A New East Sun Bldg, 18 Shing Yip St, Kwun Tong,
Hong Kong; www.moonzen.hk; +852 611 305 51

◆ Tour

◆ Transport

Mexican-Hongkonger couple Laszlo and Michele Raphael started as home-brewers after meeting when they were both living in Běijīng in 2006.

Space is at a premium in Hong Kong and their operation has grown into a converted industrial space on the second floor of a Hong Kong warehouse, where the original home-brewing kit has been converted into the bathroom sink. You ascend in a huge cargo lift to one of the few breweries in the world operating on an upper floor, with all the ventilation and drainage challenges that presents.

The brewery, which you can visit by appointment to avail of the four taps, is fitted out with traditional Chinese decor that Laszlo and Michele have collected themselves. The name 'Moonzen' stands for 'door gods' – in Chinese folklore, these spiritual guardians of entrances attract good luck and fend off evil spirits. Moonzen's brews are themed around a deity; for example, the Yama Sichuan Porter is named for the king of the underworld and brewed with smoky cherry-wood malts and numbing Sichuan peppercorns and chillies. Don't leave without trying the Dragon King Fujian Radler: a saltwater IPA named for the undersea god, nodding to his favourite fruit, honey pomelos from Fujian province.

THINGS TO DO NEARBY

Hong Kong Global Geopark
Hike among eerily-shaped volcanic rocks, or up to a ridge for amazing South China Sea views in this Unesco-listed geopark in Hong Kong's New Territories. *www.geopark. gov.hk*

Kowloon Walled City Park
This leafy park covers a 19th-century walled garrison that was technically a Chinese enclave during the period of British rule in Hong Kong.

Chi Lin Nunnery
This 1930s temple was rebuilt in 1998 in Tang dynasty style, with interlocking wood pieces and no nails. Lunch at the temple's celebrated vegetarian restaurant, located behind a waterfall.

Ladies Market
Haggling skills can be honed at this chaotic yet atmospheric street market where you can pick up anything, from socks to tawdry Hong Kong souvenirs.

MASTER GAO BEER HOUSE

Boai Square, 8 Changjiang Back Street, Nanjing;
http://mastergaobeer.com; +86 25 8452 0589

◆ Food　　◆ Bar
◆ Takeout　◆ Transport

Gao Yan spent 14 years in New England, USA, learned the ins-and-outs of beer brewing there and decided to take this knowledge back home to Nanjing. Since then, he's written a (literal!) Chinese manual on home brewing and founded a brewery, Master Gao.

The early years were tough and the government twice shut him down but his persistence paid off and Gao now brews more than 100,000 cases of his famed jasmine green tea lager and Baby IPA with hopes of exporting the beer to the US. If you're in Nanjing, it's worth visiting one of his local bars. We love the courtyard stylings of the Boai Square branch. If the weather is good, pull up a pew outdoors and sink the slightly floral Jasmine Tea lager before moving on to the mildly hopped Baby IPA.

THINGS TO DO NEARBY

Purple Mountain Area
A large swathe of land known as the Purple Mountain area is home to key sights such as Sun Yat-Sen's Mausoleum and the serene Zixia Lake.

Nanjing Massacre Memorial Hall
A sobering but well thought-out museum and memorial to the victims of the Nanjing Massacre in 1937 when the Japanese invaded the city.
www.nj1937.org

BOXING CAT

Unit 26A, Sinan Mansions, 519 Middle Fuxing Rd, Shànghǎi; www.boxingcatbrewery.com

◆ Food　　◆ Bar
◆ Family　◆ Transport

Started in 2008, Boxing Cat now pours beers in three branches around Shànghǎi, plus its sister restaurant, Liquid Laundry. Although the beer is not brewed on-site, the Sinan Mansions pub is the perfect place to sample it, in the heart of the leafy French Concession. The feel here is distinctly American – with gumbo and southern fried chicken on the menu, the sleek decor inspired by US brew-pubs, and even the brewer, Michael Jordan, hails from the US. With extensive experience at breweries in Portland and Denmark, Jordan's collaboration brews and unusual ales – including one with tongue-numbing Sichuan peppercorns – make Boxing Cat one of Asia's most exciting breweries. For something a little less fiery, try the TKO IPA, a bitter, fragrant pint with an American hop punch.

THINGS TO DO NEARBY

Propaganda Poster Art Centre
There are thousands of original propaganda posters from the 1950s, '60s and '70s on show at this small gallery – a fascinating collection. ***www.shanghai propagandaart.com***

Shànghǎi Museum
You either need several hours here, or a carefully crafted plan of which of the calligraphy, art, furniture, sculpture, ceramic or costume galleries you'd like to see. ***www.shanghai museum.net***

JAPAN

How to ask for a beer in local language?
Biru kudasai ['Beer please.' Substitute 'biru' with a brand name if you know it]
How to say cheers? Kanpai!
Signature beer style? Pale lagers are ubiquitous
Local bar snack? Edamame beans
Don't: Pour your own beer when sharing a bottle or pitcher; pour for others and let them refill your glass

Japan may not have a long history of beer making, but beyond the commercial breweries, the spirit of *shokunin* has been brought to bear on our favourite craft.

Shokunin you ask? You might see it translated as craftsman or artisan, but there's a dimension to this appellation that defies a simple definition. If you've had any experience of Japanese craft or food, you can sense it – a focus, a care, a principle of doing something the right way, of respect, of quality ... everything you want in a beer, no doubt.

Beer hit Japan around 400 years ago, courtesy of Dutch traders, and for the following two centuries was predominantly limited to foreign consumption. But in the late 19th century, three breweries that now dominate the Japanese beer trade came into being – Kirin, Asahi and Sapporo.

Like most national brewers, the Japanese big boys (along with their more recent partner in prime time, Suntory) made mainstream pale lagers as their bread-and-butter style, but in recent years they've adopted some of the craft beer world's outlook, going for the occasional seasonal special.

But that's just marketing, right?

It's at the craft end of town where *shokunin* comes to the fore. Beer brewing in Japan was, until the early 1990s, limited to mass production – licenses were restricted to just the giants who could produce millions of litres of the stuff. But when volume requirements were lowered, allowing small brewers into the market, a free-for-all resulted in a hit-or-miss approach and a lot of low-quality 'craft' beer. This tarnished the reputation of small-scale brewing; it's only since the early 2000s that the craft scene has shone. Enter the *shokunin*!

There's no obvious variation in beer-making preference from region to region, but breweries tend to have been heavily influenced by either American brewing styles, or German. That said, it's a rare brewery that doesn't offer both a hefeweizen and an IPA.

The granddaddy of American-style craft beer in Japan is arguably Baird Brewing Company. Their own journey in many ways tells the story of Japanese craft brewing – pay them a visit and get the story from the horse's mouth, while you explore their balanced, fine beers. In amongst their seasonal offerings, be sure to sample the Rising Sun pale and the Suruga Bay Imperial IPA.

The new wave of Japanese craft beer arrived around 2010, this time following the American craft beer movement

TOP 5 BEERS

- **Wabi-Sabi Japan Pale Ale** Baird Brewing Company
- **Aooni Pale** Yo-Ho Brewing Company
- **Minoh Stout** AJI Beer Inc
- **Hitochino Nest Espresso Stout** Kiuchi Brewing
- **Coedo Shikkoku Schwarzbier** Coedo Brewery

By contrast, the award-winning Fujizakura brewery show-cases a fascination with German styles – try their Rauchbier, a solid, smoky nod to the style.

Hokkaido, the northernmost of Japan's islands is home to a surprisingly large number of brewers (and spiritual home of Sapporo as well). Hokkaido Brewing, for one, has an eclectic range of fruit beers, alongside a couple of more traditional ales. Back on the main island of Honshu, it's hard to go past Kiuchi Brewing and their line of Hitachino Nest beers. Think Western styles with Japanese traditional influence and ingredients – aged in *shochu* casks, made with yuzu or red rice ... genuinely unique and well-made beers.

The list of Japanese brewers is growing quickly now that the bar has been set by the first wave of quality brewers. There's an energy and enthusiasm in the community – but now it has the wisdom and patience that comes with a *shokunin* mindset.

BEER KOMACHI

444 Hachikencho, Higashiyama-ki, Kyoto;
www.beerkomachi.com; +81 75 746 6152

◆ Food   ◆ Transport
◆ Bar

THINGS TO DO NEARBY

Chion-in
For an insight into Japanese
Buddhism, explore the
massive Chion-in complex
where you can soak up
the spiritual atmosphere
of chanting monks and
wafting incense smoke.
www.chion-in.or.jp/e/

Shoren-in
This peaceful temple is a
beautiful spot to take time
out from sightseeing in
the Southern Higashiyama
district. Savour a bowl of
matcha tea overlooking the
stunning garden.

**Kyoto Municipal
Museum of Art**
Located in Okazaki Park,
this grand old museum
regularly hosts some top-
notch art exhibitions. The
pond behind the museum
makes a great setting for
a picnic.

Maruyama-kōen
Work up a thirst strolling
around the lovely
Maruyama Park, where
paths wind through
gardens, souvenir stalls
and a carp-filled pond in
the centre.

Located in the Furokawa-cho covered shopping
arcade in the middle of the Higashiyama sightseeing
district, Beer Komachi is a tiny, hidden-away drinking den
dedicated to promoting Japanese craft beer. With just a few
seats, concrete decor and plastic sheeting at the entrance
attempting to contain the smoke and smells of the cooking
wafting from the kitchen, this is a casual affair where
beer-loving tourists and locals mingle. There are usually
seven Japanese beers on tap and generally always one from
a local Kyoto brewery, such as the popular Belgian Wheat
Ale from the Kyoto Brewing Company. The menu of beers
on tap rotates on an almost daily basis and other favourites
might include the Hyogo Stout from Kinosaki or the Ozaru

IPA by Minoh Brewery in Osaka. You'll also find around 20
bottled beers, imported mainly from the US. The experience
is rounded out by the friendly and knowledgeable staff
and an excellent bar-food menu, with such delights as
fried chicken in beer batter, deep-fried tofu pizza, tempura
veggies made with a beer batter and even a stout chocolate
gateau for dessert. See if the hoppy, malty Ise Kadoya
Imperial Red Ale from the Mie prefecture is available.

KYOTO BREWING COMPANY

25-1 Nishikujyo, Takahatacho, Minami-ku, Kyoto;
www.kyotobrewing.com; +81 75 574 7820

◆ Food   ◆ Bar
◆ Family   ◆ Transport

The small tasting room of the Kyoto Brewing Company is a 15-minute walk from Kintetsu Jyujyo, the nearest train station, but well worth the trip. You'll find its beer in many Kyoto craft beer bars, but to chat to the English-speaking knowledgeable staff, peer through glass windows to the brewery vats and experience the friendly local atmosphere, it's best sampled at the brewery site. Inspired by American and Belgian beer styles, it usually has a line-up of six beers on tap, including some year-round beers, with a couple of limited releases and seasonal specials. There's usually a food truck on-site and the tasting room is open most weekends in summer; check the website. Try the Ichigo Ichie, a refreshing Belgian-style Saison with American and New Zealand hops.

THINGS TO DO NEARBY

Tō-ji
Established in 794 to protect the city, this fine temple complex with its 5-storey pagoda (the highest in Japan) is well worth a visit.

Kyoto Tower
Shoot up to the 15th-floor observation deck of this retro, rocket-like tower for sweeping city views – as far south as Osaka – from the free mounted binoculars.

HITACHINO NEST

1257 Kounsou, Naka-shi;
www.hitachino.cc/en; +81 (0)29 298 0105

◆ Food   ◆ Bar
◆ Tour   ◆ Transport

THINGS TO DO NEARBY

Kodokan School
Ibaraki prefecture's capital, Mito, was a power base of the ruling clan during Japan's Edo period (the culturally rich years from 1603 to 1868). Key sights include Kodokan School, the largest of the Edo era.

Kairaku-en Garden
One of Japan's three great gardens is in Mito. It was commissioned by the leader of the Mito clan, who had a penchant for plum trees: there are 3000 of them in 100 varieties around the landscaped gardens.

True Brew
Hitachino Nest's Mito pub, in the train station, has Hitachino Nest on tap, fresh from the nearby brewery, in addition to a selection of craft brews from around the world.
www.truebrew.cc

Beaches
The Pacific coast of Ibaraki is known for having some of Japan's best surfing beaches, such as Oarai, accessed by train from Mito. There are dozens of beaches to choose from, most with broad sweeps of sand.

Hitachino Nest's lucky owl logo has big ambitions In 2016, the Kiuchi brewery opened a taproom in San Francisco but if you want to taste Hitachino Nest beers where they're made, and experience the local culture, you have to go to Naka, a small, low-rise city lying a couple of hours northeast of Tokyo by car (or multiple changes of train) in the Ibaraki prefecture. The beers are worth the journey: there's an excellent IPA, a lager, a saison, a stout and more. Toshiyuki Kiuchi, the current director of Hitachino Nest and the eighth generation of the Kiuchi brewery's founding family explains that the beers are made using local produce and traditional Japanese brewing methods: 'We do not simply imitate Western brews', he says.

Kiuchi brewery is well set up for visitors with a tasting bar and a soba noodle restaurant. The brewery is better known in Japan for its sake (made in the winter) than Hitachino Nest and visitors can try the rice wine too. Best of all there's the chance to be a brewer for half a day. It takes a bit more experience to craft the gold medal-winning White Ale, a wheat beer gently flavoured with coriander, nutmeg and orange peel in addition to five varieties of hops, which is highly quaffable.

HYOUKO YASHIKI NO MORI BREWERY

345-1 Kanaya, Agano, Niigata Prefecture;
www.swanlake.co.jp; +81 250 63 2000

◆ Food ◆ Takeout
◆ Bar

THINGS TO DO NEARBY

Sado-ga-shima
Catch the fast ferry 80km (50 miles) west of Niigata city to this spectacular island where the Earth Celebration takes place in the third week of August.

Furu-machi
Niigata city's nightlife district is on the north side of the Shinano-gawa River. Restaurants, bars, clubs and shops abound in this traditional neighbourhood.

Niigata Manga & Animation Museum
Turning back the clock or crank up a child's imagination with the interactive displays, mini-theatre and voice-over machines here. *www. museum.nmam.jp*

Ponshu-kan Sake Tasting Corner
Head for this cute sake bar near the west exit of Niigata train station. It serves over 90 varieties of the region's famed rice wines.

Thawed snow seeps into Niigata-*ken's* (prefecture) rich soil in a natural filtering process, forming pools of ready-to-drink spring water at numerous 'secret' wells. Niigata has long been known throughout Japan for the quality of its water and, as a result, its rice, sake, and now, craft beer. Swan Lake is the most established beer label in the prefecture and it's made here at Hyouko Yashiki No Mori Brewery.

Its products are available across the country, including at three dedicated taprooms in Tokyo and at this highly regarded brewery, roughly 30km (18½ miles) west of downtown Niigata-*shi* (city). The new premises are in the shape of a swan, but aside from that architectural quirk – and a location in the middle of Japanese nowhere – the beer remains blissfully unchanged. Young staff

are fastidious about presenting the perfect pint on long communal oak tables, and visitors may feel like they are judges in a silent drinking competition (don't even think about overlooking the reading notes). You could go for the fig and raisin tang of the award-winning Swan Lake Porter, but try to time your visit for the much vaunted ski season when the winter ales hit the menu, and take on the caramel-infused Big Daddy Imperial Red.

ASAHI BEER HALL & SKY ROOM

Sumida-ku, Tokyo Azumabashi 1-23-1;
www.asahibeer.co.jp; +81 3 5608 5277

◆ Food   ◆ Takeout
◆ Bar

The golden sculpture atop Tokyo's Asahi Beer Hall is meant to represent the foam on a fresh pint of beer, but locally it is better known, perhaps lovingly, as 'the golden turd'. The building itself, part of Asahi's HQ, is supposedly shaped like a beer glass, though thanks to its rooftop sculpture, it's also blessed with a local nickname: the 'poo building'.

Jump in the lift of the neighbouring gold-tinged skyscraper filled with Asahi office workers – topped with a crown of white, it looks a lot like a pint of beer constructed from Lego blocks. The 22nd floor is home to the Asahi Sky Room: enjoy a glass of the light, crisp, rice lager Asahi Super Dry accompanied by impressive vistas over the city.

THINGS TO DO NEARBY

Ueno-kōen
With many of Tokyo's museums, temples and shrines within its park borders, Ueno-kōen is ideal for art and history buffs, or simply wander its wide wooded pathways.

Sensō-ji
Although largely reconstructed after WWII, this Buddhist temple, founded in the 7th century still oozes character. It's overlooked by a 5-storey pagoda built in the '70s.
www.senso-ji.jp

BAIRD BEER: HARAJUKU TAPROOM

2nd fl, 1-20-13 Jingūmae, Shibuya-ku, Tokyo;
www.bairdbeer.com; +81 3 6438 0450

◆ Food ◆ Takeout
◆ Bar ◆ Transport

From little things, big things grow. Since launching with a tiny 30L brewhouse at the fish market in the regional Japanese city of Numazu in 2000, Baird Beer has grown to be one of Japan's most well-known craft breweries.

The Numazu taproom is still going strong, but Baird's distinctive labels are now seen in pubs and beer bars around the world, and its Harajuku Taproom in Tokyo is handily placed for visitors to the city. Bar snacks are served in the wood-lined Japanese izakaya pub – try the grilled yakitori-style squid – and 15 taps dispense Baird's core range and seasonal specials. On our visit our favourite was the Wabi-Sabi Japan Pale Ale, subtly infused with Japanese wasabi and green tea.

THINGS TO DO NEARBY

Takeshita-dōri
Cutting-edge youth culture, crazy mash-ups of green tea and yoghurt, and weird shopping opportunities all combine at this pedestrian street just metres from Baird Beer.

Meiji-jingū
Visit Tokyo's grandest Shintō shrine, dedicated to Emperor Meiji's reign (1867–1912), before exploring the grounds, which feature more than 120,000 trees from around Japan. *www.meijijingu.or.jp*

TY HARBOR BREWERY

2 1-3 Higashi-Shinagawa, Tokyo;
www.tysons.jp/tyharbor/en; +81 3 5479 4555

◆ Food ◆ Transport
◆ Bar

Brewing approachable ales since 1997, TY Harbor is one of Japan's longest running microbreweries. Located in a former warehouse south of the city centre, the brewery-restaurant has great views over the canal and is a fine spot to escape Tokyo's hubbub. With hop forward beers available – the IPA gets good reviews – and a range of burgers and ribs on the menu, you could almost be in an American brewpub.

The core range is fairly standard, featuring a wheat beer, a seasonal stout/porter, a pale ale, an amber ale and an IPA. But the brewer's choice keeps the regulars guessing – past beers include a Mango Ale, a Maple Rye Amber and a Peach Wheat Beer. If you're lucky, the Coffee IPA will be on tap.

THINGS TO DO NEARBY

Odaiba & Tokyo Bay
Cross the Rainbow Bridge to this collection of artificial islands on Tokyo Bay, home to theme parks, museums and shopping malls galore.

Tokyo Tower
Japan's second highest structure was built in 1958 as a communications tower. Lifts whoosh people to the viewing platforms at 145m and at 250m. *www.tokyotower.co.jp*

NEPAL

How to ask for a beer in local language?
Ek beer dinuhos? (Nepali)
How to say cheers? Nepal doesn't have a strong
tradition of toasting, but 'cheers' will do the job
Signature beer style? Pale, strong lager, or – in the
hills – thin rice beer
Local bar snack? Sukuti (deliciously spicy dried meat,
often yak or buffalo)
Do: Ask if the place serves tongba – served hot, this
traditional millet beer is a wonderful winter warmer

Nepal has a surprisingly long history of brewing for
a country that was closed off to the outside world
until the 20th century. The tribes of Nepal have been making
their own homebrews since time immemorial, but it was
mountaineers and playboy Maharajas who introduced Nepal
to European-style beer in the 1950s. In the early days, bottled
beers were trekked in from the plains of India – it took 20
years for the first brewery to open in Kathmandu, and another
40 years before things moved beyond strong, peppy lagers.

Toasting the end of a trek with an ice-cold Everest beer
is now as much a part of the Nepali trekking experience

as tying prayer flags to boulders on mountain passes, but
Everest lager and its somewhat interchangeable compet-
itors Tuborg, Carlsberg and Gorkha are facing a growing
challenge from the German-style Kölsch produced by the
Sherpa Brewery at Chitwan in the Terai plains. The fledgling
Yeti Distilling Company, based near Kathmandu, has prom-
ised new wheat beers to further weaken the stranglehold of
Nepal's lager-addicted big brewers.

But the country's most authentic brewing scene is found in
remote mountain villages, where rustic bars serve steaming
hot pots of *chang* rice beer and *tongba*, the traditional millet
beer of the eastern Himalaya. Falling somewhere between
Russian *kvass* and Japanese sake, these fermented mashes
are steeped in hot water and sucked through a bamboo straw
to filter out debris. Sipped at altitude, which exaggerates the
effects of alcohol, they can be surprisingly potent.

SHERPA BREWERY

Chainpur, Chitwan; www.sherpabrewery.com.np;
+977 981 325 5669

◆ Food ◆ Takeout
◆ Tour ◆ Transport

Once upon a time, under the shadow of Everest, a Sherpa was tired of travellers complaining about the bland beer served in his Lukla pub. Importing some home brew kits from the USA, Phura Geljen Sherpa sold out of his creation in days, and an idea was born. Getting his fledgling brewery up and running was no easy task, eventually relocating the family-owned enterprise from his mountainous Khumbu to the flat Terai, close to Nepal's main road artery and the Indian border.

With tourism in its infancy, and surrounded by rice paddies and banana groves, the brewery is refreshingly low-key and welcomes all travellers; a taxi from nearby Bharatpur (20km/12.5 miles) will cost roughly $10USD. Using imported German malt and barley, Chinese vats and Indian machinery, the brewery's signature Kölsch is crisp, light and clean tasting, unlike any of Nepal's

THINGS TO DO NEARBY

Chitwan National Park
One of Nepal's premier tourist attractions, this World-Heritage listed reserve is where to view wild elephants, one-horned rhinos or, if incredibly lucky, a royal Bengal tiger.

Devghat
Soak up the karma of this important Hindu pilgrimage site at the confluence of the Kali Gandaki and Trisuli rivers, 9km (5.5 miles) from Bharatpur airport.

Lumbini
Buddha's birthplace, and of huge religious significance to Buddhist pilgrims, this World-Heritage listed cluster of shrines, temples, pagodas and international monasteries is a peaceful retreat.

Daman
For a Himalayan panorama rivalling the one on the Khumbu Kölsch can, head back to Kathmandu via this 2322m hill station on the windy Tribhuvan Hwy.

more mass-produced brands. Currently only available in ice-axe emblazoned cans, three more beers are in the planning stages: Himalayan Red Ale, Summit Stout and Trekkers Brown Ale. Simple food is available, and accommodation and local tours are planned.

Until then, relax outside under a shady palm, with views of the breathtaking Himalayan foothills and a Khumbu Kölsch.

NORTH KOREA

 How to ask for a beer in local language?
Maekju juseyo
How to say cheers? Gon bei
Signature beer style? Crisp, smooth lager
Local bar snack? Ojingeochae – dried squid
Do: If you're drinking beer from a pitcher, be sure to pour for others, starting with the most senior drinker – they will return the favour

Back in 2012, *The Economist* declared North Korean beer to be better than the mass-produced lagers of the South. It was a proud moment for the North, whose beer culture only dates back to the start of the 21st century. In 2000, Kim Jong Il is credited – of course – with founding the country's first brewery, Taedonggang, using equipment bought from a defunct UK brewing company. The beer, named for the Taedonggang River, is a fairly full-flavoured lager that is swilled with gusto around the country. Getting hold of a bottle outside North Korea is tough, though export to China is not unheard of. While it couldn't quite be said that a beer revolution has happened in Pyongyang, the capital now has a handful of microbreweries brewing speciality ales, largely for the tourist palate.

Visitors to the country will almost definitely encounter the brewery in the Yanggakdo Hotel, while beer enthusiasts should also request a trip to the local bowling alley and department store to sample further brews. If you're really lucky, you'll be in town for Pyongyang's Oktoberfest. The country's first ever festival took place in 2016 alongside the river that gives the country's best-loved beer its name. Government dignitaries and visiting tourists rubbed shoulders while knocking back litre steins of cold lager, proving that there's virtually no barrier that can't be broken down with a couple of well-made beers.

RAKWON PARADISE MICROBREWERY

Rakwon Department Store,
Changgwang St, Pyongyang

◆ Food
◆ Bar

Trips to North Korea tend to be filled with visits to war sites and historical landmarks and you'll likely spend a decent amount of time bowing before grandiose monuments, so what a treat to step away from museums and into a microbrewery. Not to be outdone by its southern counterpart, Seoul, Pyongyang is home to a smattering of microbreweries, plus Taedonggang Brewery, where North Korea's national beer – a very palatable lager – is produced. Based in the Rakwon department store, Paradise is the city's oldest microbrewery, serving pale lager, a pretty good wheat beer and some unusual fruit-infused ales. But when you have a story as good as 'drinking in a North Korean microbrewery', who really cares what the beer tastes like?

THINGS TO DO NEARBY

Mansudae Grand Monument
Bowing before the colossal statues of Korea's Great Leader, Kim Il-Sung and Dear Leader, Kim Jong-Il, is a compulsory component on any North Korean itinerary.

Victorious Fatherland Liberation War Museum
Guided tours of this magnificently named museum tell the story of the Korean War from a northern perspective, with interactive exhibits and a diorama of the Battle of Daejon.

SINGAPORE

How to ask for a beer in local language?
A beer, please
How to say cheers? Cheers! Yum Seng!
Signature beer style? Pale adjunct lagers
Local bar snack? Salted peanuts, dried fish
Do: Drink a Tiger in situ; then find a local
IPA to shock your palate back to life

Perhaps Southeast Asia's most well known beer
arrives to the world from Singapore – Tiger beer. First
brewed in the 1930s, it's a pale lager and delivers very little
in terms of flavor. Still, hot weather can make an ice-cold
Tiger a pretty desirable experience!

Things are looking rosy on the craft beer front though.
Singapore has developed a fine local microbrew scene,
and its annual craft beer festival – Beerfest Asia – makes
Singapore the Asian hub of tasty beer drinking experiences.
To cap it all off, the imported beer scene is booming, with
specialist bars all over the island.

Brewerkz is your go-to starting point for getting crafty
with a few local brews. A strong selection of year-round
beers is complemented by a genuinely adventurous
seasonal range. On the regulars list, give their IPA a go, and
there'll almost certainly be a fruit-based seasonal on tap.

Another microbrewery to pay your respects to is RedDot
Brewery. Singapore's first locally owned microbrewery,
still going strong as it approaches 20. Try the RedDot Lime
Wheat – it's a bright tasty wheat beer with a pronounced
zing. Then take it up a notch with a visit to the world's
highest microbrewery – LeVel33. Half a dozen classic beer
styles are on offer.

Singapore is an island of beer choice in a surrounding
ocean of rice-based lagers. Definitely worth exploring!

LEVEL33

Level 33, Marina Bay Financial Tower 1, 8 Marina Blvd, Singapore; www.level33.com.sg; +65 6834 3133

◆ Food ◆ Transport
◆ Bar

There's a convention that real ale breweries should have historic, fusty premises in Benedictine abbeys or medieval farmyards.

That's so last century; LeVel33 is perched on the 33rd floor of a sleek glass skyscraper overlooking Marina Bay, yet its beers taste as hoppy and artisan as anything concocted in a 16th-century brewhouse. Using equipment and brewing know-how from Austria, this is the world's highest urban craft brewery, and the whole package is stylishly done, with gleaming copper kettles, a swish food menu and an open-air terrace for soaking up the cityscape. There's a sampling platter of the house brews with the beer paddle, but the perfect beer to go with the angular skyline is the crisp 33.1 Blond Lager.

THINGS TO DO NEARBY

Gardens by the Bay
There's a hint of *Avatar* about these futuristic gardens fronting Marina Bay, with everything from South African *fynbos* to 'supertrees' that put on a nightly light show. *www. gardensbythebay.com.sg*

ArtScience Museum
Another space-age slice of Singapore architecture, this museum hosts exhibitions, including art shows, tech installations and science-themed artworks. *www. marinabaysands.com/ museum*

RED DOT MICROBREWERY

25A Dempsey Rd, Singapore; www.reddotbrewhouse.com.sg; +65 6475 0500

◆ Food ◆ Bar ◆ Transport
◆ Family ◆ Takeout

Foamy, friendly and tenuously Bavarian, Red Dot might be an unlikely candidate for Singapore's first locally owned, independent microbrewery, but that's nothing compared to the story of its foundation. Owner and brewmaster Ernest Ng launched his first foray into beer-making after a chance encounter with two home-brew-swigging soldiers in South Africa's Kruger National Park, and he named his brewery after the label on a brewing kit purchased in Johannesburg. Two decades later, and Red Dot is producing some very credible ales, served in two busy brewhouses in historic colonial buildings in Dempsey Rd and Boat Quay. Alongside a platter of wurst, you can whet your tonsils with the Monster Green Lager flavoured with Spirulina – for a reminder that this is, after all, Singapore.

THINGS TO DO NEARBY

Singapore Botanic Gardens
Unesco-listed and almost unbelievably verdant, Singapore's botanic gardens (housing the National Orchid Garden) were coaxed from the rainforest in 1860. *www.sbg.org.sg*

Chopsuey
Step back to Thomas Raffles' time as ceiling fans swirl nonchalantly overhead at this graceful Dempsey Hill cafe, loved by expats and locals for its lunchtime yum cha. *www.chopsueycafe.com*

SOUTH KOREA

How to ask for a beer in local language?
Maekju han/du byeong butakamnida
How to say cheers? Jjan! – informal/with friends;
Gunbae! – formal/with colleagues and elders
Signature beer style? Asian lager
Local bar snack? KFC (Korean fried chicken)
Do: Try one of South Korea's many hangover cures:
haejangkook (hangover soup), medicinal drinks, or a
trip to a jjimjil-bang (sauna) to sweat out your sins

South Korea is a country that loves a tipple.
Historically, alcohol was drunk during rituals to mark
holidays, and over time developed into *hyanguemjurye*, the
Confucian drinking etiquette designed to show respect for
one's elders and superiors. There are even elements of South
Korean cooking – known as *anju* – designed just to accompany a good session. Beer with fried chicken is a pairing that
has become so popular it is known by a combined abbreviation: *chimaek* (chicken + maekju, the Korean word for beer).

The most common beer in South Korea is light,

mass-produced lager; Cass and Hite are the two major
brands that can be found everywhere. Since 2010, when
Canadian Dan Vroon started the country's first microbrewery, Craftworks, the craft beer scene has grown in spades.
But there was one hitch: South Korean law prohibited beer
to be sold by any brewery that wasn't producing at least one
million litres a year. Microbrewers found ways around this
by contracting large-scale breweries to brew their recipes.
Laws have since been relaxed, allowing small breweries to
produce their own beer, but the lag effect means that many
microbreweries in South Korea still don't produce their own
beer on-site at their taprooms.

New breweries and craft beer bars are popping up all
the time, and the large numbers of expats – particularly
from North America and Europe – living in South Korea has
meant that, from the outset, there was a market to support
microbrewers until local tastes caught on to the trend of
hoppier, more flavourful beers.

123

GALMEGI BREWING COMPANY

58 Gwangnam-ro, Suyeong-gu, Busan;
www.galmegibrewing.com; +82 070 7677 9658

◆ Food   ◆ Bar
◆ Family   ◆ Transport

The first brewery to capitalise on the recently relaxed laws allowing smaller brewers to open brewpubs in South Korea, Galmegi started as a group of home-brewers who were tired of the mass-market beers then on offer in South Korea. In 2014, they expanded into commercial brewing.

All of the beer is made on site at Galmegi's brewpub – the first of its kind to open in the southern city of Busan. Galmegi means 'seagull' in Korean, a nod to its location: just a few streets away from Gwangan (Gwangalli) Beach

in a former snowboard shop. Ten taps offer a full range of Galmegi's brews, including staple beers, seasonals and specials. Try the hoppy Moonrise Pale Ale, brewed primarily with American hops.

THINGS TO DO NEARBY

Gwangan (Gwangalli) Beach
Swim at this wide, pristine arc of sand just a few blocks from the brewery. Waterskiing, jet skiing and windsurfing are also popular here.

Igidae
Take the two-hour coastal trail walk through this nature park for excellent views across the bay to one of South Korea's most beautiful beaches: Haeundae.

CRAFTWORKS TAPHOUSE NAMSAN

651-1 Itaewon 2-dong, Gyeongridan, Seoul;
www.craftworkstaphouse.com; +82 02 794 2537

◆ Food   ◆ Bar   ◆ Transport
◆ Family   ◆ Takeout

One of the earliest microbreweries in South Korea, Craftworks was established by Canadian expat Dan Vroon in 2010, when microbrewing was simply unheard of in this country. The brewery now does a range of seven staple beers, all named for the most famous mountain peaks in South Korea.

The original taphouse in Itaewon spawned a number of similar craft beer bars to open nearby; the area eventually became known as 'Craft Beer Valley'. Craftworks now operate several other locations around Seoul, including a branch in Namsan and a cosy basement space in a high-rise building in downtown Seoul. The Seorak Oatmeal Stout is creamy and moreish but American-style Jirisan Moon Bear IPA is the brewery's most classic hoppy offering.

THINGS TO DO NEARBY

N Seoul Tower & Namsan
Take a cable car to Seoul's highest point on top of Namsan. There's also a viewing platform atop N Seoul Tower for even more lofty vistas.
www.nseoultower.com

War Memorial of Korea
This behemoth museum traces the history of the Korean War and other conflicts through thoughtful exhibits. There's a huge collection of aircraft and armoured vehicles on display outside.

PONGDANG CRAFT BEER

517-8 Sinsa-dong, Gangnam-gu; Seoul;
www.pongdangsplash.com; +82 2 790 3875

◆ Food   ◆ Transport
◆ Bar

This Seoul microbrewery began life in 2011, and in 2013 opened its first taproom on the upper floor of a corner unit in Gangnam, near Sinsa subway station. In 2014, it expanded to a second location in what has become known as 'Craft Beer Valley' in the Itaewon nightlife district. The original location remains the best: a slick, modern space with bare bulbs and a sign shouting 'LOVE BEER' in bright-pink neon scrawl behind the tiled bar. The taps are split between Pongdang's beers and Korean and international guests. There are a number of hop-forward pales and IPAs (the 6.5% Mosaic Bomb does what it says on the tin with a juicy blast of Mosaic hops), but the oatmeal smooth, bitter chocolate Breakfast Stout can battle any South Korean winter.

THINGS TO DO NEARBY

Bongeun-sa
This leafy Buddhist temple dating to 794 AD is a world away from Gangnam's K-Pop-infused streets. On Thursdays, resident monks teach lantern-making and host tea ceremonies. **www.bongeunsa.org**

Coreanos Kitchen
Straight out of Austin, Texas, this fusion joint serves up Korean tacos: think *galbi* beef ribs and kimchi pork belly wrapped in freshly made corn tortillas. **www.coreanoskitchen.com**

THAILAND

How to ask for a beer in local language?
Kaw bia krap
How to say cheers? Chai yo!
Signature beer style? Pale lagers brewed with rice
Local bar snack? Salted peanuts, fried squid
Do: Succumb to the simple pleasure of a crisp cold lager
from a beach- (or pool-) side deck chair

Like many Southeast Asian countries, Thailand's beer scene is dominated by pale lagers, light on bitterness and an easy-drinking option for the hot steamy climate. The original Thai beer is Singha, first brewed by the father of Thai brewing, 'Boon Rawd' Sreshthaputra in the early 1930s. Chang is the other national beer, though a relative newcomer on the scene, born from a partnership

with Danish brewer Carlsberg in the mid-1990s. Both beers exhibit the classic rice lager style of the region.

When the beer is this easy to drink, it becomes less about what it is and more about the experience. So picture yourself on a Thai beach, simple deck chair and a bucket of Singha bottles packed into ice. This is how to enjoy one of these simple beers. Or as a crisp accompaniment to a rich, fiery Thai curry, an antidote to the sweat the heat and chilli has brought to your brow (and most everywhere else as well!).

And what of craft beer? Restrictive brewing laws has meant microbrewing is effectively illegal. It may be some time before there's a local brew of note. In the meantime, a number of pubs have sprung up in the cities, importing fine craft beers from around the world – a sign that there's an appetite here for beers beyond the pale.

CHIT BEER

219/266 Baan Suan Palm, Ko Kret, Nonthaburi;
www.facebook.com/Chitbeer; +66 8 9799 1123

◆ Bar

◆ Takeout

In a city notorious for its tight regulation of alcohol, guerrilla brewer P'Chit has somehow managed to stay below the radar of the authorities, producing and selling innovative brews and even running back-room beer-making workshops to encourage other hopheads (in the best sense of the word) to challenge the status quo.

Brewing at Chit Beer is a cottage industry, in a country-style riverbank home on sleepy Ko Kret island (just north of Bangkok) but devotees are happy to trek out here to sip from a bar menu that runs to Porter, Pilsner and IPA, while clumps of water hyacinth float lazily by on the Chao Phraya river. Expect experimental beers, such as Pumpkin Ale, but don't miss the light, summery Kölsch, which comes plain, or scented with lemongrass.

THINGS TO DO NEARBY

Wat Poramai Yikawat
The walk to this leaning Burmese-style stupa at the tip of Ko Kret island, past rickety village-style houses, is as charming as the Buddhist temple itself.

Nonthaburi Market
Arrive early for the pick of the countryside crop at this daily old-fashioned wet-and-dry market at Tha Nam Nonthaburi pier. Most traders are gone by 9am.

TAWANDANG GERMAN BREWERY

462/61 Rama 3 Rd, Khwaeng Chongnonsi, Khet Yanna-
wa, Bangkok; www.tawandang.co.th; +66 2 678 1114

◆ Food   ◆ Transport
◆ Bar

Paying homage to all things German, Bangkok's first
microbrewery feels more pre-reunification Berlin
than bucolic Bavaria, but the owners definitely get the beers
right. The complex flavours and cloudy tones of the house
wheat beer and dunkel are sweet nectar in a city sewn up
by strong, hoppy lagers, such as Singha and Chang. Big
crowds of mainly Thai drinkers gather nightly to quaff the
brews prepared in-house to German recipes, under strict
supervision from Bavarian brewmaster Jochen Neuhaus.
And there's a bonus: adding to the Cabaret mood, the
flowing curtains at the end of the beer-hall part nightly to
reveal song and dance spectaculars with multiple costume
changes. Order a glass of confident, malty dunkel and enjoy
the show.

THINGS TO DO NEARBY

Bang Nam Pheung Market
The country-style Bang
Nam Phueng weekend
market is nominally
'floating' but it's more
interesting to wander on
land, past village-style
homes, ancient temples and
sprawling market stalls.

nahm
Ranked among the world's
top 50 restaurants, namh
serves up the creations of
feted Aussie chef David
Thompson, who learned his
trade from the Thai royal
household cooking staff.
www.comohotels.com

VIETNAM

How to ask for a beer in local language? Mot bia!
How to say cheers? Mot hai ba, vo! (mot hai ba yo)
Signature beer style? Pale lagers brewed with rice
Local bar snack? Salted peanuts
Do: Drink beer from a glass filled with ice in a bia hoi

For the most part, beer in Vietnam has been a means to a cool, refreshing end. So the mainstream beers are light in colour, light in flavour and best consumed icy cold. Often enough with ice in the glass!

The names may change, but it's classic lagers that dominate the lists. In the south around Ho Chi Minh City, 333 (Ba Ba Ba) is, arguably, the branded beer of choice. In Hanoi, it is – you guessed it! – Bia Hanoi. In the centre, around Hue, you'll invariably be served Huda.

But more important than brand is how you drink it. *Bia*

hoi – draft beer – is a firm favourite, served to tables in *bia hoi* restaurants in 2-litre plastic bottles, or jugs, or some other choice vessel – and from them into your ice-filled glass. (It can be served ice cold, but the ice in the glass experience is a right of passage.) Drink till your face turns red, keeping your hunger at bay with food designed to keep you drinking – delicious deep-fried options abound.

As for craft beer – and 'craft' here refers to beers other than light lagers brewed in the commercial style) well, it's a frontier outpost, with just a couple of years of microbrewing in its history. In HCMC, visit Pasteur St Brewing Co and try their Jasmine IPA for a little insight into how local influence might affect the craft beer scene here – it's distinct, flavoursome and a little unusual. A perfect start to a craft beer day.

PASTEUR STREET BREWING CO.

144 Pasteur St, District 1, Ho Chi Minh City;
www.pasteurstreet.com; +84 8 3823 9562

◆ Food   ◆ Takeout
◆ Bar   ◆ Transport

THINGS TO DO NEARBY

Vespa Adventures
Negotiate Saigon's neon-lit rivers of traffic on the back on a vintage Vespa scooter, drinking at hidden bars and eating the world's best street food. *www. vespaadventures.com*

Saigon Outcast
Street art, live music and outdoor cinema all feature at this bohemian and diverse space an easy taxi ride from downtown Ho Chi Minh City.
www.saigonoutcast.com

War Remnants Museum
Understand the Vietnam War's tragic legacy amid the exhibitions showcased in this structure once known as the Museum of Chinese and American War Crimes.
www.baotangchung tichchientranh .vn

Reunification Palace
Explore an underground South Vietnamese telecommunications centre as you wander through this iconic 1960s building at the heart of the fall of Saigon in 1975. *www.dinhdoclap. gov.vn*

Locate the brewery's simple chalkboard on Saigon's busy streets, ease your way past the friendly foot masseurs playing cards with bored security guards, and negotiate a narrow staircase to eventually find Pasteur Street's compact tasting room. Trimmed in warm timber and studded with casual bar tables, the hip space might echo beer bars in Portland or Berlin, but there's a strong southeast Asian influence to the brews on offer.

Months before Pasteur Street Brewing's opening in early 2015, brewer Alex Violette was bouncing around Vietnam by motorbike to source local flavours and ingredients to add to his recipes. The result is some of Asia's most interesting beers. A quaffable IPA is infused with dried jasmine flowers, and fragrant black pepper and zesty lemongrass provide a subtle kick to Pasteur Street's

Spice Island Saigon Saison. Coconut from Ben Tre province in the Mekong Delta is added to the Toasted Coconut Porter; and dragon fruit, Thai black tea, and passion fruit are used in other beers. Don't leave without pairing the fiery Nashville fried chicken with Pasteur Street's zingy wheat beer, and ask if the Cyclo Imperial Chocolate Stout, winner of the Chocolate Beer category in the 2016 World Beer Cup, is available.

UMEBOSHI (Japan)
Aka pickled plums, umeboshi are a confronting mouthful. They are pickled to within an inch of their lives, so salty and sour you'll more than likely reach for a beer to wash it down.

DRUNKEN NOODLES (Thailand)
The Southeast Asian equivalent of a bacon sandwich – wide, flat rice noodles, seafood, vegetables, chilli, soy, fish sauce and lime juice. A palate explosion that will surely take your mind off your headache.

BACON SANDWICH (UK)
In your hurtin' state, the only decision you need to face is whether it's the brown sauce (yep!) or the red sauce. Then let the squishy white bread, rich butter and smoky salty bacon do its fine, fine work. You will feel better, as long as you keep it down.

PRAIRIE OYSTER (USA)
Honestly, some hangover cures seem to be working on the principal that what doesn't kill you makes you stronger. Enter the Prairie Oyster – a raw egg dressed with salt, pepper, Tabasco and Worcestershire sauce. Slam it down hard (so it stays put).

HANGOV

Let's face it, you reap what you sow and after a night of drinking a lot of beer there's not much guaranteed to fix you the next morning. But that's not say that people haven't tried. Here are some of the better (if still scientifically unsound) ideas.

A PICKLE JUICE (Poland)
A contender with rehydration aspirations, sour, salty pickle juice could do something to your hangover, but it's not the most pleasant beginning to what is already a poor start to the day.

RICE CONGEE (Vietnam)

This is a local cure-all – when you're feeling under the weather, this comforting, thick rice soup (pork or seafood are best) is your go-to. Dressed with slivers of ginger, coriander leaf, chilli and fish sauce, it will hit a hangover too. Well worth a shot.

R CURES

SOBRIETY

We know, buzz kill – but there you have it. Avoiding drinking alcohol is 100% guaranteed to result in no hangovers. Which will leave you in a perfect state of health to go out drinking. Every cloud has a silver lining.

BEROCCA (various)

Particularly popular in Australia, this is a bright orange, fizzy, vitamin B drink. Post-session, brain aching, you drop a pale orange tablet into a glass of water, let it violently dissolve, then throw back the liquid gold. If nothing else, it removes the taste of drinker's remorse from your mouth.

HAIR OF THE DOG (global)

The ubiquitous hangover cure – it is a pearl of wisdom thrown out in every country on the planet. The extreme version of this is 'stay drunk' but that's no way to live. We recommend a Bloody Mary if you're going to try it. But any port in a storm...

EUR

TOP 5
BEER
TOWNS

OPE

BRUSSELS

You can buy many Belgian beers all over the world but it's not until you visit a Belgian city like Brussels, Bruges or Ghent that you realise quite how many incredible (and strong!) ales are made in Belgium, each with its own glass. Touring Brussels' bars is to step through the looking glass.

LONDON

London loves beer. It gave the world two core craft beer styles, IPA and porter. Long a home to big brewers such as Fuller's, the capital's craft renaissance has brought exciting beer tasting options to every neighbourhood and, best of all, it's possible to walk or travel by Tube or bus between pints.

ROME

Rome is full of great beer bars, such as Ma Che Siete Venuti a Fà, which gives plenty of options for the visiting beer tourist. Couple that with how Italy has embraced craft beer – with characteristic passion and pride – and you have the making of a fine time tasting unique brews by the likes of Baladin.

BAMBERG

Yes, Munich has a much-imitated beer festival (arguably a victim of its own success) and Berlin's bars attract hip hopheads. But for a uniquely fascinating beer culture, head to the picturesque Franconian town of Bamberg, where 300 breweries are within cycling distance of each other (see p168).

REYKJAVIK

In the dark and snowy north of Europe, several cities have strong beer scenes, especially Stockholm (check out Akkurat pub) and Copenhagen (see p153). But Iceland's compact capital gets the vote for its upbeat nightlife and the selection of local beers that never leave the island.

BELGIUM

How to ask for a beer in the local language?
Une bière, s'il vous plaît / Een pintje, alstublieft
How to say cheers? Santé!
Signature beer style? Gueuze (among many others)
Local bar snack? Kip-kap, a type of brawn
Don't: Insist on a draft pint: Belgium's remarkable beer
diversity is due in part to the popularity of bottles

No country on earth has such a diverse array of indigenous beer styles as Belgium, to say nothing of the world-class beers it produces in styles brought in from abroad. About the same size as the state of Maryland in the US and only 50% bigger than Wales in the UK, this tiny country wedged between France, Germany, the Netherlands and Luxembourg brews more different types of beer than all of its neighbours put together, creating an exceptionally dynamic range of beverages that pair particularly well with food. In fact, beer is so revered here that Belgium is even home to *la cuisine à la bière*, which means 'beer cooking' in French, one of its two major languages, with such highbrow dishes as *carbonade flamande*, which use beer as an

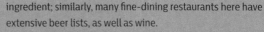

ingredient; similarly, many fine-dining restaurants here have extensive beer lists, as well as wine.

Several of the best-loved Trappist monastery breweries are located in Belgium, from funky Orval in the French-speaking south to the legendary Westvleteren in Dutch-speaking Flanders, and a number of farms that originally only made beer as a refreshment for field labourers, such as Brasserie Dupont, have since transformed into world-re-nowned farmhouse breweries.

From sour beer styles, such as Flemish Red and Oud Bruin to syrupy Golden Ales, Trappists and abbey beers, from refreshingly hoppy saisons to bitter porters and roasty stouts, Belgium is the original beer paradise. Yet despite the great variety you'll find here, it's eye-opening to discover that Belgium's current beer culture is actually much smaller than it used to be: thousands of small breweries in Belgium closed

TOP 5 BEERS

- **Saison Dupont** Brasserie Dupont
- **Taras Boulba** Brasserie de la Senne
- **Goudenband** Brouwerij Liefmans
- **Cantillon Lou Pepe Kriek** Brasserie Cantillon
- **Trappistes Rochefort 8** Brasserie de Rochefort

down over the course of the 20th century, pushed out by the growth of industrial lager and aggressive business practices. Beer fans around the world might clamour for bottles of Westvleteren 12, but the most popular beer in Belgium is actually Jupiler, a Pilsner, and its best-known export is arguably Stella Artois, brewed in the same style and often at the very same brewery as Jupiler by the world's largest brewing company. Depressingly, a number of historic beer styles like Peeterman and Bière Blanche de Louvain have more or less disappeared for good. But things are heading back in the right direction. Today, new microbreweries, such as the Brussels Beer Project and Brasserie de la Senne have brought dynamic new flavours to the country's beer scene. Even spontaneously fermented Lambic beer, long thought to be heading the way of the dodo bird, is seeing an upturn, with the first Lambic blender in 15 years, Gueuzerie Tilquin, starting up in 2009,

and a proliferation of specialist bars, including the great Moeder Lambic in Brussels. Local beer festivals are also working to revive the original diversity of Belgian beer. If you find yourself here during Zythos in April, Streekbierenfestival in August, or Kerstbierfestival in December, you'll have an amazing beer experience. The same is true if you come here any other time of year.

BAR TALK - SÉBASTIEN MORVAN

Sharing is learning. In the craft renaissance, brewers travel the world and share practices; they want to be challenged and stimulated

BRASSERIE CANTILLON

56 Rue Gheude, Brussels;
www.cantillon.be; +32 2 521 4928

◆ Family   ◆ Bar   ◆ Transport
◆ Tour   ◆ Takeout

Harking from the days when Brussels boasted over 100 breweries, the family-run Cantillon is now the lone survivor; beer fanatics flock here to tour a brewery that has never altered its methods, nor much of its machinery, in over a century.

Master brewer Jean Van Roy is most proud of his traditional, organic Lambic, a mysterious Brussels beer that relies on fermentation using 'wild' yeasts picked up naturally in the air. Lambic is aged for 18–36 months in old wooden barrels, producing a flat, cloudy beer, that is then trans-formed into fizzy Gueuze after being bottled and stored in the cellar, when bubbles are formed during a second fermentation, just like Champagne. Don't miss Cantillon's fruity Kriek 100% Lambic made with organic sour cherries.

THINGS TO DO NEARBY

Restobières
Next to the Place du Jeu-de-Balle Flea Market, every dish here is cooked with beer. Try rabbit braised in Gueuze or chocolate mousse with Hercule Stout.
www.restobieres.eu

Centre Belge de la Bande Dessinée
The country that gave the world Tintin, the Smurfs and Lucky Luke has a brilliant museum dedicated to the humble comic strip. Family fun.
www.comicscenter.net

EN STOEMELINGS

1 Rue du Miroir, Brussels;
www.enstoemelings.be; +32 489 495924

◆ Food   ◆ Tour   ◆ Takeout
◆ Family   ◆ Bar   ◆ Transport

'En Stoemelings' in Bruxellois dialect means 'on the sly', and this exciting new project by Denys van Elewyck and Samuel Languy lives up to its name. Hidden away in the funky Marolles neighbourhood, the microbrewery is no bigger than someone's living room, but is filled with enthusiasts popping in to try its latest seasonal beers as well as the signature brew, Curieuse Neus (Nosy Kid), a powerful malty Trippel. The guys are always experimenting with different hops, malted barley and herbs, and Denys insists that, 'we want everyone to watch our brewing process, to understand how beer is made, rather than keeping it some mystical secret.' Start your appreciation with Chike Madame, a refreshing Blanche (white beer), with a hint of jasmine.

THINGS TO DO NEARBY

Orybany
Almost next door to Stoemelings, this colourful boutique showcases a dozen local stylists and interior designers committed to using ethical, ethnic fashions.
www.orybany.com

Place du Grand Sablon
This majestic square, with houses from the 16th to 19th century, gourmet restaurants and the boutique of master chocolatier Pierre Marcolini, hosts a weekend antiques market.

BRUSSELS BEER PROJECT

188 Rue Antoine Dansaert, Brussels;
www.brusselsbeerproject.be; +32 2 502 2856

◆ Food   ◆ Tour   ◆ Takeout
◆ Family   ◆ Bar   ◆ Transport

THINGS TO DO NEARBY

Sainte-Catherine
This neighbourhood is in
the heart of the Brussels'
fashion quarter, with cool
boutiques showcasing
cutting-edge Belgian
designers, such as Martin
Margiela and Dries van
Noten.

Mer du Nord
A Brussels institution,
this fishmonger operates
an open-air seafood bar,
surrounded by crowds
all day. Feast on grilled
scallops, fish soup and
prawn croquettes. ***www.
vishandelnoordzee.be***

La Grand Place
Don't miss Brussels'
momentous town square,
lined with opulent
guildhouses and palaces.
Drink in the splendour
over a beer at Le Roy
d'Espagne brasserie.

À la Bécasse
Opened back in 1877, La
Bécasse, 'The Snipe', is
famed for its young Lambic
Blanche, traditionally
served in a stone jug by
waiters wearing monastic-
style uniforms.
www.alabecasse.com

This recently-opened artisan brewery, right in the
centre of Brussels, is set to shake up the traditional
Belgian beer scene. Sébastien Morvan and Olivier de
Brauwere launched their project with the backing of
enthusiastic crowdfunding, declaring that, 'while some
brewers here in Belgium are so proud to have made the
same beer for 250 years that they would never think of
changing anything, we intend to create three to four beers
a month as the whole turnaround process to come out
with a recipe is only five weeks.'

Housed in a sprawling industrial atelier, the minimalist tap room has 15 draft beers ready to taste. This is a
meeting place for enthusiasts to sip and savour weird
and wonderful ales in specially designed tasting glasses,
to discuss beer and food pairing, even music and beer
pairing. Its vast state-of-the-art Braukon vats are stored
at the back, where Sébastien and Olivier come up with
such striking brews as the IPA-style Grosse Bertha, smoky
Dark Sister made with roasted and toasted malts, and
thirst-quenching Delta IPA: hoppy, bitter, plus surprising
hints of lychee and passion fruit. Don't miss Babylone: it's
brewed with recycled bread, giving a bold, bitter, hoppy
taste. As Sébastien says, 'craft is back'.

GRUUT BREWERY

1 Rembert Dodoensdreef, Ghent;
www.gruut.be; +32 9 269 0269

◆ Food ◆ Tour ◆ Takeout
◆ Family ◆ Bar ◆ Transport

THINGS TO DO NEARBY

Sint-Jacob's Flea Market
Every Friday, Saturday and Sunday morning, the ancient square is filled with scores of tempting bric-a-brac stalls, and teeming with bargain hunters.

Herberg de Dulle Griet
This raucous tavern is perfect to sample Belgium's more classic brews. There are a mere 350 to choose from, including Gueuze, Lambic, and dozens of Trappists. *www.dullegriet.be*

Publiek
Ghent is the home of the exciting Flemish Foodies movement and the top address to try this innovative Belgian cuisine is chef Olly Ceulenaere's laidback diner. *www. publiekgent.be*

Boat in Gent
A tour of Ghent's romantic waterways is totally touristy but still the best way to get a feel for this enchanting medieval city. *www.boatingent.be*

Since 2009, the vibrant town of Ghent boasts its own craft brewery, run by Annick de Splenter, who began making her own ales in her parents' garage when still a student. She has just moved into cavernous new premises, an old leather factory hidden away down a cobbled lane, with long communal wooden tables (good for meeting the locals) or comfy leather sofas. Annick explains that 'Gruut means a mixture of herbs and that is what I use for brewing instead of hops – my brews are tasty, drinkable, aromatic and I think I can also claim they are aphrodisiac. Just don't ask me to give away any of the herb ingredients in my secret recipes!'

There are just five artisan ales on the menu, and compared to typical Belgian brews they will not knock you out with a high alcohol content. Only her latest recipe, the potent 9% Trippel Inferno, uses hops imported from California. Food is limited to snacks, but order the tasty bread, home-baked with malt residue from the brewing, perfect with tapenade and onion marmalade dips. The beer to try here is the Gruut Brown, similar to a Trappist, but with a smoked almond aftertaste.

TER DOLEN

Eikendreef 21 Houthalen-Helchteren;
www.terdolen.be; +32 11 606 999

◆ Food   ◆ Tour   ◆ Takeout
◆ Family ◆ Bar

Ter Dolen is an atmospheric Belgian brewery located in a 16th-century castle, though the estate dates back to the Middle Ages as the summer residence/refuge of the abbots of St Truiden.

There's a fine variety of beers being produced here, ranging from traditional Abbey-style brews, such as Blondes, Tripels and Flemish Dark Abbey beers, to Krieks and ales dry-hopped with Cascade flowers. Seasonally, you could luck out with the Ter Dolen Winter, which has three varieties of malt, two of hops, along with locally produced honey and cinnamon. There are guided tours of the brewery every Saturday and Sunday at 3pm. Don't miss the award-winning Ter Dolen Dark, with its rich, dark flavours and warming alcohol notes.

National Jenever Museum
Take your pick of 130 different types of Jenever (Belgian-style gin) to taste while learning all about this proudly local spirit in nearby Hasselt. *www.jenevermuseum.be*

Jessenhofke Brewery
Do your bit for the environment by drinking at Jessenhofke, an organic, family-run microbrewery powered by renewable energy, with ingredients determined by their 'low beer miles'. *www. jessenhofke.be/en*

3 FONTEINEN

Molenstraat 47, Lot;
www.3fonteinen.be; +32 2 306 71 03

◆ Food   ◆ Tour   ◆ Takeout
◆ Family   ◆ Bar   ◆ Transport

After a disastrous equipment failure followed by a four-year break from brewing, beer lovers around the world exhaled in relief when the legendary 3 Fonteinen was able to return to the production of its traditional Gueuze and Lambic in 2013. Three years later, the brewery expanded, opening a new barrel-ageing, blending, and bottling facility in the town of Lot, just 4km (2½ miles) away.

The new site is more convenient for tourists, and it includes a shop as well as lambik-O-droom, an off-the-hook beer cafe stocked with more than 30,000 bottles of vintage Geuze, Kriek and Framboise, as well as special 3 Fonteinen beers available nowhere else. (While the new site is a must-see, tours of the brewery in Beersel are available for groups with advanced reservation, and the original 3 Fonteinen restaurant still serves excellent

THINGS TO DO NEARBY

Domaine de Huizingen
This former chateau near Beersel is a grand setting for playgrounds, trampolines, tennis courts, ponds, rowboats, outdoor swimming pools and a small petting zoo. **www. kasteelvanhuizingen.be**

Oud Beersel
Founded in 1882, this historic brewery has a gift shop and a visitors centre detailing the Lambic brewing process. Book ahead for tours of the brewery. **www.oudbeersel.com**

In de Verzekering Tegen de Grote Dorst
Only open for a few hours on Sundays and church holidays, the Eizeringen village pub boasts one of the world's largest selections of Gueuze and Kriek. **www.dorst.be**

Les Galeries Royales Saint-Hubert
Opened in 1847, this elegant mall in Brussels was the first covered shopping arcade in Europe. Come for the luxury shops, stay for the amazing Italianate architecture. **www.grsh.be**

Belgian cuisine and beer on Beersel's main square.)

The Lambic region is defined by the Senne (Zenne) River; you'll cross it via a footbridge from the Lot train station, a 10-minute ride from the Gare du Midi in Brussels. When you taste your first sip of Zenne y Frontera, a Lambic aged in Oloroso and Pedro Ximénez sherry barrels, you'll know it couldn't have been made anywhere else.

WESTVLETEREN

Donkerstraat 13, Westvleteren;
www.indevrede.be; +32 57 40 03 77

◆ Food ◆ Bar
◆ Family ◆ Takeout

THINGS TO DO NEARBY

In Flanders Fields
This interactive museum offers a moving and fascinating multi-sensory insight into WWI history through videos, hands-on exhibits and more traditional displays. *www.inflandersfields.be*

National Hop Museum
Based in Poperinge, within Belgium's hop-growing region, this is the place to learn the uses, histories and legends behind beer's most fragrant ingredient. *www.hopmuseum.be*

Lakenhalle
Climb to the top of the 70m-high belfry of this magnificently reconstructed 14th-century building for great views over the pretty town of Ypres.

St Bernardus Brewery
Once the official brewer of Saint Sixtus beers, some St Bernardus ales use recipes almost identical to the celebrated Westvleteren brews. Book for a tour and tasting. *www.sintbernardus.be*

For beer nerds, the abbey of Saint Sixtus is a pilgrimage, but it's not the monastery they come for – it's the legendary ales. The Trappist monks here brew small batches of three beers – Westvleteren Blond, Westvleteren 8 and the much-revered Westvleteren 12. The beers are not distributed at all, so while priced-up bottles do make their way onto the market, the only legitimate place to buy is from the abbey and the attached cafe, In de Vrede. Purchasing from the abbey is notoriously difficult, thanks to a list of regulations – beers must be pre-ordered by telephone, though getting through requires the patience of a saint. If you're lucky enough to have your call answered, you'll need to provide the licence plate of the car collecting the order – which can't be used for pick-ups again for 60 days. Luckily, there is an easier way. Elegant six-packs of all beers go on sale at the cafe's shop each day – get there early to stand a chance of snapping up a couple, then retire to the cafe itself for a chalice of what is by many considered to be the world's best beer: Westvleteren 12, rich with robust flavours of dried fruit, plums and treacle toffee.

CZECH REPUBLIC

How to ask for a beer in the local language? Pivo, prosím
How to say 'cheers'? Na zdraví!
Signature beer style? Bohemian Pilsner, aka pale lager
Local bar snack? Nakládaný hermelín, a marinated soft cheese
Don't: Ever top up a new beer with the dregs of an old beer, or split one beer into a different glass to share with a friend – for various reasons, it's simply not done here

One of the Old World's most historic beer destinations, the Czech Republic is home to both the city of Pilsen, or Plzeň, which gave the world Pilsner, and the city of Budweis, or České Budějovice, the home of the original Budweiser. It is also the nation with the largest annual beer consumption per capita, a title it has held every year since 1993, and the source of perhaps the greatest of European noble hops, Saaz, which have been prized among beer lovers across the continent since at least the early 12th century. Other firsts here include a direct line to much of the world's brewing barley, which descends from cultivars first grown in the country's eastern region of Moravia; and one of Europe's earliest recorded breweries, Břevnovský Klášterní Pivovar, founded in the year AD 993.

Yet despite its brewing and beer-drinking history, the Czech lands have also embraced modern craft culture, so much so that almost every new brewery now offers an IPA or pale ale alongside its traditional *světlý ležák*, or pale lager, the style that is generally known elsewhere as a Pilsner. (That name is reserved for the original, Pilsner Urquell, in the country of its birth.) Globetrotting Czech brewers such as Martin Matuška of Pivovar Matuška and Honza Kočka of Pivovar Nomád have embraced IPAs, saisons, pale ales and other international styles, while foreign-born brewers like California's Chris Baerwaldt and Australia's Filip Miller have

brought in global craft influences at Pivovar Zhůřák and Pivovar Raven, respectively. In the Czech capital of Prague, craft beer bars such as Zlý Časy, Beer Geek and Pivovarský Klub make it easy to compare the country's new brews with competition from Germany, Italy or Scandinavia: the trend among younger beer drinkers is towards modern-style craft.

But for most travellers, the big draw in a country with such a deep and long-lasting relationship with what it calls *pivo* is the overwhelming sense of tradition. Trying a freshly tapped pale lager from a small producer like Břevnovský Klášterní Pivovar or Únětický Pivovar will reveal an ocean of difference between Czech pale lager and the international version: the local take is sweeter, fuller and generally far hoppier. Other

BAR TALK - JAN ŠURÁŇ

Visitors should definitely try Pilsner Urquell at a tank pub, as well as Budweiser Budvar, and compare those to smaller breweries

TOP 5 BEERS

- **Břevnovský Benedict**
  Břevnovský Klášterní Pivovar Sv. Vojtěcha
- **Únětické Pivo 12°** Únětický Pivovar
- **Pilsner Urquell** Pilsner Urquell Brewery
- **Koutská 18°** Pivovar Kout na Šumavě
- **Hop Swill IPA** Pivovar Zhůřák

great styles here include *tmavé pivo*, a bittersweet, gingery take on dark lager, as well as harder-to-find Czech porter, a rich dark beer historically brewed above 18° Plato, often resulting in 8% alcohol or more, like the gingery, almost black Koutská 18° from the cult favourite Pivovar Kout na Šumavě. Still, the vast majority of what is consumed by locals has only 4–5% alcohol, with an emphasis on sessionability: when you drink the world's largest amount of beer, there's always room for another pint. After all, the *hospoda*, or pub, has been the focus of Czech daily life for centuries, and the beer hall remains the most common meeting place for just about every element of society. It all makes for a dynamic beer scene that is both traditional and remarkably up-to-date.

BEERANEK

Ceska 7/55, České Budějovice;
www.beeranek.cz; +42 386 360 186

◆ Food ◆ Bar ◆ Transport
◆ Tour ◆ Takeout

The complete antithesis of České Budějovice's biggest attraction Budweiser Budvar, this alternative alleyway craft brewery is a great change of pace in an otherwise very traditional region. If you manage to find Beeranek, you can expect generally different versions of unpasteurised and unfiltered Czech Pilsner, labelled (as per most beers in the Czech Republic) in degrees rather than alcohol by volume. A system that has baffled visitors to the country since the beginning of time, this practice of labelling beer in degrees (Plato) is actually a measurement of fermentable material in the wort (unfermented beer) during the brewing process. Try the Beeranek 11° Světlý Ležák, a Pilsner with tasty malt notes and some pleasantly bitter, spicy Czech hops.

THINGS TO DO NEARBY

Budweiser Budvar Brewery
Not to be mistaken for the American version (in some countries the American brewer Anheuser-Busch has to remarket as 'Bud'), this huge brewery is České Budějovice's pride and joy. *www.budvar.cz*

Black Tower
It's a claustrophobic climb up a winding, narrow staircase to the top of the 73m-high Gothic-Renaissance Black Tower, but worth the best views of České Budějovice.

NOVOSAD & SON

Nový Svět 95, Harrachov;
www.sklarnaharrachov.cz; +420 481 528 141

◆ Food ◆ Tour ◆ Takeout
◆ Family ◆ Bar ◆ Transport

One of the most unusual beer makers in the Old World, the glassworks in the North Bohemian mountain town of Harrachov installed a small in-house brewery to attract visitors and provide refreshment for their glassblowers, who work in year-round blazing temperatures – even when the ski slopes outside are covered in white. Visitors to the in-house pub can watch the workers turn molten glass into works of art while sipping František, a traditional Czech pale lager dosed with plenty of spicy Saaz hops, or try the brewery's bittersweet dark lager, Čerťák, named after a nearby ski jump. The most interesting, however, is the special pale lager produced for the glassblowers: Huťské světlé výčepní pivo, a light, low-alcohol brew that's especially refreshing when temperatures rise.

THINGS TO DO NEARBY

Sportovní Areál Harrachov
The excellent wintertime pistes in Harrachov transform into hiking and mountain-biking trails in warmer weather, with summer ski jumping possible on plastic-coated slopes. *www.skiareal.com*

Rozhledna Štěpánka
The 24m Štěpánka watchtower sits on a hill at a height of 959m above sea level. Completed in 1892, it offers 360° views of the Krkonoše Mountains. *www. rozhledna-stepanka.cz*

PILSNER URQUELL

U Prazdroje 7, Plzeň;
www.prazdrojvisit.cz; +420 377 062 888

◆ Food ◆ Tour ◆ Takeout
◆ Family ◆ Bar ◆ Transport

THINGS TO DO NEARBY

Puppet Museum
A beautifully restored Gothic building on Plzeň's main square, filled with puppets and marionettes, including original versions of local favorites Spejbl and Hurvínek. ***www. muzeumloutek.cz***

Great Synagogue
The world's third-largest synagogue, this Gothic-style building was completed in 1892. Restored in 1998, it is now used for concerts and art exhibitions. ***www.zoplzen.cz***

Techmania
This interactive children's science museum offers presentations on electricity and magnetics, fun with infrared cameras, turbines and train engines, and a 3D planetarium. ***www. techmania.cz***

Patton Memorial
One of the forgotten stories of WWII is celebrated in this unique museum dedicated to the liberation of western Czechoslovakia, including Plzeň, by the US Army. ***www.patton-memorial.cz***

Few breweries can claim to have invented their own style of beer, but few breweries have the history of Pilsner Urquell. The original Pilsner from the town of Plzeň, Pilsner Urquell — or 'original source' — was first brewed on 5 October 1842, in a new 'burghers' brewery' built by the 250 local citizens who then held brewing rights. While the owners were mostly Czech, the beer was an international collaboration: the first brewmaster, Josef Groll, came from Bavaria, as did the bottom-fermenting lager yeast, while the resulting beer's pale gold colour, a novelty at the time, was due to an English-style malt kiln using indirect heat. Local influences included Czech barley and hops, as well as Plzeň's extremely soft water.

Today visitors can tour the still-functioning cooperage, dine in the immense on-site restaurant and purchase souvenirs bearing images from the brewery's 175-year history. Pilsner Urquell produces only one beer — the classic pale lager — but there is also an old-style lager, an exceptionally charismatic and sharply bittersweet version that is still fermented in wooden vessels, which is only served in the historic limestone cellars at the end of the brewery tour. Tasting it should be on everyone's beer bucket list.

DENMARK

Kept under the benevolent, Pilsner-flavoured subjugation of the big, historic Danish brewers (namely Carlsberg and Tuborg) for over a century, small-scale beer enthusiasts in Denmark recently stepped up to reclaim and reinvent their country's fine, millennia-old brewing tradition. The oldest trace of beer in Denmark dates back to 2800 BC, and Copenhagen's first brewing guild was established in 1525. Carlsberg was founded in the mid-19th century, and today is one of the world's largest brewing groups (since 1970 it has owned Tuborg, too).

About 15 years ago, bored with the lager diet from the major producers, the Danes developed an unquenchable thirst for microbrews and craft brews. There are now around 170 breweries scattered across the country (up from 21 in 2002); indeed, every small town seems to have its own *brygghus* (brewery or brewpub).

Also to emerge were nomad brewers, and the world's best-known proponent, with a cult-like following, is Mikkel Borg Bjergsø, founder of Mikkeller (www.mikkeller.dk). Based in Copenhagen but without its own physical brewery, Mikkeller collaborates with global breweries (Mikkeller devises the recipes, then uses others' facilities). Something of a mad professor, Bjergsø (formerly a high-school science teacher) explores genres by using the best raw material available – anything from *kopi luwak* coffee to chipotle chilli.

Mikkeller Bar outposts can now be found in cities from Barcelona to Seoul. And Mikkeller certainly started something: two of Bjergsø's students have created their own acclaimed nomadic brewing practice, known as To Øl.

MIKKELLER

Viktoriagade 8B-C; Copenhagen;
www.mikkeller.dk; +45 3331 0415

◆ Food   ◆ Transport
◆ Bar

THINGS TO DO NEARBY

Vesterbro's Kødbyen
The city's meatpacking district is the epicentre of Denmark's hipster scene. At its heart is the Kødbyen (Meat City), with offbeat bars, street food and fashionable eateries.

Canal Tour
This is a city carved by waterways, so the best way to take in the eclectic architecture is by boat, starting from photogenic Nyhavn canal.
www.stromma.dk

Christiania
This waterside commune on the edge of Christianshavn has been a stomping ground for nonconformists since the 1970s, with colourful graffiti, art galleries and intriguing DIY architecture.

Tivoli Gardens
Copenhagen's wacky amusement park was the inspiration for Walt Disney's own California theme park. This pleasure-garden-on-steroids is a fantasy land for young and old alike. ***www.tivoli.dk***

In true Danish fashion, Mikkeller has become a byword for innovation in the Nordic brewing scene. What started off in 2006 as a hobby for a maths and physics teacher who found himself drawn to experimentation with hops, malt and yeast in his Copenhagen kitchen, has grown to become a craft brewing mini-empire exporting to 40 countries. 'We never sit still,' jokes founder Mikkel Borg Bjergsø. 'We do new experiments and projects all the time.' The range is staggering, from pilsners to stouts, American-style IPAs to fruit beers, and gluten-free to low-alcohol brews. A recent addition is the Spontan range of fermented canned sour ales, aged in oak barrels at Mikkeller's brewery in Belgium. There's a variety of Mikkeller venues around the brewery's flagship base in Copenhagen, but two are also acclaimed restaurants: Øl & Brød and WarPigs, the former specialises in *smørrebrød* (traditional Danish open sandwiches), and the latter is a brewpub and Texan barbecue joint. 'My ambition is to open Danish chefs' and food lovers' eyes to beer as a highly competent alternative to wine,' explains Mikkel. Try the Beer Geek Breakfast, a coffee stout – the original brew that kick-started Mikkeller's meteoric rise.

FRANCE

How to ask for a beer in local language?
Une bière, s'il vous plaît.
How to say cheers? Santé, tchin tchin or just tchin!
Signature beer style? Saison
Local bar snack? Une planche or assiette – fromage,
charcuterie or mixte (a plate/board with cheese, cold
meat or both)
Do: Specify une pinte (50 cL) or un demi (25 cL);
some places will also offer un galopin (12.5 cL)

While you may not realise it sitting in a classic
Paris bar with its inevitable choice between
mass-market lager and a couple of big Belgian names,
France is a country with a proud history of *la bonne bière*
– good beer. Going back to the end of the 19th century,
there were more than 2800 breweries here. By the end
of the 1970s, that number had plunged into the double
digits, victim of two world wars and mass industrial-
isation. A strong beer tradition held in the northeast,
near the Belgian border, but elsewhere, and for obvious
reasons, the tipple of choice was wine.

But the craft beer – or *bière artisanale* – movement has
started to make itself felt. Small and slow, but insistent
and growing. There are now around 1000 *microbrasseries*
in France, and the rate of growth keeps getting faster as
the French start to discover that if they want a drink with
character, wine is not the only choice.

When you ask someone to point you to a style of beer
that's particularly French, they may indicate *bière de
garde*. The name hints that it was beer brewed to keep
(*garder* in French) or age, it's more likely that it marked the
turning point from the old-school table beer brewed in
the north of the country early in the century, to a stronger,
Belgian *abbaye*-style. And as craft beer enthusiasts will
tell you, this smooth, cereal style is a much better match
than wine for the strong cheeses and rich terrines you'll
find on the French table.

From his shop La Cave à Bulles near Les Halles, with its

impeccably curated selection of French craft beers, Simon
Thillou compares the burgeoning French craft beer movement to the Tour de France. 'There are 200 riders. Among
them, there are 20 or 30 who can make the big climbs
– they're great riders – and only two or three who could
possibly win. But they bring all the others along with them.'

Making the big climbs is one of the first brewers to
update traditional methods with modern craft beer
sensibilities, Daniel Thiriez of Brasserie Thiriez, in the
beer-loving north of the country. Known as the founding
father of French craft brewing, he started as early as 1996.
But he had to wait for local palates to catch up. As Simon
says, 'eight years ago their Etoile du Nord (a hoppy Saison)

BAR TALK - SIMON THILLOU

I compare the craft beer scene to the Tour de France. There are 200 riders. A few make the big climbs, and only two or three of them could win. But they bring all the others along with them.

TOP 5 BEERS

- **Etoile du Nord Saison** Brasserie Thiriez
- **La Bavaisienne Bière de Garde** Brasserie Theillier
- **Oyster Stout** Brasserie du Mont Saleve
- **Ernestine IPA** Brasserie de la Goutte d'Or
- **Cerberus Triple** Brasserie de l'Etre

was the hoppiest beer brewed in the country and way too out-there for normal tastes. Today, it's our best-seller'.

In big cities like Paris, Lyon and Bordeaux, *caves à bières* (beer shops) and homebrew suppliers are springing up like wild hops. Craft beer is still a small scene in a wine-centric country, which makes for a strong community brought together by the 'values of craft beer', described by Simon Thillou as 'sharing, pleasure and taste'.

Really, craft beer is made for the French – a people who support 400-odd different varieties of cheese, who invented matching food with drink, take two-hour lunches, and where regional provenance and artisanal production are already like religion.

BRASSERIE DE CHANAZ

118 Route du Canal, Chanaz; www.brasseriedechanaz.
blogspot.com; +33 04 79 52 22 19

- ◆ Food
- ◆ Family
- ◆ Tour
- ◆ Bar
- ◆ Takeout
- ◆ Transport

In the charming canal-side village of Chanaz, Pascal Moreau gradually transitioned to selling his beer after teaching himself to brew. All of his beers are produced in a tiny self-made brewery near the entrance to the village.

There are five regular beers: a blonde ale, a *blanche* (white/*witbier*), an amber, a brown and a *saison*, as well as some special one-off and seasonal brews. You can visit his brewery on weekend afternoons, and during the summer he operates a small shop in the centre of the village, where you can purchase his core range of beers (and sometimes the special brews) in bottles to take away. If it's the season, try the spring ale brewed with wild hops, which Moreau collects from nearby fields.

THINGS TO DO NEARBY

Moulin de Chanaz
This 1868 stone watermill produces oils from hazelnut and walnut. Watch artisans operate the milling crank, and purchase snacks, condiments and, of course, the oils. *www. moulindechanaz.com*

Auberge de Portout
Head 2km (1¼ miles) up the road to Auberge de Portout for local snails, cheese, and frogs' legs, washed down with Pascal Moreau's beer. *www.aubergedeportout.fr*

LES 3 BRASSEURS

22 Place de la Gare, Lille;
www.les3brasseurs.com; +33 3 20 06 46 25

◆ Food ◆ Bar ◆ Transport
◆ Family ◆ Takeout

On the frontier of French and Flemish culture, Lille is the urban centre of France's richest regional beer culture. With a climate too cool for grapes, grains and hops were grown here instead, and for centuries countless farmhouse brewers made rustic ales to keep local agricultural workers happy. So it's no surprise that some of the most vibrant new-wave *brasseurs* in France are found in this region, as traditional practices are updated by modern enthusiasts. Craft beer groundbreaker Brasserie Thiriez is further north in Esqulebecq; Brasserie du Pays Flamand makes its award-winning Saison a little west; and for a taste of tradition, look for the *bières de garde* of Brasserie Theillier, run by seven generations of the same family.

But back in Lille, Les 3 Brasseurs is the headquarters of a craft beer success story exported around the francophone

THINGS TO DO NEARBY

Vieux Lille
A warren of beautifully restored 17th- and 18th-century Flemish brick houses now home to chic boutiques, slick cafes and cosy restaurants. The quarter's architectural diversity will astound.

La Capsule
Taste your way through the beers of the region at this atmospheric bar specialising in local brews, deep in the heart of the old town.

Abbaye des Saveurs
Both French and Belgian beers line the ancient stone walls at this épicerie and beer shop deep in Vieux Lille's jumble of winding cobblestone streets.

Palais des Beaux Arts
A world-renowned fine arts museum with a first-rate collection of works from the 15th to 20th centuries, including works by Rubens, Van Dyck and Manet.
www.pba-lille.fr

world (if you ever find yourself in Tahiti in need of a decent *brune*, you're in luck). With quality beer made in-house, tasting paddles of the regular brews, a cosy settle-in-for-the-day feel and beer-friendly Flemish favourites, such as *flammekueche* (a thin-crusted tart with crème fraiche, onions and lardons) on the menu, it's a winning formula. Try a Fleur des Flandres, a gently bitter, floral Belgian-style ale.

NINKASI

Various locations, Lyon;
www.ninkasi.fr

◆ Food   ◆ Bar   ◆ Transport
◆ Family   ◆ Takeout

THINGS TO DO NEARBY

Traboules
Vieux Lyon and Croix
Rousse are criss-crossed
with a fascinating network
of secret passageways
used by 19th-century silk-
weavers to get their wares
safely to market. *www.
lyontraboules.net*

Le Garet
Eating in Lyon means going
to a bouchon, a traditional
Lyonnais bistro. Le Garet is
one of Lyon's classics, with
a devoted local clientele
and friendly service.

Musée des Beaux-Arts
France's finest collection
of sculptures and paintings
outside Paris, with works
from Rodin, Rubens,
Rembrandt, Monet,
Matisse and Picasso.
There's also a cloister
garden. *www.mba-lyon.fr*

**Les Halle de Lyon Paul
Bocuse**
This famous food market
has five dozen stalls of
gourmet delights, including
Lyonnais specialties,
such as quenelles or St
Marcellin cheese. *www.
hallespaulbocuse.lyon.fr*

How often can you do a craft beer bar crawl dedicated to a single brewery? Ninkasi is a local chain
par excellence, with nine bars in Lyon. (Aside from another
three in the region, you won't find it anywhere else.) The
beer is brewed in Tarare on the Rhône nearby, with water
from the mountains of Beaujolais, famed for its softness
and purity. The solid range of beers is complemented by a
monthly *biere de saison*; when we visited it was Buddha
Ale brewed with yuzu and kaffir lime. The award-winning
grand cru brews are cold-aged, using ingredients from the
region's winemakers – Riesling yeast, oak cask chips.

Start your tour at hilltop Croix Rousse, once Europe's
silk-weaving capital, where Ninkasi is on the buzzing
main street. Descend the impossibly picturesque staircase

Montée de la Grande Côte to Vieux Lyon and Ninkasi
Saint-Paul, just by the river.

Then drop by Ninkasi Hôtel de Ville for its stone-cel-
lar ambience. The best place to finish up is Ninkasi
Guillotière, with its enormous terrace and views over the
river to Vieux Lyon. Try the Noire – chocolate caramel
bitterness and that soft Rhône water: winner of the
world's best porter in the 2015 World Beer Awards.

BAPBAP

79 rue Saint-Maur, Paris;
www.bapbap.paris; +33 1 77 17 52 97

◆ Takeout   ◆ Tour
◆ Transport

Working hands-on and small-scale is a necessity when you're brewing in a 5-storey building in the 11th, Paris' most densely populated arrondissement. As Édouard Minart, co-founder of BapBap – *'brassée à Paris, bue à Paris'* ('brewed in Paris, drunk in Paris') – explains, it took 2½ years to find a suitable building within the city limits. You can't get a lorry into these medieval streets – fortunately a large part of BapBap's output is consumed in the hipster hangouts and craft beer bars of the 11th. It's a brewery like no other – 1800 sq m in an all-metal, Eiffel-style building. Everything happens here except the growing of the grain – malt crushing, brewing, fermenting and bottling. Try its distinctive IPA, dry-hopped with Sorachi Ace for a long-lasting, resinous bitterness.

THINGS TO DO NEARBY

Cimitière du Père Lachaise
One of Paris' most romantic places – yes, visit the graves of Oscar Wilde and Jim Morrison, but mostly just wander aimlessly through this gorgeous hilly park. *www.pere-lachaise.com*

Au Passage
Still a beloved Paris néo-bistrot, a genre invented almost single-handedly by Aussie chef James Henry, who founded Au Passage in 2011. Great wine and clever small plates. *www. restaurant-aupassage.fr*

BRASSERIE LA GOUTTE D'OR

28 rue de la Goutte d'Or, 18e, Paris;
www.brasserielagouttedor.com; +33 9 80 64 23 51
◆ Takeout
◆ Transport

Here in 'Little Africa', home to a large West and North African community and one of Paris' last thriving working-class quartiers, is Brasserie la Goutte d'Or. It has the distinction of being Paris' first microbrewery, and takes inspiration from the cultural diversity of the local community. Drop in and *brasseur* Thierry Roche will talk you through how. You'll find La Chapelle, a wheat beer infused with flavours of chai: ginger, cinnamon, cardamom. Charbonnière, a smoked amber, was inspired by Zola's description of a local street near the train station. Both gritty and romantic, these are truly Paris beers. Try Ernestine, the dry-hopped IPA with an English Pale Ale spin, and a nod to rue Ernestine, where beers were brewed in the early 1900s.

THINGS TO DO NEARBY

Marché Dejean
This chaotic local market is a vibrant introduction to African culinary culture, with exotic vegetables, such as okra and manioc, fish heads and fresh herbs.

Brasserie Barbès
Chic art deco styling, ultra-cool ambience and great food are on offer at this bar-restaurant-nightspot overlooking metro Barbès. The rooftop terrace is the place to be. *www. brasseriebarbes.com*

DECK & DONOHUE

71 rue de la Fraternité, Montreuil;
www.deck-donohue.com; +33 9 67 31 15 96
◆ Takeout
◆ Transport

Welcome to Montreuil, a little-visited Paris banlieue experiencing gradual gentrification, a wave of street art, and a beer-led renaissance. Thomas Deck and Mike Donohue have been here since 2014, after their 10-year friendship and respective Alsatian and American roots led to a vocation to create *bières fines* for the Paris market. Their handcrafted small-batch ales and IPAs are among the most popular in the city's growing number of craft beer hotspots. On Saturdays they welcome visitors to their big, bright brewery to get a taste of the range – six permanent beers and a clutch of ever-changing seasonal and special editions. Try the Vertigo, a classic American-style IPA – earthy, hoppy but approachable, a gateway beer for Kronenbourg-accustomed Parisians.

THINGS TO DO NEARBY

La Montreuilloise
Visit another of Montreuil's brasseries open on Saturdays, in the charming *Murs à Pêches* (peach-growing walls) district – or investigate one of its beer-making workshops. *www. la-montreuilloise.com*

Bois de Vincennes
Boating, cycling and mini-golf are just some of possibilities at Paris' second-biggest (995 hectares) 'green lung'. There's also a zoo, botanical gardens, and a stunning medieval chateau.

PANAME BREWING COMPANY

41 bis Quai de la Loire, Paris;
www.panamebrewingcompany.com; +33 1 40 36 43 55

◆ Food   ◆ Bar   ◆ Transport
◆ Family   ◆ Takeout

THINGS TO DO NEARBY

Canauxrama
Arrive at Paname in style, via canal. Starting at Bastille, 2½-hour tours take you through locks and under bridges for a barge-level view of the real Paris.
www.canauxrama.com

Parc des Buttes-Chaumont
This 19th-century quirky park features fake grottoes, waterfalls and a 'Roman' gazebo on a hill. Picnic on the slope with a view of Sacré-Cœur.

Belleville Street Art Tour
Gritty, rapidly gentrifying Belleville is a street art hotspot, with lanes filled with temporary masterpieces – take a tour to see the latest. *www.streetartparis.fr/street-art-tours-paris*

Le Baratin
This wine-focused bistro is a Belleville institution, offering simple, heartfelt cooking and a lunch menu that's one of the greatest deals in the 20e.

Breweries within Paris city limits are rare; breweries with waterfront views are almost nonexistent. But Paname Brewing Company, Paris' first micro-brewpub, has a prime spot on the Bassin de la Villette, where Canal St-Martin turns into Canal d'Ourcq and continues its flow north out of the city. Paname is a slangy nickname for Paris from the early 20th century, when the *bassin* was a thriving commercial transport hub. The brewery is in a 19th-century warehouse with industrial remnants and a set of dazzling stainless steel tanks taking pride of place at the back of the big, open taproom. The regular beers are named for the canal's *Belle Époch* heyday: Le Barge du Canal, the big, hoppy IPA; Oeil de Biche, the crisp, fruity pale ale. Limited-

edition monthly brews might include a Double IPA or an Imperial red ale. The menu is beer-centric – think pizza, burgers, pulled pork, charcuterie. Head for the spacious terrace that floats on a pontoon out front, with a view of the canal-side pétanque players and boat cruisers, and settle in. The must-try beer here is the Casque d'Or, the floral saison, brewed with 100% French hops, orange rind and candied ginger.

TRIANGLE

13 rue Jacques Louvel Tessier, Paris;
www.triangleparis.com; +33 1 71 39 58 02

◆ Food   ◆ Bar
◆ Family   ◆ Transport

Taking the concept of microbrewing to the extreme, the tiny 'brewhouse' at Triangle consists of three little kettles that manage to pump out an impressive 300L of handcrafted beer each week. Depending on its fermentation schedule, you'll find between two and four house beers on the list at this exquisite brewery–bar–restaurant in a hip corner of Paris' 10th arrondissement. This is a new concept in Paris, created by a trio of young Quebecois: light and bright French-bistro-meets-Scandi interior, house-brewed beers (bolstered by a changing list of guest beers), and a seasonal menu to accompany them. You'll be at the mercy of the tight brewing schedule, but if the big, treacly India Dark is on offer, don't hesitate to try it.

THINGS TO DO NEARBY

Musée des Arts et Métiers
Dating back to 1794 and housed in an 18th-century priory, Europe's oldest science and technology museum is full of fascinating historical machines and gadgets.
www.arts-et-metiers.net

Marché des Enfants Rouges
Built in 1615, this is Paris' oldest covered market. Stroll through the maze of food stalls then lunch with locals at big communal tables. **www.marchedes enfantsrougesfr.com**

BRASSERIE DES SOURCES DE VANOISE

124 montée Château Feuillet, Villarodin-Bourget;
www.brasserievanoise.com; +33 6 70 46 52 94

◆ Tour
◆ Takeout

This tiny alpine brewery makes a staple range of four organic beers – an amber, a brown, a blonde and a white ale – all of which are infused with saffron that is native to the high mountains nearby. The brewery space is located in a thoughtfully converted stone house in the village of Villarodin-Bourget at the foot of the French Alps. The brewery is open throughout the year, offering tours that take in how the beer is made and, crucially, how the house was ingeniously altered to make room for the brewing kit.

Tastings and take-away bottles are available in a teeny tasting room. If you can time your visit for spring, try the spring blonde ale infused with wild thyme and yellow gentian flowers.

THINGS TO DO NEARBY

Val d'Isere & Valloire
A number of nearby resorts, including Val d'Isere and Valloire, cater to winter sports enthusiasts, offering skiing, snowboarding, ice climbing, and ice driving. **www.valdisere.com; www. valloire.net**

Col du Galibier
The Col du Galibier is one of the notoriously steep alpine ascents on the Tour de France. Mere mortals can zip up on e-bikes hired in Valloire.

GERMANY

How to ask for a beer in local language?
Ein Bier, bitte
How to say cheers? Prost!
Signature beer style? Pilsner
Local bar snack? Pretzels, cheese and bread
Don't: Be afraid to have one before noon: an early beer at Frühschoppen is a cherished tradition in many parts of Germany

Get ready to be overwhelmed: a quick dive into German beer culture could easily take up a whole summer, if not your entire life. Home to over a thousand years of beer-soaked history, Germany is the country that perfected large-scale brewing, from dark lager, Pilsner and Hefeweizen in Bavaria to fruity Kölsch in Cologne and bittersweet Alt in Düsseldorf. This is the country whose emperor once declared, in all seriousness, 'Give me a woman who loves beer and I will conquer the world.' This is the land of the Reinheitsgebot, one of the world's first food purity laws, which defined what could and could not go into beer way back in the year 1516 – and which still rules today.

Not content to have created some of the world's most recognised and beloved beer styles, Germany is also home to true oddballs, like the sour ales Berliner Weisse and Gose, or the smokey Rauchbiers from Bamberg. And while getting your head around the grand traditions of Germany can require years of study, bear in mind that the country has an entire new generation of craft brewers now making world-class pale ales, Imperial stouts and saisons – styles that have nothing at all to do with Germany's highly enviable beer history.

In a city like Munich, you can visit an old-school beer hall like the Hofbräuhaus, enjoying the same lagers as customers there did over a hundred years ago, and then move on to a craft beer bar like Tap-House, which boasts 42 draft lines and hundreds of bottles from local craft producers, as well as renowned Italian, Danish or American imports.

In Cologne, a city dedicated to its own indigenous style of Kölsch, you can have a traditional late-morning snack of Kölsch with *Halve Hahn* – rye bread with cheese – at Früh am Dom, right by the massive cathedral, then visit the brew-pub Braustelle, a palace of experimentation and innovation where tradition is largely thrown out the window.

While excellent craft breweries can be found around the country, the coolest new scene is, unsurprisingly, found in Berlin, one of Europe's hippest cities. Here, expat-owned craft breweries, such as Vagabund and Stone, offer authen-

BAR TALK - MANUELE COLONNA

The Berlin beer scene is growing really fast, though it started just few years ago, and there's much more interest among locals

TOP 5 BEERS

- **Schneider Weisse TAP 1 Meine Helle Weisse**
  Schneider Weisse
- **Wöllnitzer Weissbier** Gasthausbrauerei Talschänke
- **Spezial Ungespundet** Brauerei Spezial
- **Gänstaller Kellerbier** Gänstaller Bräu
- **Kellerbier Ayinger Celebrator Doppelbock** Brauerei Aying

tic, American-style brews, while local heroes Schoppe Bräu, Eschenbräu and Heidenpeters are turning out their own innovative beers.

German hop growers have responded to the explosive popularity of craft flavours as well, supplementing their traditional noble hops from Hallertau, Spalt and Tettnang with new, wildly aromatic cultivars, such as Mandarina Bavaria, Polaris and Hüll Melon. It all adds up to one of the world's greatest places for beer travellers: in a country just slightly larger than New Mexico, there are now over 1300 breweries, with over 300 great beer makers in Franconia alone, and the tiny village of Aufseß has a total of four breweries for just 1300 inhabitants. Yes, a beer tour of Germany might be overwhelming, and you certainly won't be able to see everything. But it'll be so much fun to try.

MAHR'S BRÄU

Wunderburg 10, Bamberg;
www.mahrs.de; +49 951 915 170

◆ Food   ◆ Tour   ◆ Takeout
◆ Family   ◆ Bar   ◆ Transport

In a city as jam-packed with world-class beer-drinking spots as Bamberg, it's hard to stand out from the crowd, but for the small family-run brewpub Mahr's Bräu, set near to the river, the secret to success lies with one of its most popular brews: U-Beer. Mahr's also produce great Bocks, Weissbiers and seasonals, such as its popular Christmas beer.

Aside from amazing beer, you can expect a cosy pub with a crackling fire in winter, or a quaint little flower-adorned beer garden in summer and some of the finest traditional Franconian food in town. Of course you have to try the famed U-Beer (or Ungespundet-hefetrüb, to give it its full name): the smooth, silky, malty flavour is really quite delicious and unique to this region.

THINGS TO DO NEARBY

UTracks Bavarian Beer Trail Cycle
With its flat terrain and closely spaced towns, this region of Franconia is the ultimate place to tour by pedal power, with refreshing brewery stops, of course.

Altstadt
Having largely avoided the destructive bombs during WWII, the Altstadt, or Old Town of Bamberg still stands and is, in its entirety, a Unesco World Heritage site.

SPEZIAL KELLER

Sternwartstraße 8, Bamberg;
www.spezial-keller.de; +49 951 54887

◆ Food   ◆ Bar   ◆ Transport
◆ Family   ◆ Takeout

With its leafy, breezy beer garden, delicious traditional cuisine, tasty beer and lofty views across Bamberg's medieval skyline, Spezial Keller is a favourite for most Bamberg locals. While you do have to walk about 15 minutes from the city centre (and up a small hill), the hike is definitely worth it. While Bamberg is a beer mecca in itself, the traditional brew of this old city is a malty, smoky brew called *Rauchbier*. Spezial's version isn't as intensely smoky as Bamberg's other well-known *Rauchbier* (Schlenkerla), so it's a good introduction to the style and it still carries all those delicious malty flavours. To accompany your Spezial Rauchbier, you won't go wrong with the prehistoric-sized pork knuckle in a swimming pool of sauerkraut.

THINGS TO DO NEARBY

Weyermann Maltings
White malt bags sporting the Weyermann logo can be found in breweries all around the globe, and it all begins right here. Regular tours on Wednesdays. *www.weyermann.de/in*

Naturkunde-Museum
This natural history museum's collection of stuffed birds and animal skeletons, as well as seashells, crustaceans and fish, is impressive. *www. naturkundemuseum. berlin/en*

SCHLENKERLA

Dominikanerstrasse 6, Bamberg;
www.schlenkerla.de; +49 951 560 60

◆ Food   ◆ Bar   ◆ Transport
◆ Family   ◆ Takeout

The German hinterlands are home to a number of unusual beer styles, but few compare to the remarkable *Rauchbier* from Bamberg in northern Bavaria. *Rauch* means smoke, and Bamberger Rauchbier uses barley malt that has been dried over a beech-wood fire, which gives the grain its charismatic smoky, vanilla like flavours and aroma.

It is produced by several breweries in Bamberg and the surrounding region, including the excellent Brauerei Spezial, as well as at Schlenkerla, a pub and brewery dating back to 1405. Also known as Heller-Bräu Trum or Brauerei Heller-Trum, Schlenkerla occupies a timbered building in Bamberg's Unesco World Heritage–listed city centre, with arches from the Gothic era still clearly visible inside the wood-lined, flower-festooned beer hall. Several types of *Rauchbier* are produced at Schlenkerla, all of which pair deliciously with the kitchen's meat-and-potatoes fare, including homemade

bratwurst and stuffed onions with beer sauce. But the pinnacle of any Bamberg beer trip has to be the first sip of Aecht Schlenkerla Rauchbier Märzen, a smoky-sweet, rich amber lager with 5.1% alcohol, which is dispensed in the Schlenkerla taproom from gravity-drawn, small oak casks.

THINGS TO DO NEARBY

Bamberg Cathedral
Founded in the year 1002, Bamberger Dom mixes Romanesque and Gothic styles into an architectural masterpiece. The large, carved wooden nativity altar dates from 1520. ***www.bamberger-dom.de***

Fränkisches Brauereimuseum
Located in the vaults of a former Benedictine monastery brewery from 1122, this museum tells the story of beer in the region of Franconia. ***www. brauereimuseum.de***

STONE BREWING WORLD BISTRO & GARDENS

Im Marienpark 23, Berlin;
www.stonebrewing.eu; +49 30 212 3430

◆ Food ◆ Tour ◆ Takeout
◆ Family ◆ Bar ◆ Transport

THINGS TO DO NEARBY

DDR Museum
The former East Germany (aka DDR) is long-gone, but its unusual kitschy style lives on forever in this fun museum dedicated to the Communist era.
www.ddr-museum.de

Bauhaus Archive
This expansive collection documents the influence of Walter Gropius and the Bauhaus School, a movement of design, crafts and fine arts that operated from 1919 to 1933.
www.bauhaus.de

Pergamon Museum
One of the world's most important archaeological museums, the Pergamon includes thousands of artifacts, including its massive, eponymous Greek altar dating from 170–159 BC. ***www.smb.museum***

Berliner Fernsehturm
The symbol of modern Berlin, the 368m television tower has risen over the city since 1969, offering 360° views as far as 42km (26 miles) away.
www.tv-turm.de

The race among America's craft brewers to branch into Europe ended with three different winners claiming to be the 'first' in one way or another. Brooklyn Brewery launched the Nya Carnegiebryggeriet brewery with its partner, Carlsberg, in Stockholm in 2014. The next year, Urban Chestnut bought an established brewery in Wolnzach, Germany, and rebranded it under its own name. Just after that, San Diego's Stone Brewing staked its claim as the first American craft brand to build its own European outpost when it launched its massive brewery and restaurant in southwestern Berlin.

This gorgeous converted industrial site, a former gasworks from 1901, features the main building's original brick facade and art deco–style rose window, as well as a space for concerts and events in a former train repair shop. Beers are sold at the on-site restaurant, styled after the original Bistro & Gardens in California, and tours in English and German are available. Though bottles are far more common in Europe, Stone remains an iconoclast, and its to-go beers are pre-packed in cans, while the draft offerings include prototypes, rare barrel-aged versions and specialty brews, such as Stone Imperial Black Belgian IPA, a drink quite unlike anything traditionally produced in Pils-loving Germany.

BRAUHAUS ZUR MALZMÜHLE

Heumarkt 6, Cologne;
www.muehlenkoelsch.de; +49 221 921 6061

◆ Food   ◆ Transport
◆ Bar

THINGS TO DO NEARBY

The Dom
Cologne's colossal cathedral, Germany's largest, has an irresistible gravitational pull. Don't just stand and stare; there are treasures inside, such as Gerhard Richter's stained-glass window of 11,500 panels.

Brauhaus Peters
Kölsch converts are spoiled for choice in Cologne's centre. Sample more bars, such as this characterful 19th-century pub, which features one room with a stained-glass ceiling. *www.peters-brauhaus.de*

Kölner Philharmonie
This modern (built in 1986) concert hall, close to the cathedral, is one of the best in the world for acoustics. It hosts contemporary and classical music concerts. Thursday's Tripclubbing nights offer Kölsch and a DJ.

Rhine River cruise
The Rhine plays a large role in Cologne's life, although its trading barges are being gradually replaced by river cruises. Take a boat trip to explore Cologne's beaches and the revitalised docklands.

Kölsch is a pale, dry, beguiling beer that doesn't bash you over the head with hops but offers a refreshing and subtly floral experience instead. Breweries in the US and Australia produce some excellent interpretations (see 4 Pines in Sydney, p254, for example) but its German hometown of Cologne (and the only place in Europe permitted to call its beer Kölsch) remains the best place to quaff it.

The lanes around the city's famous twin-spired cathedral are full of bars and *brauhausers* serving beer and brätwurst and one of the oldest is Brauhaus zur Malzmühle on Heumarkt, just south of the cathedral and a short walk from the Rhine. Beer has been handmade at this family-owned beer hall since 1858 according to the age-old recipe of barley and wheat malt, spring water, hops and yeast. Few things have changed: blue-clad waiters still beetle between tables delivering foamy glasses of Kölsch fresh from the barrel. The custom is to place a coaster over the top of your empty glass if you don't require a refill. Brewer Andree Vrana has also started a craft beer bar at the same venue where a wider range of world beers are available. But start first with the Schwartz family's own Kölsch.

BRAUHAUS ZUM SCHLÜSSEL

Bolkerstrasse 41-47, Dusseldorf;
www.zumschluessel.de; +49 211 135 159

◆ Food ◆ Bar
◆ Tour ◆ Transport

THINGS TO DO NEARBY

Rheinturm
Get an overview of North Rhine-Westphalia's capital from the observation desk (open until late, when it becomes a neon-lit landmark) of this 1980s tower on the Rhine. Decode the dots to read the clock.

MedienHafen
Düsseldorf's harbour area, adapting to post-industrial purposes, is home to a lot of modern architecture, including some typically twisted buildings by Frank Gehry, with bars, restaurants and hotels.

Kunstsammlung Nordrhein-Westfalen
This region's modern art collection is divided between three locations, primarily a granite edifice on Grabbeplatz (K20) and the Ständehaus (K21). *www.kunstsammlung.de*

Nordpark
For fresh air, venture to the city's largest park, which is packed with themed gardens linked by paths. Highlights include the Japanese Garden and the Lily Garden. Kids might enjoy the Aquazoo.

Welcome to the dark side. Cologne and Düsseldorf are divided by just 40km of Autobahn but, in beer terms, the gulf between the two west German cities runs deep. Cologne favours its own pale and delicate Kölsch but Düsseldorfers drink the dark and brooding *Altbier*, a literal translation of which is 'old beer'. This style of beer arose when the city combined the long, cool conditioning period of lager with ale-type yeasts (and ale-levels of hopping). Perhaps think of Altbier as a halfway house between heavy winter beers and lighter summer ales. They vary a fair bit, even within this single city, but you should generally expect a clear copper-brown colour topped by bright white foam; look for toffee, bready, sometimes earthy notes and a much hoppier aroma.

There are numerous *brauhausers* in Düsseldorf's Altstadt (old town) all serving Altbier and very little else (whatever you do, don't order a Kölsch unless you're ready for a lot of ribbing). One of the more interesting venues is Brauhaus Zum Schlüssel on Bolkerstrasse in Düsseldorf's historic heart. Its Altbier is a darkly roasted and complex example but with no shortage of other bars in the Altstadt, make sure to sample a few during your visit.

STAATSBRAUEREI WEIHENSTEPHAN

Alte Akademie 2, Freising;
www.weihenstephaner.de/en; +49 8161 5360

◆ Food   ◆ Tour   ◆ Takeout
◆ Family   ◆ Bar   ◆ Transport

THINGS TO DO NEARBY

Dom St Maria und St Korbinian
This twin-towered cathedral in the middle of Freising is exquisite inside and out, with a restored interior in whitewash, ochre and delicate rose.
www.freisinger-dom.de

Mariensäule
The quaint town square is a pretty spot to sit in the sun with a coffee or a cold drink and chat with the friendly locals.

Freisinger Wochenmarkt
This is the local street market where you can find a wide range of seasonal food and produce, including homemade bread, honey and fruit.

Munich Oktoberfest
Munich is only 20 minutes away, so why not plan your trip in late September/ early October to enjoy this famed festival, one of the largest in the world.
www.oktoberfest.de/en

Sitting in the leafy Weihenstephan beer garden with a tall frothy glass of fresh Hefeweizen in your hand, it's hard to fathom that this brewery is close to 1000 years old. Originally inhabited by Benedictine monks, this site has been operating as a commercial brewery since the year 1040, making it the oldest continually working brewery on earth. Located just outside Munich, it is an easy 20-minute train ride to Freising, but well worth the journey. Not only do you have this incredible history seeping out of every wall and in the very ground below you, but if you love your German brews – your Hefeweizens, Helles, Pils and Dunkels – then you are in for a treat, because they don't get much better, or more original than at Weihenstephan.

All its beer is brewed according to the Beer Purity Law of 1516 (the Reinheitsgebot) that states beer can only be produced using four ingredients – water, malt, hops and yeast, so you know you are drinking the good stuff here. Make sure you become acquainted with its multi-award winning Weizenbock, the Vitus: a magnificently crafted brew lends flavour notes of banana, citrus, clove and dried apricot.

BAYERISCHER BAHNHOF GOSEBRAUEREI

Bayrischer Pl. 1, Leipzig;
www.bayerischer-bahnhof.de; +49 341 124 5760

◆ Food   ◆ Tour   ◆ Takeout
◆ Family   ◆ Bar   ◆ Transport

THINGS TO DO NEARBY

Spinnerei Art Gallery
A huge 19th-century cotton mill, this building is now a hub of artistic creativity: it's home to 10 galleries and at least 80 individual art studios.
www.spinnerei.de/

KarLi
The street-art-adorned, alternative district in the city's south, Karl-Liebknecht-Straße (or 'Karli' as it's known) is jam-packed with bars and pubs of all styles and sizes.

Eat The World tour
Take a culinary walking tour through Leipzig's blossoming food scene and sample traditional Saxon pot-roasts, street food, and high-end gastronomy.
www.eat-the-world.com/ en/food-tours-leipzig.html

Auerbachs Keller
Founded in 1525, this famous restaurant attracts crowds but it's the place to go for a traditional Saxon feed and a few frothy German brews.
www.auerbachs-keller-leipzig.de

The region of Leipzig is renowned for Gose, a sour and saline beer style that is not only one of the most polarising in all of Germany, but also one of the oldest, having been brewed since the early 16th century in Goslar, on the northeast edge of the Harz Mountains, to the west of Leipzig. Economic decline in the early 18th century saw the Gose move its spiritual homelands to the trade city of Leipzig, where it has been brewed ever since.

Nowadays, Gose is crafted with an addition of salt in order to replicate the mineral-rich water of the Gose River and local Goslar aquifers, which were traditionally used to brew these beers. To achieve its signature sour note, Gose is fermented with lactic bacteria and then spiced with hops and coriander. While this style isn't for everyone, the best place to try it is Bayerischer Bahnhof. Located in the oldest preserved head railway station in the world, this impressive brewery is a must-see for any visitor to the city, beer lover or not. Of course you have to try the Gose: a refreshing, slightly sour, slightly saline brew with a lovely spice profile.

BRAUEREI IM EISWERK

Ohlmüllerstraße 44, Munich;
www.brauerei-im-eiswerk.de; +49 89 39292350

◆ Food ◆ Bar ◆ Transport
◆ Tour ◆ Takeout

This tiny craft brewery tacked onto the edge of the huge Paulaner beer institution proves just how far you can take the four key ingredients of the Beer Purity Law (water, malt, hops and yeast) and get away with it. Have a taste of the almost brandy like Comet Ale (an American strong ale) and have your mind blown to think all these beers have been brewed strictly according to the Purity Law decree. If you're looking for a crafty alternative to the never ending Weissbiers, Dunkels and Helles Lagers of Munich, then this is your oasis.

The beer to try? With its deep orange hue the Eiswerk Weizenbock Mandarin has a hoppy, slightly fruity yet intense taste, and aptly demonstrates this out-of-the-ordinary brewery's creativity.

THINGS TO DO NEARBY

Englischer Garten
Munich's English Garden is one of the largest city parks in Europe. Head for Kleinhesseloher See, the pretty lake at its centre, and the beer garden Seehaus. *www.muenchen.de*

Alte Pinakothek
Renowned for the quality and depth of its collection, this important museum houses canvases from many of the Old European Masters in an impressive neoclassical building. *www.pinakothek.de*

ZOIGL

Windischeschenbach (and four other villages), Oberpfalz; www.zoiglbier.de

◆ Food ◆ Tour ◆ Takeout
◆ Family ◆ Bar ◆ Transport

A medieval holdover that somehow survived into the 21st century, Zoigl is brewed in communal brewhouses in just five villages in Germany's remote Oberpfalz region, then fermented, conditioned and served in different brewpubs in each. When the beer is ready to drink, a sign —also known as a Zoigl – is hung before the pub, which is often just a family home. The taste varies, but every Zoigl is a bottom-fermented lager, deep gold to dark amber, with a prickly bitter finish. Hardcore fans might seek out samples in villages Eslarn, Falkenberg and Mitterteich,

but Zoigl's heart lies in Neuhaus and Windischeschenbach, where pubs such as Günter Zimmermann's Zum Posterer serve endless glasses of Zoigl alongside table-size platters of local sausages, ham and pâte.

THINGS TO DO NEARBY

Waldsassen Abbey
This Cistercian convent houses a remarkable rococo library, built in 1726, as well as a basilica featuring real skeletons, dressed in extravagant 18th-century royal costumes. *www.abtei-waldsassen.de*

International Ceramic Museum
This branch of Munich's Neue Sammlung design museum displays ceramics spanning eight millennia, from Qing Dynasty porcelain to art nouveau objets d'art. *www.dnstdm.de*

HUNGARY

How to ask for a beer in local language?
Egy sört, kérem
How to say cheers? Egészségedre!
Signature beer style? Pale lager
Local bar snack? Lángos, a type of fried sour dough
Don't: Clink beer glasses to say cheers – clinking has
been a faux-pas here since 1848

Make no mistake, Hungary is wine country, home to an enviable history of viticulture that includes some of the oldest classified vineyards in Europe. Yet a new craft beer scene has absolutely exploded here, with over 50 vibrant craft breweries – often only a few years old – which most beer lovers outside the country have never heard about. In the romantic capital of Budapest, cool new beer bars, such as Élesztőház ('Yeast House'), Jónás and Csak a Jó Sör ('Only Good Beer') serve rotating brews from regional producers, and the semi-annual Főzdefeszt craft beer festival has become a major event, filling Budapest's historic streets and squares with a huge, beer-loving crowd.

While wine remains the more common drink, annual beer consumption is growing, led largely by products from small producers. Perhaps due to the flavours of the country's legendary sweet wines, Hungarian craft brewers were early into the trend of brewing with fruit. Local standouts include the *Meggyes Sör* sour-cherry beers from cult favourites Szent András Sörfőzde, Rizmajer and Stari Brewery – the former's Szent András Könnye (Saint Andrew's Tears), made with real blueberries – and the Alulu Coconut Pale Ale from Hopfanatic Brewery. And at least one beer, Korty from the Serforrás brewery in Miskolc, actually includes a dose of sweet Tokaji aszú wine. Still, the country's most common style remains pale lager, aka Pilsner, with historical examples such as Dreher, originally created by the great 19th-century father of industrial lager brewing, Anton Dreher, still in production.

ÉLESZTŐ

Tűzoltó utca 22, Budapest;
www.elesztohaz.hu; +36 30 970 3625

◆ Food   ◆ Bar   ◆ Transport
◆ Family   ◆ Takeout

THINGS TO DO NEARBY

Museum of Applied Arts
If you only go to one museum it has to be this temple to art nouveau design, exhibiting furniture, textiles, glass and metalwork.
www.imm.hu

Jewish Quarter
Visit the opulent synagogue of the ancient Jewish Quarter, then discover a maze of hip boutiques, foodie bistros, and packed craft beer bars in Budapest's hottest neighbourhood.

Hungarian National Museum
The columns of this neoclassical building dominate the Museum Quarter, and the collection is a great introduction to Hungary's complex history.
www.hnm.hu

Ráday Utca
This long pedestrianised street is lined with galleries, gourmet diners, cafe terraces, bars and clubs. Here you'll find food influences from all over the world.

The genius behind Élesztő, which means 'yeast', is Daniel Dart, who founded Budapest's annual craft beer festival, Főzdefeszt, and also creates craft beers around the world. Élesztő opened in 2013 in a vast abandoned glass-making factory, and looks at first like another of Budapest's remarkable Ruin Pubs, but it's clear the whole place revolves around artisan beers. In the dark taproom, there are 21 different ales from around Hungary, including five of Élesztő's own labels, such as Black Mamma stout. A lone brewer, Daniel creates his own recipes then works in collaboration with outside microbreweries.

But there's more to Élesztő than just the beer. At the Grill Kitchen there's cheap and cheerful pork chops and sausages, which diners eat at long communal tables. Upstairs, enthusiasts can take a session at Brew Studio or book an evening of hands-on cooking/beer pairing in the Apartment-Restaurant. And the latest project is Élesztő's Hopstel, a cosy room to spend the night, rather than looking for a taxi, with hop-filled pillows and a minibar of craft brews. But if you're looking for a truly enlightening beer it's the Egymilliard Megawatt, an explosive, spicy, ginger-infused double IPA, which was brewed as an anti-nuclear protest.

JÓNÁS CRAFT BEER HOUSE

Fővám tér 11-12, Budapest; www.balnabudapest.hu/
shop/jonas-craft-beer-house; +36 70 930 1392

◆ Food ◆ Tour ◆ Takeout
◆ Family ◆ Bar ◆ Transport

One whole wall of this buzzing beerhouse is dedicated to a graphic mural explaining the process of brewing. Ok, it's in Hungarian but the friendly staff are always willing to explain it to foreigners, and afterwards you feel more confident ordering something called Monkey Funky Yeah, actually a very drinkable hazy amber sour wheat beer, brewed by Hara'Punk. Jónás takes its name from the location: the futuristic whale-like glass and metal Bálna building, a new icon on the Budapest skyline. In summer, the waterside terrace hosts concerts, beer and street food parties, with perfect views across the Danube. There's a sophisticated food menu, which reinterprets Hungarian cuisine, often using beer. Don't miss the Ravasz Hordó (Cunning Beaver), an award-winning creamy, hoppy American brown ale.

THINGS TO DO NEARBY

Great Market Hall
Hundreds of stalls fill this immense glass-and-metal food market with paprika, foie gras and smoked sausages. The first floor houses inexpensive buffet bars serving Hungarian home cooking.

Gellért Baths
These divine art-nouveau thermal baths and spas are a labyrinth of steam and sauna rooms, indoor pools decorated with azure mosaics, sculptures and stained glass. *www. gellertspa.com*

RIZMAJER BEERHOUSE

Táncsics Mihály utca 110, Csepel, Budapest;
www.rizmajersor.hu; +36 1 277 2395

◆ Food ◆ Tour ◆ Takeout
◆ Family ◆ Bar ◆ Transport

The godfather of the Budapest craft beer revolution, Josef Rizmajer creates a host of exciting, experimental ales and regularly invites other young brewers to realise their own creations.

Visitors get a warm welcome at the suburban beerhouse where there is a sunny garden, and the microbrewery is just around the corner in Josef's garage. Rizmajer admits, 'I am a malt rather than hop fanatic. I always wanted to make my own Guinness, but I never liked the bitterness, so instead I made Édes Élet, a chocolate stout, where cocoa beans soaked in alcohol are added into the mix.' Don't miss the Hippie Terror – a pale lager made with brewer armando_otchoa; this mixes the tastes of lager with IPA.

THINGS TO DO NEARBY

Nehru Part
Recently opened, Budapest's newest park is perfect for a lazy waterside walk along the mighty Danube River, or sports in the recreational areas.

Bubi Bikes
Pick up a green rental bike from one of 76 docking stations around the city, cross the Danube and explore the Buda side of the city.
www.bkk.hu/bubi/mol-bubi

ICELAND

In Iceland, the first day of March is known nationally as Beer Day. Why? It wasn't until that day in 1989 that full-strength beer was legalised after Icelanders voted in a 1915 referendum to ban all alcohol. After being prohibited for the best part of the 20th century, Icelanders could finally mark events such as the fall of the Berlin Wall with a beer.

From a standing start (although one suspects some home-brewing went on during the dry years), Iceland's craft beer scene has accelerated at an impressive rate. There are about a dozen craft breweries today and, remarkably, they're not all located in the capital city, where much of Iceland's population of 330,000 live: one of the first craft

breweries, Ölvisholt Brugghús, was founded by two farmers in Selfoss, southern Iceland. And perhaps the country's most well known brewery, Einstök, is on the north coast. The beers they're making stand up to scrutiny. Ölvisholt's most lauded ale is a smoky imperial stout and Einstök's most successful brews are widely available abroad.

As a stop on our global beer tour, Iceland has much to recommend it: otherworldly natural scenery; a compact and accessible capital city whether you're travelling from Europe or America; engaging, English-speaking locals. And beer tourists should be reassured that prices are not as high as might be feared: expect to pay less than US$10 for a local brew if you take advantage of the 'happy hours' that most of Reykjavík's bars offer. The city's nightlife is strong, with a hint of Danish influence (Mikkeller & Friends opened in the old town in 2015), and on Beer Day the party lasts all night.

EINSTÖK BEER COMPANY

Furuvellir 18, Akureyri;
www.einstokbeer.com; +354 462 1444
◆ Tour
◆ Takeout

Just a snowball-throw from the Arctic Circle, Einstök Beer Company brews its craft ales from some of the purest water on the planet, melted from glaciers that were frozen when woolly mammoths still walked the earth. Filtered through prehistoric lava flows, this pristine H2O gives a crisp, clear base to everything from porter to bilberry-flavour *Witbier*.

Beer aficionados can see the process – conducted with scientific, Icelandic efficiency at its Akureyri premises – but only on specialist beer tours. It's just as much fun to sip the glacial brews at the nearest Icelandic beerhall, preferably outside under the summertime midnight sun. If you have to pick one brew, make it the Icelandic Toasted Porter, infused with rich notes of malt, coffee and chocolate.

THINGS TO DO NEARBY

Akureyrarkirkja
Akureyri's landmark church plays architectural homage to the volcanic landscape, with buttresses and organ pipes like basalt columns and an ice-white, glacial interior. ***www.akirkja.is***

Lystigarðurinn
A garden thriving on the edge of the Arctic Circle? Yes: the world's most northerly botanic gardens hosts everything from Alpine shrubs to Icelandic summer blooms. ***www. lystigardur.akureyri.is***

BORG BRUGGHÚS

Ölgerðin Brewery, Grjótháls 7-11, Reykjavík;
www.borgbrugghus.is; +354 412 8000
◆ Tour
◆ Takeout

The impulsive, creative child of the Ölgerðin brewery – brewers of Iceland's leading lagers, ciders and fizzy pop – the Borg microbrewery weaves its magic from Western European brewing know-how and pure, unpolluted Icelandic water. Despite being the progeny of big brewing, Borg is dedicated in its pursuit of excellence, with a range of award-winning pilsners, pales ales, porters and stouts. Visiting the brewery involves joining a dedicated beer tour, but any Icelandic bar worth its pickled herring carries a range of Borg bottles. Adventurous palates may care to sample the Fenrir Taðreyktur IPA Nr. 26, prepared with sheep-dung smoked malt, which conjures up some of the sensation of sitting inside a smoke-filled Viking longhouse. Or perhaps play it safe with the Surtur Imperial Stout.

THINGS TO DO NEARBY

Árbær Open-Air Museum
Reykjavik's quaint working village of traditional Icelandic homes and tradesfolk offers a glimpse of the tough existence of islanders before the modern age. ***www. reykjavikcitymuseum.is***

Laugardalur
Translated as 'Hot Springs Valley', here's a soothing sprawl of pools, gardens, and hot springs surrounding Reykjavik's biggest thermal swimming pool and the city's former wash house.

IRELAND

How to ask for a beer in local language?
Pionta Guinness, le do thoil
How to say cheers? Sláinte!
Signature beer style? Irish stout
Local bar snack? Keogh's crisps, made from homegrown potatoes (or Tayto if there are no Keogh's)
Do: Carry cash (that's Euros) and don't expect to pay for one drink on a credit card

Take a stroll upstream alongside the River Liffey and then bear left towards the tall red-brick building with what looks like a neatly parked UFO atop it. This is the Guinness Storehouse, one of Dublin's top tourist attractions and a landmark that dominates much more than just the skyline of the Irish capital. For few breweries can be said to hold sway over the market of not just a city but a

country as Guinness. The pint of black stout with a crisp white head is shorthand for Ireland and, until very recently, it has squeezed out independent brewers to a calamitous degree. But on Ireland's west and south coasts, far from the gaze of this remorseless brewing behemoth, craft brewers have returned and there are now more than 70 alternatives to Arthur Guinness's global brand. In County Galway, stop by Galway Bay Brewery (see p207), in County Cork look for beers from Eight Degrees (their Sunburnt Irish Red Ale is the perfect partner to some morsels of Irish cheese).

Dublin too is emerging from stout's shadow with a slew of new craft beer pubs opening in recent years. Beer tourists ought to venture away from Temple Bar and visit Against the Grain on Wexford Street close to St Stephen's Green in the south, P. Mac's in the city centre, L. Mulligan Grocer in the city's northwest, and The Black Sheep on the Northside.

FRANCISCAN WELL

14b North Mall, Cork; www.franciscanwellbrewery.com; +353 21 4393 434

◆ Food ◆ Transport
◆ Bar

One of Ireland's longest-running microbreweries, Franciscan Well was founded by experienced bar manager Shane Long, back in 1998, when you might have received a raised eyebrow from local publicans if you asked for a 'craft beer'.

Located on the site of an ancient monastery, which gives the brewery its name, Franciscan Well does a range of four core beers – brewed in a space adjacent to the pub – and serves pizzas and bar snacks. These days, Franciscan Well's beers are available all over Ireland, as well as the UK and beyond, as the brewery was bought by Molson Coors in 2013. Start with a pint of Franciscan Well's signature Rebel Red, an Irish-style malty Red Ale with lots of flavour.

THINGS TO DO NEARBY

English Market
Pick up a picnic of cured meats, Irish cheeses and fresh breads or simply wander and admire the market's beautiful vaulted ceilings and wrought-iron fixtures. ***www.englishmarket.ie***

St Fin Barre's Cathedral
Explore the French Gothic architecture – mosaic tile floors and chancel ceiling – and don't miss the 17th-century cannonball that once destroyed one of the cathedral's spires, enshrined inside.

GALWAY BAY BREWERY

Oslo Bar, 226 Upper Salthill, Galway;
www.galwaybaybrewery.com; +353 91 448 390

◆ Food   ◆ Transport
◆ Bar

Galway Bay Brewery was born in the wake of Ireland's financial crisis in 2009. Co-founders Niall Walsh and Jason O'Connell initially just wanted to start a pub to cater to drinkers with expanding tastes, but soon saw the desire for new beers, and began brewing on-site at the Oslo Bar in Galway's Salthill neighbourhood.

Today the company has expanded to nearly a dozen locations around Ireland, but its original Salthill bar is as good as ever. Galway Bay's core range of five beers includes a Red Ale, a Porter, a dry-hopped IPA and a Chocolate Milk Stout, but its award-winning Of Foam and Fury Double IPA, brewed with five varieties of hop, is easily one of the best beers being brewed on the island; a must-sample when you visit.

THINGS TO DO NEARBY

McDonagh's
Best fish 'n' chips in the world? Certainly a contender, especially after sampling a few of Galway Bay's beers and a bracing walk down the Salthill prom. *www.mcdonaghs.net*

Crane Bar
A stalwart but friendly local pub on Galway's north side, where you can settle in for one of the best traditional music sessions in Ireland. *www.thecranebar.com*

BURREN BREWERY

Kincora Rd, Lisdoonvarna, Co Clare;
www.roadsidetavern.ie; +353 65 707 4084

◆ Food   ◆ Takeout
◆ Bar

The Curtin family have owned and run the Roadside Tavern in the small Clare town of Lisdoonvarna (home to a rather famous matchmaking festival) since 1893. Publican Peter Curtin has maintained the pub, and in 2011 he founded a microbrewery on-site. Burren Brewery, which is named for the special karst ecosystem that covers much of this part of Clare, produces three beers, which are available almost exclusively at the Roadside Tavern. The family's other venture, the Burren Smokehouse, is also worth a visit for its smoked fish. And the beers? The Gold is a delicious lager, Black is a creamy stout that's nuttier than its more famous Irish counterpart, but you won't go wrong with the malty Red, which is a perennial favourite.

THINGS TO DO NEARBY

Cliffs of Moher
Ireland's most famous natural sight, the 120m-high Cliffs of Moher, rises up from the Atlantic just a few kilometres down the road from Lisdoonvarna.

The Burren
This unique karst ecosystem covers 250 sq-km around Lisdoonvarna and makes for great cycling and walking. A number of loop trails connect through the area.

ITALY

How to ask for a beer in local language?
Una birra, per favore
How to say cheers? Cin-cin!
Signature beer style? Italian grape ale
Local bar snack? Large plates of antipasti
with cheese, ham and salami
Don't: Worry about leaving a big tip.
In Italy, service is included

What a difference a few years makes. Not long ago, 'Italian beer' was almost a punchline, limited to very little beyond boring lagers and other bog-standard international styles, with no discernible beer culture of its own. But then things changed. Perhaps due to the lack of a strong, indigenous beer culture like that of Germany or Belgium, early craft brewers Teo Musso of Le Baladin and Agostino Arioli at Birrificio Italiano felt free to come up with their own quirky creations, producing idiosyncratic brews, such as Baladin's powerhouse Xyauyù barley wine, a top-fermented beer which is exposed to the open air of the Langhe region during ageing, or Birrificio Italiano's Cassissona, a wine-like, bottle-conditioned beer made with blackcurrants.

In Rome, great pubs Ma Che Siete Venuti a Fà and Brasserie 4:20 introduced fans to the country's new arrivals

as they appeared, serving them alongside international craft superstars, while dozens of new brewpubs, such as Lambrate in Milan, Grado Plato in Chieri and Carrobiolo in Monza brought great beer – often paired with great Italian meals and snacks – to the furthest corners of the country.

Today, Italian craft beer is celebrated and recognised as its own quirky thing around the world, with specialty pubs such as the Italian Job in London and Birra in Berlin giving the new wave of Italian craft brewers a presence in international markets, while the country's brewmasters frequently consult and collaborate with their friends around the globe, creating destinations such as the Eataly Birreria in New York, a collaboration between Teo Musso of Le Baladin and Sam Calagione of Dogfish Head Brewery in Delaware. The result is a country that has gone from a near-punchline with no discernible beer culture to an absolute paradise for craft beer travellers. Where once there were only industrial lagers and other international standards, there are now dozens of unusual brewing styles, including at least one indigenous beer that has joined

BAR TALK - AGOSTINO ARIOLI

What should you expect from Italian craft beer? What you get from Italian food and Italian fashion: you'll have some of the best craft beers on the planet

TOP 5
BEERS

• **My Blueberry Nightmare** Birrificio del Ducato
• **Tipopils** Birrificio Italiano
• **Ghisa** Birrificio Lambrate
• **Strada S. Felice** Birrificio Grado Plato
• **Xyauyù** Le Baladin

the guidelines of the international Beer Judge Certification Program: Italian Grape Ale, a vinous, fruity style that plays with the country's great winemaking traditions.

Meanwhile, Italian farmers working with brewers have begun the country's first hop-breeding and malt-growing programs, beginning to create indigenous basic ingredients for brewing, most of which have long been imported. As might be expected in such a food-loving part of the world, Italian craft beer is intimately connected with cuisine. Many craft brewers in Italy consider themselves part of the Slow Food movement, which was originally founded in the country, and beer is often presented not on draft but in stylish bottles, which compete with great Italian wines in stately appearance, and sometimes in terms of their prices as well. When you go, keep an eye out for beer bars and brewpubs offering *aperitivo*, the local equivalent of happy hour. In this case, it doesn't mean a discount on drink prices, but, rather, the presence of snacks, sometimes stretching into dozens of plates piled high with delicious things to munch. This is Italy, after all.

BIRRIFICIO INDIPENDENTE ELAV

Via Autieri d'Italia 268, Comun Nuovo, Bergamo;
www.elavbrewery.com; +39 035 334 206

◆ Food
◆ Bar

THINGS TO DO NEARBY

Accademia Carrara
East of Bergamo's city walls is one of Italy's great art repositories, containing an exceptional range of Italian masters. Raphael's *San Sebastiano* is a highlight. *www. lacarrara.it*

Torre del Campanone
Bergamo's colossal Torre del Campanone soars 52m above the city; take the lift to the top for expansive views of the town and across the Lombard plains.

Italian Lakes
Depart Bergamo for a weekend of exploring Lake Garda (for mountain biking and other adventurous actvities at the north tip) or Lake Como (for celebrity house hunting).

Cascina Elav
Enjoy outdoor eating, drinking and culture at Elav's country farmhouse, southwest of Bergamo city centre in Grumello del Piano.
www.cascinaelav.com

As the Italian craft beer revolution marches forward, this innovative brewery is in the advance guard. It was founded by Valentina Ardemagni and Antonio Terzi in 2010 in the city of Bergamo, a satellite of Milan in Lombardy. Over recent years they have grown both their range of beers and their presence in the city: while you can't visit the brewery, you can drink the beers in two pubs they own in the area. Their first outpost was The Clock Tower pub in nearby Treviglio, originally an Irish pub but now known for its good food, great beer and live music. The Elav empire expanded with the Osteria della Birra in Bergamo itself, which is where you can sip Elav's own beers, accompanied by platters of local cured meats. The next project is the renovation of Cascina Elav, which will include a new microbrewery that visitors can tour. The core of the range are the 'musical beers': try the fruity Amber Indie Ale, the English-style Punks Do It Bitter and the Grunge IPA before turning it up to 11 with the Dark Metal Imperial Stout, rich in dark chocolate and coffee flavours. Save space for some of the brewery's rarities, such as the medal-garnering Queen of Winter Porter.

BIRRA DEL BORGO

Piana di Spedino, Borgorose;
www.birradelborgo.it; +39 6 9522 2314

◆ Food ◆ Tour ◆ Takeout
◆ Family ◆ Bar

THINGS TO DO NEARBY

Tivoli
A summer retreat for ancient Romans, this hilltop town is home to two Unesco World Heritage sites: the country estate of Emperor Hadrian and the Renaissance-style Villa d'Este.

Parco Naturale Regionale Monti Simbruni
On the route from Rome to Borgorose, this Apennine park, Lazio's largest, is wild with wolves, wildcats and eagles. Hike the hills of its seven villages. *www.parks.it/parco.monti.simbruini*

Brasserie 4:20
To get in the mood for a trip to Birra del Borgo, try one of the best craft beer bars in Rome. There's even a Hopsburger, made with hops flour. *www.brasserie420.com*

Open Baladin
Allied to Birra del Borgo, Open Baladin in Rome has more than 40 beers on tap and a wall of bottles from which to select. *www.openbaladinroma.it*

In early 2016 this much-loved and highly regarded Italian brewery was bought by an international beverage conglomerate. But fear not, commercial beer isn't on the menu. Instead, it is hoped that founder Leonardo Di Vincenzo will continue making many of Italy's best beers. He began in 2005 by developing a core range of three classics: the Duchessa Saison made with spelt; ReAle, a citrus-accented American IPA; and the DucAle, a strong and fruity Belgian-style ale. But, as you'd guess from a brewer who has collaborated with Sam Calagione of Dogfish Head Brewery in Delaware, USA, Leonardo isn't afraid to get a little freaky: one self-proclaimed 'bizarre' beer is brewed per month (check out September's autumnal CastagnAle, made from malt smoked with orange peel, lemon myrtle, coriander and chestnuts). And Birra del Borgo is still based in its small hometown in the Apennine mountains northeast of Rome, though it has opened the New Brewery, where on one Saturday or Sunday per month a brewer hosts a free tour (with tastings; book online). Meanwhile, in the Old Brewery, Leonardo Di Vincenzo's 'weirdest experiments' continue. In the shop (open daily), stock up on the ReAle Extra, a hopped-up IPA, one of Italy's best.

ARCHEA BREWERY

Via de'Serragli 44, Florence,
www.archeabrewery.com; +39 328 425 0315

◆ Food   ◆ Transport
◆ Bar

 Appraising Florentine frescoes can be thirsty work and the crowds at the Uffizi gallery can drive a traveller to seek respite from the Renaissance. So thank a higher power for Archea Brewery on the south side of the River Arno.

   This cosy backstreet brewpub is renowned for the warmth of its welcome, with friendly locals and knowledgeable bar staff happy to help visitors negotiate the varied list of guest beers, which may include Mikkeller's Danish delights (see page 153), American Ales or Lambic Belgian beers. But

Archea also brews its own and the bar's blackboard may offer IPAs, Double IPAs, Pilsners and Golden Ales. The go-to brew is the strong, malty Bock, erring on just the right side of caramel sweetness.

THINGS TO DO NEARBY

**Museo di Storia Naturale –
Zoologia La Specola**
A couple of streets east, the University of Florence's natural history museum is enthralling; don't miss the taxidermied hippo, once a 17th-century Medici pet. *www.msn.unifi.it*

Oltrarno
Also south of the river is Florence's revitalised artisan quarter: check out the ancient art of Florentine bookbinding and paper making at Erin Ciulla's Il Torchio studio. *www. legatoriailtorchio.com*

BIRRIFICIO ARTIGIANALE FOLLINA

Via Pedeguarda 26, Follina, Veneto;
+39 0438 970437

◆ Family   ◆ Takeout
◆ Tour   ◆ Transport

 Situated among vine-clad hills lining the Strada del Prosecco, the bustling town of Follina has a new attraction, tempting travellers to sample more than just the region's renowned bubbly. This tiny microbrewery is the labour of love of renowned winemaker, Giovanni Gregoletto. Inspired by Belgium's famed Trappist brews and Follina's historic abbey, Gregoletto is developing his own 'abbey' style. The Follinetta comes in a bottle inspired by the monastic Duvel, while Giana rivals the strongest Belgian ales with a heady 8% alcohol content. Visit the adjoining

Wine & The Grape museum, where Gregoletto explains how his natural beer fermentation follows the same principles as when he makes Prosecco. Try the Sanavalle: a quirky pure malt, re-fermented in the bottle, just like Prosecco.

THINGS TO DO NEARBY

Abbazia di Follina
Built in 1170 and splendidly preserved, the romantic Cistercian cloisters of Follina's Romanesque abbey is worth a wander, featuring a basilica decorated with ornate frescoes.

Bar Alpino
Even beer lovers need to taste some Prosecco along the wine route. This tiny enoteca (wine bar) in Valdobiadenne, Prosecco's capital, stocks 50 different producers. *www.baralpino.it*

GÄSSL BRAU

Gässl Brau, Gerbergasse 18, Klausen;
www.gassl-braeu.it; +39 472 523623

◆ Food ◆ Tour
◆ Takeout ◆ Bar

Though it's officially part of Italy, for much of its history the province of South Tyrol belonged to Austria, and there's still a strongly Teutonic feel to life here – not least in its enduring love for beer.

Gässl Brau, a small restaurant and microbrewery, is in the little town of Klausen, overlooked by centuries-old farms, terraced vineyards and the serrated peaks of the Dolomites. There's a cosy bar inside where you watch the copper vats at work, or down a few brews on the cobbled terrace outside. The house speciality is Kastanienbier –

brewed with chestnuts, a renowned product of South Tyrol, and a key ingredient in the local autumnal feasts known as *torgellen*. It's a delicious example of seasonal brewing with local ingredients.

THINGS TO DO NEARBY

Neustift Abbey
South Tyrol's wines aren't well-known outside Italy, but they're appreciated by oenophiles. Neustift Abbey runs tasting sessions in its medieval cellar, including local vintages.
www.kloster-neustift.it

Alpe di Siusi
In winter, Alpe di Siusi, Europe's highest meadow, is beloved by skiers and 'boarders, but in summer, it's a hikers' paradise. Scores of trails crisscross the mountainsides.
www.seiser-alm.it

PFEFFERLECHNER

4 Via San Martino, Lana;
www.pfefferlechner.it; +39 0473 562 521

◆ Food   ◆ Tour   ◆ Takeout
◆ Family   ◆ Bar   ◆ Transport

Hidden away in the mountains of the Italian Tyrol, this traditional osteria is now brewing craft beer for the loyal clientele that crowd in every evening. The ancient wooden farm of the friendly Laitner family, includes a dining room with windows looking directly into an adjoining stable filled with horses, cows and goats, another that has a copper alambic where grappa is distilled each week, and now Martin Laitner has converted the garage into a fully equipped microbrewery.

Apart from German-influenced lagers, Pfeffer 100% is made from local barley, while the bubbly Pfeffer Spumante has hints of orange and coriander. If you can time it right, don't miss the Pfeffer Kastanie, a tasty chestnut beer brewed every autumn.

THINGS TO DO NEARBY

Merano Terme
Merano is famous for its palatial spa hotels, but anyone can use the municipal thermal baths, with state-of-the-art pools, saunas and hammams. *www.termemerano.it*

Castel Trauttmansdorff
Surrounding a medieval castle, these spectacular avant-garde botanical gardens include everything from tulips to Mediterranean olive groves and ancient vines. *www.trauttmansdorff.it*

FABBRICA DELLA BIRRA PERUGIA

Via Tiberina 20, Pontenuovo di Torgiano, Perugia;
www.birraperugia.it; +39 75 988 8096

◆ Tour   ◆ Takeout
◆ Bar   ◆ Transport

An old name revitalised by a youthful zest for adventure: this 'beer factory' is one of Italy's first breweries (founded in 1875) but until recent years it was turning out forgettable industrial lagers. Today, however, under the guidance of its new owners, wine journalist Antonio Boco, marketeer Matteo Natalini and brewer Luana Meola, it has rebooted its repertoire with a Golden Ale, a Red Ale, a Chocolate Porter and more. Their efforts were rewarded in 2016 with the accolade of Brewery of the Year at Italy's national Birra dell'Anno competition.

Saturday tours are an opportunity to explore the historic building, talk to the team and taste some of Luana's creations, including the Calibro7 Pale Ale, with its blend of Galaxy, Citra, Sorachi and Chinook hops.

THINGS TO DO NEARBY

Palazzo dei Priori
The focal point of Piazza IV Novembre, this Gothic palace constructed between the 13th and 14th centuries harbours some of Perugia's finest museums, including the Galleria Nazionale dell'Umbria.

Elfo Pub
On Via Sant'Agata awaits Perugia's most popular beer bar and longest-standing 'public house', with a global selection of 200 beers and a cosy ambience.

BALADIN

Piazza 5 Luglio 1944, Piozzo, Piedmont;
www.baladin.it; +39 0173 795431

◆ Food   ◆ Tour   ◆ Takeout
◆ Family   ◆ Bar   ◆ Transport

THINGS TO DO NEARBY

Hot-air ballooning
With its medieval villages and sprawling vineyards, the best way to see this stunning pocket of Italy is on a sunrise or sunset balloon ride. ***www.in-balloon.it/#!/ita-home***

Wine tasting
Piozzo is located in the middle of the Piedmont region, which, in turn, is famed for its Piemonte wines; a good excuse to taste Barolo and Barbaresco.

Alba
Only a 30-minute drive northeast from Piozzo, this picturesque village with its medieval watchtowers is known as the gourmet capital of Piedmont for good reason.

Truffle hunting
In Alba you can join a professional truffle hunter and a specially trained dog on a quest for these subterranean gourmet treats. ***www.lebaccanti.com/en/tour/Truffle-Hunt-in-Alba***

To understand Baladin, you have to meet its creator, Teo Musso. This is a man who spent three years playing specially composed music through huge speakers to his beer as it fermented. This is a man who built a specially dedicated 'beer duct' through his home town and even named a number of his beers after his own children and family members, making sure each beer developed in style and flavour as each family member changed in real life. Not only does Teo's life story play out like a romantic Italian novel, complete with tales of love, loss and even a chapter where he ran away with the circus, but he transformed the sleepy little Italian village of Piozzo into the beating heart of his world-famous brewery. Visiting Piozzo is like no other experience you'll have in the beer world. The medieval town centre revolves around Baladin's quirky circus-themed brewpub, the main hotel in town is the beautiful Casa Baladin, and to spend a day and a night in Piozzo is to experience the story of Teo Musso, a true pioneer of Italian craft beer. Try his Nora, a Moroccan-inspired beer that is spiced with myrrh, and is dynamic paired with a spicy dish.

BIRRERIA ZAHRE

50 Via Razzo, Sauris di Sopra, Friuli;
www.zahrebeer.com; +39 0433 866314

◆ Food   ◆ Tour   ◆ Takeout
◆ Family   ◆ Bar   ◆ Transport

Sandro Petris is more at home speaking mountain dialect than Italian, but he can just manage a little English to enthusiastically explain the artisan brewery he founded with his brother Massimo back in 1999 in the stables of their parents' farm. Zahre ales are sold all over northern Italy, but the microbrewery is hidden away in a hamlet high in the wild Carnia mountains near the Austrian border. You have to be serious about beer to make the expedition out here, but it's worth it for the welcome travellers are given. The brewery has recently expanded to include a cosy wooden taproom serving hearty plates of local cheeses and smoked ham; a school offering beer-making courses, where you create a personal recipe and go home with a 50L keg of your own homebrew; as

THINGS TO DO NEARBY

Pesariis
This tiny village is surprisingly one of the world's clockmaking capitals. There's a museum dedicated to the art, but you can easily wander the 14 monumental clocks displayed outdoors.

Lago di Sauris
Sauris sits above a wood-fringed lake, perfect for fishing, canoeing, windsurfing and picnics of local ham, cheeses aged in traditional malga stone huts, and Zahre beer.

Prosciuttificio Vecchia Sauris
Less famous than San Daniele or Parma, Sauris produces prized air-dried ham. Discover the artisan secrets – and amazing aromas – with a free visit.
www.vecchiasauris.it

Borgo degli Elfi
Deep in the woods surrounding Sauris, Simone Franzone has created a bucolic Bike & Hike Hotel, where guests are led along nature trails on foot or mountain bike. **www. saurisborgodeglielfi.it**

well as three rustic B&B apartments. And the beers are sensational. The brothers roast their homegrown barley malt before brewing Zahre Affumicata, a smoky brown porter and, apart from a classic Pils and an American Pale Ale, there's Zahre Rossa Vienna, an intense, aromatic amber lager made from an ancient Viennese recipe. Don't leave without trying Canapa: not exactly cannabis beer, but hemp leaves and flowers are used in the fermentation.

NETHERLANDS

How to ask for a beer in local language?
Een biertje, alstublieft
How to say cheers? Proost!
Signature beer style? Bok, a dark lager
Local bar snack? Bitterballen; crisp-coated, deep-fried meat balls served with mustard
Do: Take care not walk on the bike paths after a few beers or expect to hear some bike bells being rung

People visit Amsterdam for all sorts of reasons – such as to see paintings by the Old Masters in the city's fabulous Rijksmuseum – but tasting the beer has not been one of them. Until now. There is, it seems, space for more than just a couple of big-name brewers (Heineken, Amstel and Grolsch) in Amsterdam and the wider Netherlands.

Craft breweries in the Netherlands now number more than 200 and it's still the early days of the scene, relative to other nations. As a result, there isn't a settled Dutch craft beer characteristic yet – a lot of brewers produce the international recognised staples of pale ale, imperial

stout and IPAs plus Belgian-style dubbels and tripels, but brewers are working on it. The closest that the Dutch have to a national beer is *bokbier*, which is a strong, dark lager that was traditionally produced in October to herald in the gloomy winter months.

In addition to the two breweries featured here, check out also the tasting room of Brouwerij de Prael in Amsterdam's red-light district and Brouwerij de 7 Deugden in the west of the city. And there are now more than a dozen craft beer bars in Amsterdam alone, such as Gollem, the Beer Temple, In de Wildeman and Troost. It's the same in Utrecht, Rotterdam and other Dutch cities. When you've got Belgium and Germany as neighbours, there shouldn't be any problem sourcing interesting beers to put on tap but, increasingly, a lot more popular craft beers will be made in the Netherlands.

OEDIPUS BREWING

Gedempt Hamerkanaal 85, Amsterdam;
www.oedipus.com

◆ Family   ◆ Bar   ◆ Transport
◆ Tour   ◆ Takeout

There's a huge line of colourful beer taps sitting underneath a huge painting of a giant pink pig, but what else would you expect from a new-generation craft brewery in Amsterdam? Oedipus is quirky, youthful and fun.

As for the beers, it seems as if a new one pops up every few days. You can expect anything: rhubarb Weissbiers, smoked porters, IPAs, Saisons, Imperial Stouts, Gose, Sours... and then pay attention because by the end of your visit, they will have probably tapped another. The best way to visit this canal-side brewery is undoubtedly by boat and before you cruise off again try the Thai Thai: a refreshing, not too spicy Trippel with galangal root, coriander, chilli and orange peel.

THINGS TO DO NEARBY

Amsterdam Craft Beer Tours & Events
Whether you choose to tour the Dutch breweries by bike or, for something distinctly 'Amsterdam', by canal boat, there are plenty of options. *www.amsterdam craftbeertours.com*

Brouwerij De Prael
In the middle of Amsterdam's infamous Red Light District, this multilevel tasting room offers organic beers and well-priced stews to a mostly young crowd. *www.deprael.nl*

BROUWERIJ DE MOLEN

Overtocht 43, Bodegraven;
www.brouwerijdemolen.nl; +31 172 610 848

◆ Food ◆ Tour ◆ Takeout
◆ Family ◆ Bar ◆ Transport

THINGS TO DO NEARBY

Gouda Cheese Market
While the historic Gouda cheese market is only held Thursday mornings from April till August, you can still find places to taste local cheese here year-round. *www. welkomingouda.nl*

Kamphuisen
Experience a traditional *bruin café* in Gouda, with hearty food and ancient wooden tables inside, or head outdoors and drink under the atmospheric eaves of the old fish market. *www.kamphuisen.com*

Wierickerschans Fort
Explore this picturesque part of the Dutch waterline (used right up to the 19th century), which allowed large parts of the country to flood, defending towns from invading forces. *www. fortwierickerschans.nl*

Gouda By Candlelight
Thousands flock to Gouda in mid-December to see the entire town lit up by countless candles, a tradition since 1956, with a programme of events expanding each year. *http:// eng.goudabijkaarslicht.nl*

De Molen has made some huge waves in the international craft beer world over the past few years, becoming the go-to brewery for mammoth Imperial Stouts as well as some world-class IPAs and big, boozy barrel-aged brews. It's hard to picture this hard-hitting craft brewery operating in such a quiet little Dutch country town as Bodegraven, but the beer world works in mysterious ways.

While De Molen's brewery is located in a warehouse space on the edge of town, the best place to drink these beers is in the Brouwcafè de Molen, which is a little tasting room, restaurant and beershop all in one, tucked underneath an iconic 17th-century windmill within easy eyeshot of the brewery. The beers are usually big and full flavoured – piles of hops, stacks of malt and heaps of booze, but somehow they all fit together in perfect balance and harmony. While you can find some De Molen beers below 5%, most sit between 6.5% and 12% ABV, so driving here would almost definitely be a one-way trip (take the train). Try the Heaven & Hell Imperial Stout: a big, well-balanced stout that oozes flavours of dark fruit, coffee and bitter cocoa, with a chesty warmth to finish.

PORTUGAL

How to ask for a beer in local language?
Uma imperial, se faz favor
How to say cheers? Saude!
Signature beer style? Pilsner
Local bar snack? Tremoços (lupin beans, often marinated in chilli and/or bay leaves)
Don't: Ask for an imperial in a craft beer bar — ordering this way is for everyday bars; order by craft beer name

Modern Portuguese beer history can be summed up in just two words: Sagres and Super Bock. These two everyday lagers created during military dictatorships have dominated the country's beer landscape for decades, but Portugal-produced beer actually predates the country itself, going all the way back to pre-Roman Lusitania (despite the fact that the country is overwhelmingly devoted to wine). But during the *Estado Novo*, an authoritarian regime that lasted some 42 years, outside influence was stifled, and aggressive marketing tactics that exist to this day allow one brand to monopolise an establishment. The Portuguese love their Sagres and Super Bock, though — these pale

amber, easy-drinking lagers do indeed go hand-in-hand with one of Europe's loveliest summer climates.

But despite being late to the craft beer brew fest, things began to change in the 2010s, when many Portuguese who had bolted for greener pastures during the brutal European recession (the country lost some 600,000 of its younger workforce) began returning. Armed with a bevy of boozy ideas and a thirst for the craft beers they became accustomed to drinking in other parts of Europe and North America, the tapgates opened. Porto-based Sovina, considered the country's first true craft beer brewery, hit the market in 2011 with an amber, a Helles, an IPA, a stout and a wheat and there was no turning back. In just four short years, Lisbon now counts two brewpubs, at least five dedicated craft beer bars, nearly a dozen established microbreweries and numerous contract and home brewers among its craft arsenal.

DOIS CORVOS CERVEJARIA

Rua Capitão Leitão 94, Lisbon;
www.doiscorvos.pt; +351 914 440 326

◆ Food   ◆ Bar   ◆ Transport
◆ Tour   ◆ Takeout

THINGS TO DO NEARBY

Alfama
Immersed in the waft of grilled sardines and a fado soundtrack, the narrow alleys, winding streets and whitewashed architecture of labyrinthine Alfama makes for a most cinematic neighbourhood.

Mosteiro dos Jerónimos
There's usually a 'wow' moment when visitors first fix their eyes on this Unesco-recognised monastery in Belém, a marvel of Manueline architecture. *www. mosteirojeronimos.pt*

Chimera Brewpub
An 18th-century coach tunnel in Alcântara has been transformed into a beautiful stone-walled drinking den, churning out small batch brews on 12 taps. *www. chimerabrewpub.pt*

Mercado da Ribeira
Trading since 1892, Lisbon's urban market had half of it transformed by *Time Out* into a gourmet food court in 2014, with several stalls run by Michelin-starred chefs. *www.timeoutmarket.com*

While Portugal was traditionally tied down under the dominance of just two industrial beers for decades, the craft beer explosion finally reached Lisbon in 2014, when its first craft beer bar opened. A year later, the fermentation tanks were fired up at Dois Corvos, founded by husband-and-wife team Susana Cascais and Scott Steffens, and it was the first to offer a taproom experience in the city. An American transplant, Steffens brings his Seattle experience to Marvila, an up-and-coming warehouse district turned artistic and hipster enclave, brewing just 10,000L per month.

The brewery, which debuted 26 beers in its first year alone, is constantly experimenting and producing one-off beers and filling style gaps. 'Like anywhere, Portugal has unique ingredients available, such as Portuguese fruit, spices and local wine and spirits barrels (re-used for

ageing beer) and wild native yeast – these are just a few of the things that we play with,' says Steffens.

The taproom has a dozen taps – often featuring pilot batches, infusions and barrel-aged exclusive beers – and growler service. Tours of the brewery and the nearby barrel-ageing warehouse debuted in 2017. Definitely try the Finisterra Porter, especially if a barrel-aged version is on tap.

DUQUE BREWPUB

Duques da Calçada 49, Lisbon;
www.duquebrewpub.com; +351 213 469 947

◆ Food ◆ Takeout
◆ Bar ◆ Transport

Lisbon's first brewpub didn't start pulling pints until 2015, but Duque in the stylish Chiado district is eager to make up for lost time. On any given day, you'll find Lisbon-area brews, such as Bolina, Dois Corvos, Passarola, Oitava Colina, LX, Musa, Mean Sardine, Against the Tide and Amnesia flowing from the 10 taps, along with staples and one-off creations from Cerveja Aroeira, the house label (there's also a small but thoughtfully curated bottle selection). The cosy space has a conventionally bar-like atmosphere, with its hardwood tables and burlap-draped bar stools, and the outdoor terrace is hard to beat. Don't miss trying Look, I'm Your Lager, an Aroeira–Bolina collaboration Imperial Pale Lager with a spectacular hoppy punch.

THINGS TO DO NEARBY

Convento do Carmo
The ruins of Convento do Carmo soaring above Lisbon put the 1755 earthquake into perspective; shattered pillars and wishbone-like arches remain exposed to the elements.

Núcleo Arqueológico da Rua dos Correeiros
Under the Millennium BCP bank are ruins dating from the Iron Age. Fascinating archaeologist-led tours descend into remnants of a Roman sardine factory.

CERVEJA LETRA

Ave Professor Machado Vilela 147, Vila Verde;
www.cervejaletra.pt, +351-253 321 424

◆ Food   ◆ Bar   ◆ Transport
◆ Tour   ◆ Takeout

Around 13km (8 miles) north of the beautiful city of Braga in unexceptional Vila Verde is Portugal's first brewpub, Letraria, which opened in 2015 inside an abandoned municipal government building. A worth-a-trip stop on the Portuguese beer trail, Letraria brews Cerveja Letra, one of Portugal's first three craft beers (in production since 2011) and easily one of its best brew experiences. True to its name, Letra's brews by the letter: A for Weiss, B for Pilsner, C for Stout and D for Red Ale, which monopolise four of the seven taps here; an expansion to 12 is in the works. Flowing from the remaining three taps are special edition, barrel-aged and collaboration brews, some fermented in a homemade makeshift 100L fermenter, others concocted with local ingredients,

THINGS TO DO NEARBY

Parque Nacional Peneda-Gerês
Portugal's only national park, the 703-sq-km Parque Nacional Peneda-Gerês, 52km (32 miles) northeast of Braga, shelters boulder-strewn peaks, pine forest, and ancient granite villages.

Bom Jesus do Monte
Reached via a cinematic zigzagging baroque staircase, in itself reached via a lush forest stone stairway, this iconic cathedral is tucked into the hillside high above Braga. *www.bomjesus.pt*

Bira dos Namorados
Braga has a well-documented gourmet burger scene and this adorable cafe, with its decor inspired by the popular folk traditions from Minho, is the spot to indulge. *www.biradosnamorados.pt*

Guimarães
Unesco World Heritage–protected Guimarães, 25km (15½ miles) southeast of Braga, is a medieval warren of labyrinthine alleyways, plazas and well preserved 14th-century edifices.

such as *Casca de Carvalho* melon or the brewery's own hops (25 rhizomes of American Cascade hops have been planted in a field next door: a Portugal first). The inviting taproom does excellent Northern Portugal bar food (stout-laced pulled pork, toasted Barroso ham and Gerês mountain cheese sandwiches) and free Saturday afternoon tours include a healthy sampling of 'the alphabet'. Don't miss the Letra On Oak Port Barrel Aged Sour Ale.

SLOVAKIA

How to ask for a beer in local language?
Jedno pivo, prosim
How to say cheers? Na Zdravie!
Signature beer style? Bohemian-style Pilsner
Local bar snack? Various pickles, normally gherkins; and hermelin, a Camembert-like cheese
Don't: Complain about the head of foam – it's standard practice, and can be a sign of quality

The Slovaks excel at producing alcohol. While potent homemade fruit brandies and amber-hued Tokaj wines are the most singular tipples the country concocts, the lofty mountains in the north of Slovakia channel high-quality water down into flat, warm, arable land where hops can thrive, which provides conditions conducive for making beer too. Weave in a shared history with the famously beer-savvy Czechs, and the fact that Slovak capital Bratislava has topped out 'cheapest city to buy beer' indexes in 2015 and 2016, and it's easy to see why beer is the nation's favourite booze.

Beer production in Slovakia has a prestigious history that has perhaps been overshadowed by its brewery-rich

neighbour, the Czech Republic. The production of beer here can be traced directly back to at least the 15th century, with Hungarian monarch Matthias Corvinus preferring beer from the Eastern Slovak city of Bardejov for his wedding. Members of the Knights Templar formed Slovakia's first brewery in Banská Bystrica region in 1473, initiating a healthy relationship between beer and Slovakia's mining districts (some Slovak miners even called beer 'liquid bread') that is still alive and kicking.

It was another mining centre, Banská Štiavnica, which would play a part in breaking the stranglehold on Slovak beer that the industrial-scale breweries had enjoyed since the mid-20th century. In 2010, the opening of smaller breweries, such as Banská Štiavnica's Pivovar Erb and Bratislava's Bratislavský Meštiansky Pivovar paved the way for a new generation of brewers that prioritised quality over quantity.

PIVOVAR ERB

Novozámocká 2, Banská Štiavnica;
www.pivovarerb.sk; +421 45 692 2205

- ◆ Food
- ◆ Tour
- ◆ Takeout
- ◆ Family
- ◆ Bar
- ◆ Transport

The Unesco-listed medieval mining town of Banská Štiavnica once had ten breweries. Pivovar Erb, ensconced in a fetching rose-pink building in the historic centre, is sole survivor. The brewery's beamed restaurant–bar, thick with the scent of malt, centres on the two burnished copper vats used to produce the four main brews made here. Relax on the drinking terrace with its view of undulating photogenic old town rooftops. Or there's a dinky theatre, where you can often catch a performance before sinking some cold ones. Pivovar Erb's brew master travels throughout Slovakia and Central Europe sourcing select ingredients for his beer, and the brewery's finest offering is also arguably Slovakia's best: a nuanced, hoppy 12% smoked lager with a deep caramel hue.

THINGS TO DO NEARBY

Kalvaria
Straddling a pea-green hill overlooking town, Banská Štiavnica's calvary is a complex of 22 baroque churches and chapels vividly depicting the Passion of the Christ.
www.en.kalvaria.org

Slovak Mining Museum
Some beautifully preserved wooden mining buildings outside Banská Štiavnica guard the entrance to a mine shaft, štôlňa Bartolomej, which you can visit on a guided tour.
www.muzeumbs.sk

BRATISLAVSKÝ MEŠTIANSKY PIVOVAR

Drevená 8, Bratislava;
www.mestianskypivovar.sk; +421 944 512 265

- ◆ Food
- ◆ Bar
- ◆ Tour
- ◆ Transport

Unfazed by the brewing clout of the nearby Czechs, Bratislava has been beer-making for 500 years, and has had a brewery-restaurant since 1752. The town's burgesses commissioned the brewery's building to match the best Bavarian beer houses and so Bratislava's Burgess Brewery (Bratislavský Meštiansky Pivovar in Slovak) became a drinking and dining destination of distinction.

Today's brewery was founded in 2010 and put Slovak craft beer back on the map. An urbane crowd sprawls across two spacious floors with soaring vaulted ceilings. As for the beer, it's pilsner-style, with a *ležiak* (light lager) and a *bubák* (dark beer) available, but the signature way to drink is to have a half-and-half mix of both: fruity, chocolatey, surprisingly superb.

THINGS TO DO NEARBY

UFO
Thus do locals call this surreal flying saucer suspended above Nový Most, Bratislava's main bridge over the Danube. Ascend it for wondrous city views.
www.u-f-o.sk

Slovak National Gallery
Slovakia's premier art collection, showcasing 16th- to 19th-century Central European works, plus important Slovak art from the 20th century, including iconic modernist Ľudovít Fulla. *www.sng.sk*

UNITED KINGDOM

How to ask for a beer in local language? A beer, please
How to say cheers? Cheers!
Signature beer style? Pale ale
Local bar snack? Peanuts and potato crisps
Do: Order half pints if tasting lots of beers

Britain may be synonymous with beer – having invented most of the styles of beer prevalent today – but the relationship hasn't always been a happy one. In fact, far from being a brewing powerhouse, for much of the 20th century British beer was lacklustre. In the middle of the last century, for a variety of reasons that include government legislation and taxation dating from WWI, a dominance of mediocre mass-market brands, and weak demand from consumers, British beer was at a low ebb. There were few independent, creative breweries left in the country (just a couple in London) and British pubs – the cornerstones of civilised society – were closing at a rapid rate. Even real ale advocates had a curiously myopic view of what constituted good beer.

But then, around 20 years ago, something happened to jolt British brewing back to life. The Americans started making good beer. In fact, not just good beer but incredibly fantastic beer. Then the Australians and New Zealanders followed suit. And they were making beer in British styles: pale ales, porters, stouts (Imperial and standard) and India Pale Ales (IPA). This could not stand.

It's necessary to unearth the origins of these signature styles of beer briefly. Let's start with pale ale and IPA, arguably the most widespread style of craft beer today. Pale ale first appeared in Britain in the 17th century when malted barley was able to be lightly roasted. Hops, yeast and local water were added to the brew and a pale ale was the result. A century later and a whole load of extra hopping plus a higher alcohol level helped ensure pale ales survived shipping to India. Looking around rural Britain today and there's plenty of evidence of the brewing industry, with pointy-hatted oast houses for drying hops common in southern counties of Kent, Sussex and Hampshire.

Porter evolved in London as a pick-me-up for workers loading and unloading cargo beside the Thames. A stronger, stouter version became known as stout, but they are essentially the same beer: dark, roasted malted barley with a generous quantity of hops giving a toasted, sweet but bitter flavour, often with hints of coffee and chocolate. A stronger version was sold to Russia, hence Imperial Russian stout.

But it took Britain's colonies to remind the mother country how great beer was made for independent British craft brewers to rediscover these lost arts. Thankfully, demand for tasty beer has more than kept pace with the explosion of British craft breweries over the last decade. London now has

The UK has always had a proud brewing heritage but the use of New World hops and innovation within styles is changing the way people view beer

211

TOP 5 BEERS

- **Black Betty IPA** Beavertown
- **Best Bitter** Harvey's
- **Citra** Oakham Ales
- **IPA Citra** The Kernel
- **Even More Jesus VIII** Siren/Evil Twin

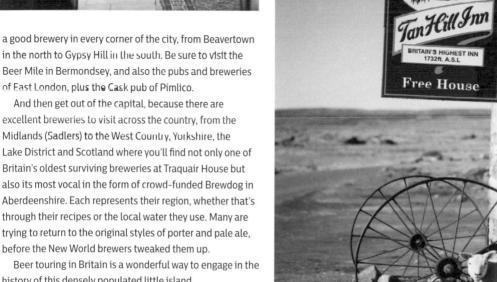

a good brewery in every corner of the city, from Beavertown in the north to Gypsy Hill in the south. Be sure to visit the Beer Mile in Bermondsey, and also the pubs and breweries of East London, plus the Cask pub of Pimlico.

And then get out of the capital, because there are excellent breweries to visit across the country, from the Midlands (Sadlers) to the West Country, Yorkshire, the Lake District and Scotland where you'll find not only one of Britain's oldest surviving breweries at Traquair House but also its most vocal in the form of crowd-funded Brewdog in Aberdeenshire. Each represents their region, whether that's through their recipes or the local water they use. Many are trying to return to the original styles of porter and pale ale, before the New World brewers tweaked them up.

Beer touring in Britain is a wonderful way to engage in the history of this densely populated little island.

BARNGATES BREWERY

The Drunken Duck Inn, Barngates, Ambleside, Cumbria;
www.drunkenduckinn.co.uk; +44 1539 436347

◆ Food   ◆ Tour   ◆ Transport
◆ Family   ◆ Bar

This small brewery is based at one of the Lake District's most famous dining pubs, the marvellously named Drunken Duck Inn, perched on a crossroads between Hawkshead and Coniston, near the picturesque lake of Tarn Hows. Housed in old outbuildings, the brewery has a range of bespoke ales, all brewed using traditional techniques, with catchy titles such as Tag Lag, Catnap and Cracker. You'll find all on tap inside the pub, accompanied by a bistro menu. Chesters Strong & Ugly is our choice here – both for its superb moniker and its rich, dark, roasted-malt flavours.

THINGS TO DO NEARBY

Grizedale Forest
There are miles and miles of bike trails to explore in this pretty woodland, and on your way around, you can spot one of dozens of outdoor sculptures.

Beatrix Potter Gallery
Avoid the crowds at Beatrix Potter's house at Hill Top by heading for this fascinating little gallery in Hawkshead, which displays lots of her original paintings. *www. nationaltrust.org.uk*

BATH ALES

Hare House, Southway Drive, Warmley, nr Bath;
www.bathales.com; +44 117 947 4797

◆ Food   ◆ Bar   ◆ Transport
◆ Tour   ◆ Takeout

Bath and Bristol drinkers are well-acquainted with this stalwart brewery, whose running hare logo can be seen racing across the taps of many local pubs. It has good gold, red, dark and bitter ales, plus a hearty porter made with Fuggles hops, but it's the special edition brews we especially like – flavoured with ginger, chocolate malt, toffee and even ghost chillies. It owns several pubs – in Bath, our favourite is The Salamander, a friendly, old-fashioned pub just a short walk downhill from the world-famous Royal Crescent. You really can't go wrong with a pint of Gem, a fruity best bitter.

THINGS TO DO NEARBY

Royal Crescent
This magnificent semi-circle of thirty Georgian mansions was built between 1767 and 1775. Glimpse how Bath's upper crust lived inside No 1, which has been redecorated in grand period style *www. no1royalcrescent.org.uk*

Thermae Bath Spa
A visit to the original Roman Baths (www. romanbaths.co.uk) is a must, but if you actually want to soak in Bath's thermal waters, this flashy spa is the place. *www. thermaebathspa.com*

THREE TUNS BREWERY

Station St, Bishops Castle, Shropshire;
www.threetunsbrewery.co.uk; +44 1588 638392

◆ Food   ◆ Tour   ◆ Takeout
◆ Family   ◆ Bar   ◆ Transport

THINGS TO DO NEARBY

Ludlow Castle
The stones of Ludlow
Castle were laid just 20
years after the Norman
conquest; come for
the history but stay for
the foodie offerings in
epicurean Ludlow.
www.ludlowcastle.com

Shrewsbury Abbey
This lovely red sandstone
Norman abbey has seen a
lot of action since 1086,
but it's maybe best known
as the home of history lit
sleuth Brother Cadfael.
*www.shrewsburyabbey.
com*

Ironbridge Gorge
Stroll or cycle through this
peaceful World Heritage
site, where the Industrial
Revolution came steaming
to life with the world's first
iron bridge.
www.ironbridge.org.uk

Long Mynd
Forget the Peak District,
Shropshire's most famous
hill, Long Mynd (517m)
offers the same rolling
landscapes with smaller
crowds, and, many would
argue, better beer.

Claiming to be the oldest licensed brewery in Britain is quite a statement, but in the case of Shropshire's Three Tuns, it has the paperwork to prove it. The Three Tuns Brewery was granted the first official brewing licence in British history in 1642, and the brewers are still working their magic in the same timber-framed premises, albeit with some Victorian-era modifications. When the Campaign for Real Ale launched its crusade to save proper beer in the 1970s, Three Tuns was one of only four pubs still brewing its own ale in the whole of the UK, and the whole enterprise almost faltered in the early years of the new millennium, before real ale aficionados leapt to its rescue in 2003, updating some of the machinery, but not the ethos or ingredients.

Today, brewers still brew to the same age-old recipes, with a few playful nods to the modern era (check out the ginger and lemon tones in the Faust Banana spiced beer). Next door at the Three Tuns Inn, regulars wobble unsteadily by the bar and bearded folk singers fill the back room with medieval harmonies. The wobbling regulars insist that the house XXX Pale Ale is the quintessential Three Tuns brew.

BRISTOL BEER FACTORY

The Old Brewery, Durnford Street, Bristol;
www.bristolbeerfactory.co.uk; +44 117 902 6317

◆ Food   ◆ Bar   ◆ Transport
◆ Tour   ◆ Takeout

Creative, quirky and alternative, Bristol is often touted as the southwest's coolest city, so it's no surprise to discover the place is awash with indie breweries (not to mention plenty of craft beer bars, including the superb Small Bar, www.smallbar.co.uk).

The Bristol Beer Factory has been around for over a decade now, but it's become a favourite for Bristol's ale aficionados; there are five core beers plus a dozen-odd specials, including the Oatmeal Porter, Milk Stout and Bristol Rye. The best place to try them is the brewery's own Grain Barge, a converted riverboat moored along the harbourside, or the cosy Barley Mow, its taphouse-cum-community pub, a short walk from central Temple Meads train station.

THINGS TO DO NEARBY

SS Great Britain
Designed by Isambard Kingdom Brunel, the *SS Great Britain* was launched in 1843 as the world's largest passenger ship. The city icon is restored and moored in Bristol's docks.
www.ssgreatbritain.org

Clifton
Bristol's upmarket quarter has boutiques and cafes galore. Don't miss Brunel's other Bristol masterpiece – the graceful Clifton Suspension Bridge across the Avon Gorge, which offers fabulous city views.

NATIONAL BREWERY CENTRE

Horninglow St, Burton upon Trent, Staffordshire;
www.nationalbrewerycentre.co.uk; +44 1 283 532 880

◆ Food ◆ Tour ◆ Takeout
◆ Family ◆ Bar ◆ Transport

THINGS TO DO NEARBY

Last Heretic
Although Burton's beer heyday has passed, microbreweries are again popping up. This small pub is a good place to sample a selection from the area. **www.thelastheretic.co.uk**

Barton Marina
This pleasant canal-side development south of the town has a few artsy shops and a large pub serving hand-pulled real ale. **www.bartonmarina.co.uk**

National Memorial Arboretum
With 30,000 trees planted in remembrance of those who have died while serving in the armed and emergency services, this is a sombre spot to wander. **www.thenma.org.uk**

East Midlands Aeropark
Alongside East Midlands Airport and 15½ miles (25km) east of Burton, the Aeropark is a plane-lover's paradise, with dozens of historical planes on display. **www. eastmidlandsaeropark.org**

Once upon a time, Burton was considered the most important brewing city in Britain. Its location on the edge of the Trent and Mersey Canal positioned it perfectly for shipping to the harbours of Hull and Liverpool. Add to that mineral-rich waters ideal for brewing pale ales and you start to see why Burton has often been referred to as 'Beer Town'.

Sadly, from its heady days as 'beer capital of the world', counting over 30 breweries in its small town centre, Burton's importance diminished and breweries closed or merged. The whole story, alongside the tale of arguably Burton's most important brewery, Bass, is told at the National Brewery Centre. You can also get superb pub lunches here, and there's a shop with beers from around the world – real kid-in-a-candy-store stuff for beer nerds. Guided tours kick off with an overview of the brewing process before leading into the tale of how Burton became great and the factors that contributed to its decline. Tours end, as all brewery tours do, with a tasting in the attached pub, where you can sample beers brewed at the on-site microbrewery. Tuck into a pint of White Shield IPA, a beer with a 180-year-old pedigree.

SULWATH BREWERY

209 King Street, Castle Douglas, Scotland; www.sulwathbrewers.co.uk,
www.cd-foodtown.org; +44 1556 504 525

◆ Tour
◆ Transport

THINGS TO DO NEARBY

Kirroughtree Forest Visitor Centre
An hour's drive west from Castle Douglas is the best mountain biking trail centre in the Scottish Borders, Kirroughtree 7 Stanes. Bikes can be rented here. *www.scotland.forestry.gov.uk*

Kirkcudbright
Explore the colourful town of Kirkcudbright, 10 miles away on the River Dee, which is famed for being a creative community and home to lots of artists.

Threave Garden and Estate
The mild climate in this corner of Scotland has helped the gardens at this country estate thrive. Wildlife has followed suit: track the bat trail or visit the osprey viewing platform. *www.nts.org.uk*

Threave Castle
Take a boat across the River Dee to see the historic home of the Black Douglases, a massive tower built in 1369 by Archibald the Grim. *www.historicenvironment.scot*

In the centre of the Scottish Borders, Castle Douglas would have been a stronghold of the Douglas clan since the Middle Ages, contending with marauding reivers (raiders). Today, things are more sedate in this market town. Rather than war, its inhabitants make food; Castle Douglas has been designated a food town, surrounded by fertile farms – each week there's still a livestock market here. Among the 50 or so food businesses in the town is a family-run brewery, Sulwath, named after the Solway Firth just to the south, whose waters create a warm micro-climate along this coast.

The Henderson family's brewery, established in 1996, makes a number of traditional cask ales, all using the soft local water. The Galloway Gold adds Saaz hops for Sulwath's only lager, and the Grace is a good example of 'mild', one of the oldest styles of beer in Britain and emphasising fruity and sweet malts over the hops' bitterness. The award-winning Black Galloway uses British Maris Otter barley to achieve its chocolatey flavour. Try them in Sulwath's no-frills taproom, adjoining its brewery. Tours are often available on Mondays and Fridays at 1pm. On our visit, the Criffel IPA (named after a local granite mountain), with more restrained flavours than American interpretations, was the beer of the day.

HOOK NORTON BREWERY

Brewery Ln, Hook Norton, Oxfordshire;
www.hooky.co.uk; +44 1 608 730 384

◆ Food ◆ Bar
◆ Tour ◆ Takeout

THINGS TO DO NEARBY

Rollright Stones
Far smaller than Stonehenge, but also less crowded, the Rollright Stones on the Oxfordshire–Warwickshire border date back to the Neolithic and Bronze Age eras.
www.rollrightstones.co.uk

Stow-on-the-Wold
Drowse for antiques, enjoy cream tea in a quaint cafe or grab a pint and a pub lunch in this picture-perfect town, the highest in the Cotswolds (244m).

Bourton-on-the-Water
Attractions in this riverside village include a vintage car museum, a brewery, a maze and a miniature replica of the village, just in case the original isn't cute enough.

Blenheim Palace
Themed trails through the grounds of this 18th-century stately home bring it alive – choose TV/ film locations or follow the Churchill route; the PM was born here in 1874.
www.blenheimpalace.com

It looks like something straight out of a Dickens novel, and considering the pedigree of this village brewery, that's no great surprise.

Dating back to the 1850s, Hook Norton is one of a handful of surviving Victorian tower breweries – designed to use gravity in the brewing process, removing the need for pumps. The excellent tour takes you around a brewery that's about as traditional as it gets – you can even peep into the stables, home to the shire horses that to this day deliver beer to nearby pubs on a traditional dray. You'll find Hook Norton's real ales on tap in most pubs here and in surrounding Cotswolds villages.

Beer-wise, the emphasis is on 'sessionability' – that is, sinking a few pints in one sitting. Traditionally a cask ale brewery, it has a separate line for its so-called 'crafty ales' – served in keg rather than cask. Stronger ales, in both flavour and alcohol, do feature, and the list of seasonal, speciality and collaboration brews is constantly growing. But the beer that properly sums up this traditional brewery is Hooky Bitter: at 3.5% ABV and offering malty, floral flavours with a crisp finish, it's designed to be quaffed in an old Cotswold pub all afternoon.

NORTHERN MONK

The Old Flax Store, Marshall's Mill, Leeds; www.north-ernmonkbrewco.com; +44 (0)113 243 0003

◆ Food   ◆ Tour   ◆ Takeout
◆ Family   ◆ Bar   ◆ Transport

In an until-recently abandoned area of Leeds, there stands a Grade II-listed mill thick with the aromas of malts and hops. The mill is at the heart of Holbeck Urban Village, now a regeneration zone, thanks in part to community pioneers, such as Northern Monk. Founder Russell Bisset explains: 'For me the vision from the outset was to create something that was quintes-sentially British and Northern but that was still very progressive.' The theme of the brewery is a nod to the centuries of monastic brewing heritage that exists in the north of England, but a generous dose of inspiration also comes from the hophead craft beer scene across the pond in America. Russell's focus is very much on the evolution of tradition and he has an eye for collaborations; Northern

THINGS TO DO NEARBY

Royal Armouries
The UK's national military museum has more than 8500 artefacts, including suits of armour from around the world, and rifles dating back to the 16th century.
www.royalarmouries.org

Wapentake
A traditional Yorkshire shop on what is claimed to be Leeds' oldest street has been restored to its former glory and transformed into a cafe-cum-bar.
www.wapentakeleeds.com

Corn Exchange
Leeds' Corn Exchange (completed 1864) is a cultural icon; instead of corn it's now vintage threads, crafts and coffees being sold under its domed atrium. ***www. leedscornexchange.co.uk***

Leeds' Shopping Arcades
Nineteenth-century industrialist wealth generated a series of ornate covered shopping arcades in Leeds, many still in use, in the alleyways either side of Briggate. ***www.victoria-quarter.co.uk***

Monk was the first brewery to produce an Anglo-Indian beer, in partnership with a tiny brewery in Mumbai. Upstairs at the mill, the informal bare-brick tap room is The Refectory, serving up to 20 draft beers including some guest names. Food is also a highlight, focusing on British small plates that pair well with the beers.

Don't leave without sampling the flagship new-world Session IPA, Eternal.

HILDEN BREWING CO.

Hilden House, Grand St, Lisburn, Northern Ireland;
www.taproomhilden.com; +44 28 9266 3863

◆ Food   ◆ Tour   ◆ Takeout
◆ Family   ◆ Bar   ◆ Transport

The oldest independent brewery in Northern Ireland, Hilden is owned and operated by husband-and-wife team Seamus and Ann Scullion. The Scullions have been brewing at their home, Hilden House – a 19th century linen baron's Georgian estate in Lisburn, 7½ miles (12km) south of Belfast – since 1981. They expanded their brewery to include a taproom in the estate's former stables, and later opened Molly's Yard, a Hilden-branded taproom and restaurant in Belfast. In addition to beer sampling, the taproom at Lisburn has a well-rated restaurant and on Wednesday nights runs traditional Irish music sessions. Hilden excels at IPAs – the Buck's Head Double IPA packs a punch of bitter hops – but the Hilden Halt is a boozy 6.1% red ale that's not to be missed.

THINGS TO DO NEARBY

Irish Linen Centre & Lisburn Museum
Explore this museum for an understanding of how the linen industry shaped this part of Northern Ireland. Hands-on exhibits help bring the past to life.
www.lisburnmuseum.com

Titanic Belfast
Covering the history of Belfast's most famous ship, these thoughtful, interactive exhibits encompass the sights, sounds and even smells of early 20th-century industry.
www.titanicbelfast.com

BEAVERTOWN BREWERY

Units 2, 17-18, Lockwood Industrial Park, Mill Mead Rd, Tottenham Hale,
London; www.beavertownbrewery.co.uk; +44 208 525 9884

◆ Food   ◆ Takeout
◆ Bar   ◆ Transport

THINGS TO DO NEARBY

Birdwatching
The ten Walthamstow reservoirs next to Beavertown attract a variety of wetland birds, including herons, cormorants, various ducks, warblers and the great crested grebe. *www.visitleevalley.org.uk*

Dukes
Deep in De Beauvoir Town, Duke's Brew and Que marries Logan's beers with barbecue meat cooked low and slow. Open evenings and weekend lunchtimes. *www.dukesbrewandque.com*

Dennis Severs' House
Just a bus ride (the 149) south in lively Shoreditch is one of London's most enthralling museums, the house of a family of 18th-century Huguenot silk weavers. *www.dennissevershouse.co.uk*

Stoke Newington
Halfway between Shoreditch and Tottenham, hop off at Stoke Newington to explore this appealing neighbourhood: check out Church Street's independent boutiques and bars.

Wedged between Walthamstow and Stoke Newington in North London, Beavertown is off the beaten path (unless you're on your way to Tottenham's IKEA store) but there's an excellent reason for making the trip up here: a taproom is open on Saturday afternoons and it sells, arguably, London's most highly rated craft beers (in cans that bear the best artwork in town too, by creative director Nick Dwyer). Beavertown was brought to life in 2011 by Logan Plant (work out the Led Zep connection for yourself), who looked to the US and brewers such as Dogfish Head (see p80) for inspiration rather than traditional British cask ales.

Head brewer Jenn Merrick has led Beavertown to numerous awards including the accolade of Supreme Champion Brewer in 2015. She has built a core range of seven beers but the brewery is continually trying new collaborations with the likes of Mikkeller (see p153), Dogfish Head and Odell (see p74). The Barbarian IPA series turns the hops up to 11. All in all, with the taproom's regular events, it's a stimulating sort of place. Highlights are the Gamma Ray American Pale Ale, dry-hopped for days with Amarillo and Citra hops among others, and the Black Betty IPA, with West Coast hops underpinned by a roasted malt.

BREW BY NUMBERS

79 Enid Street, South Bermondsey, London;
www.brewbynumbers.com; +44 207 237 9794

◆ Bar   ◆ Transport

◆ Takeout

Begin your Bermondsey beer odyssey at BBNo, conveniently located just south of Maltby Street Market. In common with many of the breweries on the famed 'beer mile', Brew by Numbers' taproom is open on Fridays and Saturdays.

Similarly, its founders, friends Dave Seymour and Tom Hutchings, were inspired by their beer-quaffing trips in Australia, New Zealand, the US and Belgium. They've continued that spirit of adventure in the beers they make, becoming known for their saisons (farmhouse ales) but

also trying witbiers, barrel-aged beers and more. A new brewhouse has freed up their original kit for more experiments. Their excellent Double IPA marries British malt and American and New Zealand hops.

THINGS TO DO NEARBY

Maltby Street Market
Maltby St is small but perfectly formed: with a delectable selection of places to eat and drink under the railway arches, this is a good place to start your beer adventure.

Borough Market
In this tale of two artisan food markets, Borough is the big deal on the block, but that means it is always busy. Find a quiet time and it's very enjoyable. *www. boroughmarket.org.uk*

FOURPURE BREWING CO.

22 Bermondsey Trading Estate, Rotherhithe New Road,
London; www.fourpure.com; +44 203 744 2141

◆ Tour ◆ Takeout
◆ Bar ◆ Transport

THINGS TO DO NEARBY

Deptford art galleries
South London's Deptford
has inherited Shoreditch's
mantle as the affordable
base for artists, who
exhibit in galleries such
as BEARSPACE and at the
Deptford X festival.

**Copeland Park and Bussey
Building**
Art studios, theatres and
creative pop-ups occupy this
trading estate at the end of
Rye Lane in Peckham. Also
find indie shops and eateries
in the Holdrons Arcade.
www.copelandpark.com

Imperial War Museum
It's a couple of stops away
on the Underground but
the Imperial War Museum
(free admission) on
Lambeth Road is one of
South London's unmissable
institutions. *www.iwm.
org.uk*

Dulwich Hamlet FC
Fourpure might be in
Millwall FC's backyard but
we'd suggest watching a
Dulwich Hamlet match a
fair hop to the south (train
required) – there are better
beers available. *www.
dulwichhamletfc.co.uk*

It takes a bit of searching to reach but the schlep
is worth it (historian Simon Winchester described
19th-century South London as a place to which 'few
respectable Londoners would ever admit to venturing'
and some would say that the region has been slow to
change). Awaiting you in a trading estate at the gritty
southern end of the Bermondsey Beer Mile are, in our
opinion, some of its tastiest beers. The founders of
Fourpure, brothers Dan and Tom Lowe, were inspired
by their travels around the world and encounters with
American craft brewers such as Pfriem (see p77), before
they started Fourpure in 2013. They developed a core
range of beers including a pale ale, a session IPA at a
manageable 4.2%ABV and a full-powered, West Coast-
style IPA with abundant mango, pineapple and grapefruit
flavours from the Citra and Mosaic hops. With up to 16
beers on draught at the taproom (open Friday afternoons
and most of Saturday) there are also guest appearances
from the rest of the range.

It's an unvarnished experience – a corner of the factory
has a few benches and tables and there's a Portaloo outside
– but on the plus side, it is close to South Bermondsey rail
station. However, it's all about the beer and on our wintry
visit the Oatmeal Stout was particularly welcome.

225

HOWLING HOPS TANK BAR

9A Queens Yard, White Post Ln, London;
www.howlinghops.co.uk; +44 203 583 8262

◆ Food   ◆ Tour   ◆ Takeout
◆ Family   ◆ Bar   ◆ Transport

THINGS TO DO NEARBY

Queen Elizabeth Olympic Park
Cycle, stroll or take a boat tour through this 227-hectare park, the heart of the 2012 Olympic Games. It also features the world's tallest, longest slide: ArcelorMittal Orbit.

Rough Trade East
Dig through the vinyl bins for indie, soul, electronica, or don the listening-station cans and find your next favourite at London's most beloved record store. *www.roughtrade.com*

Old Spitalfields Market
Peruse the shops and stalls, score an antique, or sit down for lunch at this 350-year-old converted fruit and veg market, trading daily. *www. oldspitalfieldsmarket.com*

Santander Cycles
Hire a bike from one of the many stands and cycle along Regent's Canal, lined by houseboats. Start in Little Venice for the whole 9.3km (6 mile) route. *www.tfl.gov.uk/modes/ cycling/santander-cycles*

Howling Hops Tank Bar was the first, and remains one of the only places in the UK that serves all of its beer directly from the tank, rather than out of kegs or casks. The bar has a whopping 10 tanks of beers, ranging from fresh pale ale to smoked porter. Long bench tables and outdoor seats not far from Regent's Canal, and a small pop-up kitchen doing smoked barbecue make this one of the best and unique places to drink beer in the UK. Howling Hops (the name is an homage to bluesman Howlin' Wolf) started life brewing hoppy, New World-style beers in the basement of the Cock Tavern in Hackney. In the interests of space and effort-saving,

it served the beer directly from the tanks in the cellar, via pipes that connected them to the taps on the bar. This streamlined approach, which eliminated the step of putting the beer into kegs, inspired the idea of opening the full tank bar. One or two experimental brews, such as the recent double chocolate coffee toffee vanilla milk porter, are usually on offer, though its 6.9% West Coast-style IPA goes down well on almost every visit.

JERUSALEM TAVERN

55 Britton St, Clerkenwell, London;
www.stpetersbrewery.co.uk/london-pub; +44 207 490 4281

◆ Food   ◆ Takeout
◆ Bar   ◆ Transport

From the moment you step in through the panelled wooden doors, the Jerusalem Tavern seems splendidly ancient. You could easily imagine Pitt the Younger and Charles Fox arguing in the snug, or Samuel Johnson stopping by for a pint, gout allowing, on the way home from urgent dictionary business in the city. Buried somewhere beneath the foundations are even older relics from the Priory of the Knights of St John of Jerusalem, honoured in the pub's name.

The Bible-thumping knights weren't averse to a drop or two, and the tradition is still enthusiastically continued behind the tavern's bowed, Curiosity Shoppe-esque windows, within easy staggering distance of the Square Mile. The lines of barrels behind the bar swish agreeably with the full-flavoured brews produced by St Peter's Brewery near Bungay in Suffolk, which channels the spirit of a medieval monastic ale-maker, despite only arriving on the scene in 1996. While the ales taste just like you'd imagine beer to taste in the time of Pitt and Johnson, this historic watering hole is looking to the future, with everything from honey porter to gluten-free and organic beers behind the bar. Enthusiasts swear by the Organic Ale, served on tap, or in distinctive green-glass bottles, inspired by 18th-century gin bottles.

THINGS TO DO NEARBY

Museum of London
London's patron museum tells the whole story of the British capital, from the Roman camp at Heathrow to the Great Fire and the Blitz. *www.museumoflondon.org.uk*

St John
Nose-to-tail eating is the motto at chef Fergus Henderson's pioneering restaurant and their crusade to bring forgotten offal back to the capital's tables. *www.stjohngroup.uk.com/smithfield*

Smithfield Market
From the early hours, London's atmospheric wholesale meat market buzzes with energy. Visit by 7am at the latest to see it in full swing. *www.smithfieldmarket.com*

Church of St Bartholomew the Great
London's oldest church dates from 1123. Its interior has stood in for Elizabethan England in more films than you can shake an ermine robe at. *www.greatstbarts.com*

MEANTIME BREWING

Lawrence Trading Estate, Blackwall Lane, London;
www.meantimebrewing.com; +44 208 293 1111

◆ Food   ◆ Bar   ◆ Transport
◆ Tour   ◆ Takeout

THINGS TO DO NEARBY

Old Royal Naval College
Generations of sailors were trained at this gorgeous building, designed by Christopher Wren. It's now the heart of Greenwich's Unesco World Heritage Site. Check out the chapel.
www.ornc.org

Royal Observatory
Learn about the wonders of time and straddle the Meridian Line, where east meets west, at this institution founded in 1675. The astronomy exhibitions in the planetarium are ace.
www.rmg.co.uk

National Maritime Museum
Occupying several buildings (designed by Christopher Wren and Inigo Jones), this museum houses a remarkable collection, including Lord Nelson's coat from the Battle of Trafalgar.

The Cutty Sark
It's strange to see this sleek sailing ship, once the fastest way to get from Britain to Australia, on dry land, just metres from the Thames. *www.rmg.co.uk*

At one point in history, Greenwich was the centre of the world, or at least the British Empire. The nation's 19th-century sailors calculated their longitude and thus their location based on the time at the Greenwich Meridian. The legacy today is a remarkable collection of fascinating places clustered around Greenwich in the southeast of London (see below). And in 1999, Alastair Hook started brewing beer there under the name Meantime. The new brewery heralded a return to craft brewing in the capital after bleak decades when London brewers had shut up shop. Today, London's brewing scene is healthy and Meantime (although it is now owned by Asahi, see p113) is still making beers that draw on traditional local ingredients: hops from Kent, malting barley from East Anglia.

The brewery itself is in no-man's-land midway between the O2 dome and Greenwich Park. But it lures visitors with a two-hour tour (£20) and a tasting room. Another option is to visit (and eat at) Meantime's own pub on Royal Hill, the Greenwich Union, which has a superb range of beers. A good starting point is Meantime's IPA, which uses Fuggles and Goldings hops from Kent and harks back to when Britannia ruled the waves.

KIRKSTILE INN

Loweswater, Cumbria;
www.kirkstile.com; +44 1900 85219

◆ Food   ◆ Transport
◆ Bar

You won't find many breweries that feel more out-of-the-way than this one, located at a tiny pub in the valley of Buttermere. There's been an inn here since Tudor times, and the building is packed with history – beams, inglenooks, vintage black-and-white photos and the odd stuffed animal or two. Outside, there's a classic whitewashed, slate-topped façade; inside, there are low ceilings, old carpets and well-worn wooden furniture, plus a largely local clientele. In-house brews include hoppy Esthwaite Bitter, dark Grasmoor and smooth Loweswater Gold.

THINGS TO DO NEARBY

Honister Slate Mine
Delve into the depths of the Lake District's last working slate mine, where you can take an underground mine tour, brave the hillside via ferrata or browse for slate-themed souvenirs.
www.honister.com

Haystacks
This hill was the favourite of the famous fell-walker and author Alfred Wainwright, who penned the classic series *A Pictorial Guide to the Lakeland Fells*. He loved it so much, he even had his ashes scattered here.

BLACK SHEEP BREWERY

Wellgarth, Masham, North Yorkshire;
www.blacksheepbrewery.com; +44 1765 689227

◆ Food   ◆ Tour   ◆ Takeout
◆ Family   ◆ Bar

Once upon a time there was a family brewing dynasty called T & R Theakston, born and raised in the Dales village of Masham, North Yorkshire. After five generations the family sold out to mega brewing company Scottish & Newcastle Breweries. It was a move that one Theakston couldn't quite square with himself. Preloved brewing equipment was salvaged from other defunct breweries and a breakaway brewery was created: Black Sheep – Paul Theakston's vision. His team's passion and dedication electrifies the brewery's excellent brewery tours, bulging beer shop and popular on-site family Bistro & Baa...r (get it?). Beers are bursting with malty flavour backed by the bitterness of English hops: try Riggwelter, a classic, strong ale with a silky mouthfeel.

THINGS TO DO NEARBY

Theakston's Brewery
The original Theakston brewery was bought back by the family in 2003. Tour the tower-style brewery from top to bottom and visit the fireside tap room.
www.theakstons.co.uk

Yorkshire Dales National Park
Green valleys, heather moors and stone villages, such as Wensleydale, are the fabric of this North Yorkshire park, beloved by walkers and cyclists. ***www.yorkshiredales.org.uk***

SALTAIRE BREWERY

Dockfield Rd, Shipley, West Yorkshire;
www.saltairebrewery.co.uk; +44 1274 594 959

◆ Family   ◆ Takeout
◆ Bar   ◆ Transport

Saltaire's makeshift canal-side tap room in the brewery's back yard is a manifestation of the way this craft brewery has taken the market by storm – with quiet confidence and a down-to-earth focus on community. The brewery's monthly Beer Club (£5), held on the last Friday of every month, has ticket-holders seated cheek by jowl with beer tanks and equipment in and around the working brewery and treated to 13 pumps' worth of Saltaire ales and guest beers at £2 a pint.

Saltaire's focus is on both traditional-style British ales and heavily hopped craft beers. Its award-winning brews are crowd pleasers: the flagship beer, Saltaire Blonde, is a real easy drinker with a crisp flavour from German and Czech malts.

THINGS TO DO NEARBY

Salts Mill
This giant, Unesco-listed mill – the centrepiece to a 19th-century utopian vision for the workers' village of Saltaire – now houses an expansive shopping and culture complex.
www.saltsmill.org.uk

Bradford: Curry Capital
Large numbers of Bangladeshi and Pakistani workers immigrated to Bradford in the 20th century, and as a result the city is known for superb curries.

ST AUSTELL BREWERY

63 Trevarthian Road, St Austell, Cornwall;
www.staustellbrewery.co.uk; +44 1726 66022

◆ Food ◆ Tour ◆ Takeout
◆ Family ◆ Bar ◆ Transport

 This is Cornwall's big-boy brewer. In business since 1851, St Austell Brewery now owns pubs all the way from Land's End to Bristol, and its cask ales are available right across the Westcountry (apparently, the company is on the brink of serving its billionth pint). It makes some of Cornwall's best-known ales – notably Tribute, a smooth, drinkable golden pale ale, and Korev, a zesty and refreshing lager. Tours are available, and there's a flashy visitor's centre, an 'inter-active' brewing experience. Our tip is the company's newly developed stout, Mena Dhu (from the Cornish for black hill).

THINGS TO DO NEARBY

Eden Project
Built inside a disused clay-pit just outside St Austell, Eden's three gigantic biomes look like something from a sci-fi movie, and recreate natural habitats from across the globe. *www.edenproject.com*

Fowey Estuary
Take a guided kayak trip downriver and keep your eyes peeled for kingfishers, herons, cormorants and – if you're lucky – a seal or two near the sea. *www. encountercornwall.com*

HAWKSHEAD BREWERY

Mill Yard, Staveley, Cumbria;
www.hawksheadbrewery.co.uk; +44 1539 822644

◆ Food ◆ Bar ◆ Transport
◆ Tour ◆ Takeout

THINGS TO DO NEARBY

Lake Windermere
England's largest lake is a must-see: cruise boats putter around the wooded islands, or you can explore in your own wooden rowing-boat. *www.windermere-lakecruises.co.uk*

Orrest Head
Hike up this hill for a wrap-around view of Windermere and its surroundings. On a clear day, you'll have an unbeatable panorama over England's most popular national park. *www.lakedistrict.gov.uk*

Lakeland Motor Museum
This collection of vintage automobilia includes replicas of the Bluebird boats used by father-and-son speedsters, Malcolm and Donald Campbell. *www.lakelandmotormuseum.co.uk*

The Lakeside & Haverthwaite Railway
Travel back to steam age aboard the carriages of this heritage train, as it puffs along a scenic track between Haverthwaite and Newby Bridge. *www.lakesiderailway.co.uk*

From whitewashed inns to oak-beamed hikers' bars, pubs are a cornerstone of life in the Lake District, slaking the thirst of farmers and fell-walkers alike. There are several fine breweries here – but for connoisseurs, Hawkshead Brewery is the cream of the crop.

Based in the village of Staveley, surrounded by drystone walls and green, sheep-spotted fells, this renowned brewery was founded in 2002 by Alex Brodie, an ex-foreign correspondent for the BBC. Its *raison d'être* is 'beer from the heart' – traditional, cask-brewed ales made with crystal-clear Lakeland spring-water and a variety of hops and malts from across the globe.

From its amber Gold and fruity Red to its rich, treacly stout, Brodie's Prime, Hawkshead's beers are designed to be served in the 'northern manner', poured through a tight sparkler to create a rich, creamy head. You can sample them in the onsite Beer Hall, accompanied by Lakeland tapas, venison burgers and huntsman's pies. Best of all, the rolling Lakeland fells are ideal for working up a thirst – and there's no better post-hike quencher than Hawkshead Bitter, with a citrus tang and floral notes.

ST IVES BREWERY

Trewidden Road, St Ives, Cornwall;
www.stives-brewery.co.uk; +44 1736 793488

◆ Food   ◆ Tour   ◆ Takeout
◆ Family   ◆ Bar   ◆ Transport

Another Cornish newcomer, this start-up only began bottling beers in 2010, but it's earned a loyal following and a bevy of awards. It's located in the quaint town of St Ives, famous for its stunning seafront location and artistic heritage. The beers here include a classic gold, a good pale ale and a boozy, intense Belgian-style wheat beer. The brewery doesn't offer tours, but it has recently opened its own café, where you can sample the brews and enjoy cracking views over the brilliant blue waters of St Ives Bay. Try the golden, hop-forward Boilers Golden Ale.

THINGS TO DO NEARBY

Tate St Ives
After a major expansion, St Ives' foremost art gallery reopens in 2017, with a focus on local artists such as Barbara Hepworth, Patrick Heron, Terry Frost and Alfred Wallis.
www.tate.org.uk

Gwithian beach
Shed that nascent beer belly with a surf lesson on the golden sands of Gwithian, renowned for having some of the county's most reliable waves.
www.surfacademy.co.uk

TRAPPIST BREWS OF BELGIUM

No beer lover can pass up the opportunity to make a pilgrimage to Belgium and with 450 or so brews to experience in a relatively small space, it makes complete sense. But being reasonable, let's apply a filter and narrow the journey to the six genuine Trappist breweries – surely the pilgrimage of pilgrimages. Put them on your list: Orval, Westvleteren, Chimay, Rochefort, Achel and Westmalle. Now go, fill your holy grail with these other-worldly, rich, strong ales.

With so many new breweries and beers to explore, it's possible to create extended beer trails around a region, or follow one of the new signposted routes. Here are five of our favourite ideas for finding beervana.

GREAT A

CYCLE NEW ZEALAND'S BEERY HEART

Nelson, in the north of the South Island, is a wine and food wonderland, and craft brewing has flourished too. There's more than 20 brewers in the region, including McCashin's in Stoke and Moa in Blenheim. It's a beautiful region, made better by all the palate pleasing to be done. Bittersweet perhaps, but these are beers you'll probably only ever find in the region.

E TRAILS

HIKE A BEER TRAIL (Germany)

Franconian Switzerland – a region of Bavaria in Germany – has 70 breweries, and at its heart is a municipality called Aufseß. It claims a Guinness Book of Records entry for highest brewery density – four breweries for just 1500 people. Get your hiking boots on and discover them on a 14km (8½-mile) hike through the forest. Kathi Bräu, Stadler, Reichold and Rothenbach are your stopovers, and you can print out a certificate to take around with you, which the breweries will stamp as proof of your intrepid beer exploration.

YOUTHFUL YARRA VALLEY (Australia)

Long known as a wine-making district, the Yarra Valley, barely an hour's drive from Melbourne, is home to a growing band of beer makers. There are operators who'll take you around for the day and at the same time expand your knowledge of beer making. Must tries: Napoleone, in Coldstream, with a variety of styles; Coldstream Brewery and Hargreaves Hill in Yarra Glen – also a good spot for lunch.

HARD WORKING BEER (Detroit, USA)

We know about Oregon, we know about California – honestly, the whole of the USA could be a beer tour if you had the time. So let's go to Detroit, a solid American city, jam-packed with breweries. Speaking of which, try Traffic Jam, the city's first brewpub. Then head to South Main St and 4th – there's a handful of breweries and restaurants that will keep you busy. Motor city it may be – but find a designated driver!

OCEA

TOP 3 BEER TOWNS

ANIA

MELBOURNE

It shouldn't be a surprise that Melbourne excels at brewing, selling and drinking craft beer. It's clearly Australia's ale capital, with breweries ranging from the mainstream (Mountain Goat) to the obscure but brilliant (La Sirène), and a ton of great indie beer bars in such neighbourhoods as Brunswick and Fitzroy.

PERTH

Home to some of Australia's first craft brewers, Matilda Bay and Little Creatures, and one of its most lauded, Feral Brewing in the northeast, Perth thoroughly deserves its place here. It's also the departure point for any beer tours south to Margaret River (highly recommended). Western Australia's beer scene is alive and kicking.

WELLINGTON

It might be wet and windy for much of the year in Wellington but there are always sunny fruit flavours in a pint glass to banish the blues with New Zealand's distinctively tropical take on pale ale and IPA. Wellington has an extremely strong array of breweries and craft beer bars, making it a compact and cool city to tour.

AUSTRALIA

How to ask for a beer?
I'd like a pot/pint/schooner of beer please
How to say cheers? Cheers!
Signature beer style? Australian pale ale
Local bar snack? Salted potato crisps and peanuts
Don't: Turn up to a party with less than a
six-pack of stubbies

Uncharitable observers might suggest that the reason Australians like their beer numbingly cold – to the extent that insulating stubby holders are commonplace – is so that they can't taste it. They may have had a point in the age of industrial 1980s lagers such as Castlemaine XXXX and Fosters but the theory couldn't be further from the truth today. Over the last decade Australia has established itself as the source of some of the most inventive, interesting and high-quality beers in the world, produced by around 200 craft breweries across the country.

Geographically, Australian craft brewing reaches from Murrays on the east coast to Feral on the west, from big city breweries such as Mountain Goat in Melbourne and Four Pines in Sydney to breweries that are important parts of the community in small country towns such as Woodend, Beechworth and Bright. And that means, when the hot summer sun is setting and the sound of the cicadas is ringing in your ears, you're never far from a great local beer.

It wasn't always so. Australia, like New Zealand and Britain, had relatively restrictive drinking laws and taxes during much of the 20th century – as was common, such regulations were introduced during wartime but never relaxed afterwards. The 'six o'clock swill' was a feature of Australian towns and cities as patrons rushed to finish their beers before closing time. Taxes based on alcohol content and limited appetite for flavourful beer meant that

BAR TALK – BEN KRAUS

In the past decade Aussie beer has had a hop-driven renaissance and ale enthusiasts will find unique experiences in every corner

TOP 5 BEERS

- **Robohop Golden IPA** Kaiju!
- **Saison** La Sirène
- **Temptress** Holgate Brewhouse
- **Pale Ale** Bridge Road Brewers
- **Pacific Ale** Stone & Wood Brewing Co.

mass-produced beers were ubiquitous. There was one outlier, a family-owned brewery called Cooper's in Adelaide, which remains one of Australia's largest and still produces its iconic 'red' and 'green' bottled ales.

For many Australians, wine became their preferred drink during these doldrums. But Australia, as a colony peopled by British, Irish, Scottish and, near Adelaide, German settlers, had a rich beer-drinking heritage to fall back on. Indeed, the man credited with founding the first brewery in Australia was James Squire, a London-born convict transported to the island in 1788. As gold mining and exploration sparked settlements across the nation, each town had several (often many) public houses, often doubling as hotels. Today, Australia's beer culture still revolves around handsome old pubs – except that the taps are often pouring a variety excellent guest ales from local breweries. There's

also a new wave of beer bars, such as the Alehouse Project in Melbourne, to investigate.

Australia's signature beer styles stem from Britain, its northern relation. pale ales, porters and IPAs are all standard for most craft brewers. But they're usually given a southern twist. Take Murray Brewing's Angry Man pale ale: it uses Australian, British and German malts plus Motueka hops from near neighbour New Zealand and Centennial hops from the US. It's a classic Australian pale ale, taking the best of all its influences and delivering something delicious.

So, how best to approach beer touring in a country where you'll be spoiled for choice? Aside from our recommendations – there are many more brilliant breweries to visit – the best strategy is to meet and talk to as many Australian beer fans as you can; you'll find them friendly, eager to offer local tips, and as passionate about finding and drinking great beer as you.

BRIDGE ROAD BREWERS

Old Coach House, Ford Street, Beechworth, Victoria;
www.bridgeroadbrewers.com.au; +61 3 5728 2703

◆ Food　　◆ Bar
◆ Tour　　◆ Takeout

THINGS TO DO NEARBY

Beechworth Mountain Bike Park
These trails twist and turn around the rocky slopes on the outskirts of town. They're a fun way to pass half a day but you'll need to bring your own bike. *www.beechworthchaingang.com*

The Provenance
Michael Ryan's restaurant is renowned for using locally sourced and seasonal produce. Set in a grand old former bank, it's one of Australia's top dining experiences. *www.theprovenance.com.au*

Swim in the gorge
On a hot, dry day – of which there are many in these parts – dip into the swimming holes along Beechworth's gorge to cool down. Access is via a slow-and-scenic road. See also: Woolshed Falls.

Indigo Gold Trail
www.indigogoldtrail.com
The corner of Victoria marked out by Beechworth, Chiltern, Yackandandah and Rutherglen was prime gold-rush land. Explore its handsome towns on this road-trip.

More than 15 years ago, an Australian viticulturist discovered European beers while working and studying in the continent, and returned to his hometown of Beechworth dreaming of hops not vines. Fortunately, Ben Kraus was from northeast Victoria, where mountain waters, fertile soils and benign climate, made for an ideal place to start a brewery with wife Maria, using local ingredients. 'We work and live in a hop growing region, and have always championed our local hop growers,' he says.

Bridge Road Brewers is now a much-loved part of Australia's best-preserved 19th-century gold-mining town, about three hours' drive from Melbourne. Venture into the bar's cool interior (note the hop-shaped light fittings) to check out the beers on tap and view the tanks. The flavour profiles (malty and hoppy) of each beer are described, from the mellow Golden Ale to the medal-winning Bling IPA,

helping your choice. The perfect companion to a couple of pints is some of the best pizza in the state from Maria's kitchen, such as the gorgonzola with apples from the orchards of Stanley, up the road.

Kraus's favourite beer is his Beechworth Pale Ale, but we're going to go with the seasonal Fat Man, Red Suit, Big Sack, a dark and malty India red ale that uses Australian hops: worth the wait for Christmas.

MOO BREW

MONA, 655 Main Road, Berriedale, Tasmania;
www.moobrew.com.au; +61 3 6277 9900

◆ Food   ◆ Bar   ◆ Transport
◆ Family   ◆ Takeout

Admittedly, this is more of a bar than a brewery, since brewing operations moved off-site after expansion. No matter, you won't be short of things to be amazed by, since Moo Brew is based at the Museum of Old and New Art (MONA), along with the long-established winery Moorilla Estate. MONA, probably the southern hemisphere's most challenging, eclectic and impressive contemporary art gallery is the creation of one man, self-made millionaire and collector of avant-garde art, David Walsh. It occupies a peninsula just up the Derwent River from Hobart and you can reach it by boat, bus or bicycle. If you need a fortifying beer before or after your tour in the incredible subterranean complex, Moo Brew has a range of pale ales, a Pilsner and a wheat beer. The Winter Stout is especially good.

THINGS TO DO NEARBY

Tasmanian Devil Unzoo
Ever wondered what those eerie yowls are in the Tasmanian bush? Find out at a rambunctious feeding time at this Tasmanian Devil sanctuary on the Port Arthur road. *www.tasmanian devilunzoo.com.au*

Lark Distillery
A dram of Lark's world-class single malt whisky at its waterfront bar in state capital Hobart will take the edge off a winter evening at the edge of the world. *www.larkdistillery.com*

MURRAYS BREWING COMPANY

3443 Nelson Bay Rd, Bobs Farm, New South Wales;
www.murraysbrewingco.com.au; +61 2 4982 6411

◆ Food   ◆ Tour   ◆ Takeout
◆ Family   ◆ Bar

THINGS TO DO NEARBY

Port Stephens Winery
The region's oldest winery shares a location with Murrays so if your discerning beer palate extends to wine you'll be very happy here. *www.murraysbrewingco.com.au /psw*

Red Ned's Gourmet Pie Bar
Not your average pie shop, this is pastry nirvana for adventurous foodies who'd fancy a crocodile pie in mushroom and white wine sauce, among other gourmet delicacies. *www.redneds.com.au*

Worimi Conservation Lands
Explore via 4WD, quad bike or horse the longest moving sand dunes in the southern hemisphere or surf them on a sandboard. *www.portstephens.org.au /see-and-do/the-sand-dunes*

Nelson Head Lighthouse Cottage
For a tearoom with a view, visit this historic lighthouse built in 1875. There's a small museum where you can learn about the local area's history.

Flying a simple, but to-the-point mantra of 'No boring beer', Murrays really does keep its word. Having bought the iconic Pub With No Beer in the tiny town of Taylors Arm, owner Murray built a brewery on-site and 'Murrays Brewing' was born. Outgrowing the original digs, Murrays moved to the current location at Bob's Farm and well and truly established itself as a must-do experience for any visitor to the region.

Located just outside Nelson Bay on the beautiful mid north coast of NSW, Murrays can lay claim to around 98 beers, which rotate seasonally through its line of 10 taps and bottle sales. This list, while it is long, is also brain-tinglingly diverse, and includes a seasonal seaweed beer, a

hoppy pale ale, a wheat beer, a pumpkin ale, IPAs of all descriptions, Pilsners, wild fermented sours, brown ales, a Habanero chili beer, a Schwarzbier, a coffee stout, a porter, and just about every style and twist your imagination can conjure. The hardest part about visiting this place is deciding what to order. Try the Punch and Judy amber ale: a fine brew with piles of delicious, nutty caramel notes, and at 3.9%, it's a great option for those not looking to overindulge.

BRIGHT BREWERY

121 Great Alpine Road, Bright, Victoria;
www.brightbrewery.com; +61 3 5755 1301

◆ Food   ◆ Tour   ◆ Takeout
◆ Family   ◆ Bar

THINGS TO DO NEARBY

Mystic Mountain
Rent a mountain bike at the local cycle shop and try the trails at Mystic Mountain Bike Park or simply pedal the riverside rail trail.

Mount Buffalo
Just outside town lies the access road to Mount Buffalo National Park. At the top of the peak are 90km of hiking tracks, plus skiing and rock climbing in season.

Bright Chocolate
Crazy about quality cacao? Visit Bright Chocolate's factory, backing onto the Ovens River in the town centre, to try its handmade, single-origin chocolate bars. *www. brightchocolate.com.au*

Sweetwater Brewing
Make it a hat-trick and visit Sweetwater in Mount Beauty, a short drive from Bright. Its ales are brewed with water from the Kiewa River. *www. sweetwaterbrewing. com.au*

Follow the Great Alpine Road into Bright, a small town on the Ovens River (east of Beechworth) in northeast Victoria. The town has evolved into an adventure sports hub for Australia's Alpine National Park, and its excellent brewery, owned by avid skier and cyclist Scott Brandon, has expanded to meet demand. What first impresses is the size of the venue – adjacent to the working half of the brewery there's a large bar area with tables for diners, and outside overlooking the river is a terrace, over which hop vines grow. The place is so family friendly there's a playground just below the terrace.

Bright produces a solid range of brews, from standards such as the pale and amber ales to rarities such as Rule 47, a witbier-IPA hybrid using experimental hops from nearby Rostrevor Hop Gardens and, like all Bright beers, water from the Ovens River. The brewery also has a full schedule of events and tours: you don't have to be a beer geek to want to join Bright's Be a Brewer for A Day programme, but you should expect to get hands-on with a commercial-scale batch of beer. The brightest of the beers? The Blowhard Pale Ale, named after a local mountain, is a refreshingly fruity example.

CASCADE BREWERY

131 Cascade Road, Hobart, Tasmania;
www.cascadebreweryco.com.au; +61 3 6224 1117

◆ Food   ◆ Tour   ◆ Takeout
◆ Family   ◆ Bar

Tasmanian loyalties are divided between the island's two mainstream beer companies. In Launceston, in the north of the island, there is James Boag's. And in the south there's Hobart's Cascade Brewery, established in 1824. Both are big businesses and neither can pass themselves off as craft breweries, but we've included Cascade for the simple reason that it's the oldest working brewery in Australia and, boy, does it look the part. Set in the ominous shadow of Mount Wellington and looking like the sort of Gothic building where there's plenty of hair-raising goings-on, Cascade's

home is worth savouring from the outside. Inside, the two-hour tour is an interesting journey through the brewing process, followed by tastings. The Cascade Pale Ale is made with Tasmanian mountain water and Pride of Ringwood hops.

THINGS TO DO NEARBY

Battery Point
The historic maritime village of Battery Point – named after the guns that protected Hobart harbour – is a tight nest of lanes and 19th-century cottages. Explore it on foot.

Mount Wellington
Continue up the road to explore Hobart's very own mountain: there are hiking trails, views over the entire bay and a mountain bike track. *www. wellingtonpark.org.au*

EAGLE BAY BREWING CO

Eagle Bay Rd, Dunsborough, Margaret River,
Western Australia; www.eaglebaybrewing.com.au

◆ Food   ◆ Bar
◆ Family   ◆ Takeout

Eagle Bay Brewing is the most northern of Margaret River's craft breweries, and it also celebrates one of the region's most spectacular locations. Set on a farm that has been in the d'Espeissis family since the 1950s, both brewing and Eagle Bay Vineyard wines have created diversification on the coastal property. Eagle Bay's beers are well-balanced and true to style, with a core range including a crisp and refreshing kölsch and a bold pale ale. Shared outdoor tables provide glimpses of the Indian Ocean through rolling farmland, and the wood-fired oven turns out great Mediterranean-inspired pizza and slow-cooked Moroccan lamb. Ask about the Brewer's Series seasonal beers, especially the cacao stout made with Margaret River artisan chocolate makers, Bahen & Co.

THINGS TO DO NEARBY

Bunkers Beach Cafe
Negotiate a winding down-hill road to Bunkers' beach-front location. Get there when it opens at 8.30am to see intrepid surfers heading off into morning waves.
www.bunkersbeachcafe.com.au

Cape Naturaliste Lighthouse
Constructed in shimmering white limestone, this 20m-high lighthouse offers brilliant coastal views. Nearby, walking trails explore the serried coast-line in more detail.

BOOTLEG BREWERY

Puzey Rd, Wilyabrup, Margaret River, Western Australia;
www.bootlegbrewery.com.au; +61 8 9755 6300

◆ Food   ◆ Bar
◆ Family   ◆ Takeout

In 1994 when the Bootleg Brewery was first launched – then crafting a single brew called 'Bitter Beer' – the verdant salt-kissed land of the Margaret River region was known as one of Australia's finest wine-producing areas. Now there's around 10 breweries in the region, and craft beer is the hottest game in town. Still owned by descendants of the Reynolds family who first arrived in the area in 1841, Bootleg's range has expanded to six core beers, and seasonal brews – including regular collaborations with Perth's Mane Liquor, one of Australia's best beer shops – keep fans of bold and hoppy brews coming back. Weekends see the property lined with century-old trees filled with both local regulars and visitors from Perth, and blues and country musicians provide an easy-going soundtrack to the quintessential Aussie ambience.

THINGS TO DO NEARBY

Cycling in Bramley National Park
Bounce along on two knobbly wheels amid the dappled shade of Bramley National Park. Mountain bikes can be hired from nearby Margaret River Cycles & Repairs.

Lake Cave
More than 300 steps descend to Lake Cave, where limestone formations reflected in an underground stream make it one of Margaret River's most appealing caverns.

Prevelly Beach
Ease into an Indian Ocean state of mind around the region's wildly spectacular coastline. Prevelly Beach's sweeping bay stretches from Rivermouth south to rugged Gnarabup.

Margaret River Farmers Market
Held Saturday morning, this laid-back affair features everything from local kombucha, organic honey and artisan cheese, through to stonking bowls of pho (Vietnamese noodle soup).

Margaret River is a big destination for both surfers and mountain bikers, and in early July there's action-sports thrills when the pastures around the brewery host the South West Mudfest, a gloriously gluggy cross between a cross-country run, an obstacle course and an army boot camp. Competitors get to shower at the brewery before recharging on Bootleg's renowned Raging Bull, a robust 7.1% porter, first brewed in 1995.

GOODIESON

194 Sand Rd, McLaren Vale, South Australia;
www.goodiesonbrewery.com.au; +61 409 676 542

◆ Family   ◆ Bar
◆ Tour   ◆ Takeout

After falling in love with traditional German and Austrian beers during their travels, Jeff and Mary Goodieson decided they wanted to recreate these delicious brews at home using natural Australian ingredients. After researching the Australian beer industry for a while, they decided to set up their dream in the gourmet food and wine region of McLaren Vale. The result was Goodieson, a family-run craft brewery that sits on a pretty green slice of rural South Australia. With its old-fashioned copper kettles, quaint little tasting room and friendly, knowledgeable staff,

it's already popular on itineraries. The seasonal Christmas Ale brewed with the spices of Christmas and slightly higher alcohol volume is a true winter warmer... even in the middle of an Australian summer.

THINGS TO DO NEARBY

Wine Tasting
Home to around 65 wineries and some of the planet's oldest grapevines, McLaren Vale is renowned as one of Australia's best wine producing regions. *www.mclarenvale.info*

Blessed Cheese
The starting point for the McLaren Vale Cheese & Wine Trail, but also a hotspot for great coffee, food and, naturally, fabulous cheese. *www.blessedcheese.com.au*

MOON DOG

17 Duke St, Abbotsford, Melbourne, Victoria;
www.moondogbrewing.com.au; +61 3 9428 2307

- ◆ Food
- ◆ Family
- ◆ Tour
- ◆ Bar
- ◆ Takeout
- ◆ Transport

Wander down a street of car mechanics and, by accident or purpose, you might stumble across Moon Dog, a tiny cult-like brewery hidden in the backstreets of industrial Abbotsford that churns out craft beers, such as Chocolate Salty Balls (a stout), Perverse Sexual Amalgam (a sour ale) and Henry Ford's Girthsome Fjord (an American strong ale). Tasty sourdough pizzas (also with snazzy names: David Hassle Hock is a braised ham hock delight, there's a Leonardo DiCapricciosa and a sublime Return of the Mack, with truffled mackerel, no

less) are served out of a retro truck, to add to the unique atmosphere. Don't miss the incredibly polished Jukebox Hero IPA: a frontrunner as Australia's cleanest, most well balanced IPA.

THINGS TO DO NEARBY

Abbotsford Convent
This beautiful 19th-century convent, along with 10 other buildings on almost 7 hectares of riverside land, is an artistic hub of creativity, hosting markets and cultural events. *www. abbotsfordconvent.com.au*

Mountain Goat Brewery
A 15-minute walk down the road from Moon Dog is the hugely popular Mountain Goat Brewery, which has a great little bar and free brewery tours on Wednesdays. *www. goatbeer.com.au*

MOUNTAIN GOAT

80 North Street, Richmond, Melbourne, Victoria;
www.goatbeer.com.au; +61 3 9428 1180

◆ Food ◆ Bar
◆ Tour ◆ Transport

THINGS TO DO NEARBY

Moon Dog
Since you're in the neighboourhood it would be rude not to drop into Moon Dog (see previous page) for a beer or three. *www.moondogbrewing. com.au*

Melbourne Museum
See 600 million years of Melbourne's history, from dinosaurs onwards, in a building in Carlton Gardens. The wildlife displays are great (or spot possums outside at dusk). *www. museumvictoria.com.au*

The MCG
The Melbourne Cricket Ground is central to sports-mad Melbourne, hosting Australian Rules Football in the winter, with stadium tours and a sports museum to visit on non-match days. *www.mcg.org.au*

Yarra Trail
You can follow the Yarra River on this cycling and walking trail from the ocean, past Mountain Goat and all the way into Melbourne's suburbs; look out for the flying foxes!

When this airy warehouse on a Richmond backstreet throws open its doors twice a week on Wednesday and Friday evenings, it fills up pretty quickly with a thirsty after-work crowd, all eager to see what's on the distinctively antlered taps. Mountain Goat was founded in 1997 by Cam Hines and Dave Bonighton (but is now owned by Japan's Asahi corporation), after Cam returned from Vancouver with mouthwatering tales of the city's microbreweries. As one of the first independent breweries in Melbourne, Mountain Goat has seen tastes change over the past 20 years. Out went bland fizzy lager and Victoria Bitter (VB) and in came the more challenging flavours of bitingly hoppy American pale ale, rich amber ale and other beer types

from around the world. Many are represented in Mountain Goat's herd, while the brewery's Rare Breeds are limited releases such as the Rye IPA and the Surefoot Stout. You can see where they're all made on the free tour at 6.30pm each Wednesday. Mountain Goat's first beer was the amber Hightail Ale, a malty beer with a spicy hop edge inspired, so brewer Dave Bonighton says, by Anchor Steam's Liberty Ale and English ale, and it's still one of the best in show.

TWO BIRDS BREWING

136 Hall St, Spotswood, Melbourne, Victoria;
www.twobirdsbrewing.com.au; +61 3 9762 0000

◆ Food ◆ Tour ◆ Takeout
◆ Family ◆ Bar ◆ Transport

The clue is in the name: Two Birds is the creation of two craft beer-loving ladies, Jayne Lewis and Danielle Allen. Australia's first female-owned brewing company, Two Birds has gone from strength to strength in recent years. Following their initial success, the two best friends decided to open up their very own brewpub, smack bang in the middle of their hard-working brewery, between Footscray and Williamstown.

Here in 'The Nest' you can sit, drink and eat, while flanked on either side by towering brew kettles and fermentation tanks, as the brewers drag around bags of malt and buckets of hops, preparing their next tasty creation. Don't miss the Sunset Ale, a lovely amber ale with tropical fruit and grapefruit hop flavours.

THINGS TO DO NEARBY

Scienceworks
Designed for curious minds (young and old), this museum in Williamstown is a great place for an interactive, mind-opening experience with science and technology. *www. museumvictoria.com.au*

Yarraville
Wander this quaint little urban village, just north of Spotswood. It's far enough out of the Melbourne city centre to have adopted its own unique, laid-back vibe. *www.visitvictoria.com/ Regions/Melbourne/*

LITTLE CREATURES

40 Mews Rd, Fremantle, Perth, Western Australia;
www.littlecreatures.com.au; +61 8 6215 1000

◆ Food ◆ Tour ◆ Takeout
◆ Family ◆ Bar ◆ Transport

In sun-kissed WA, overlooking the boat-filled harbour in central Fremantle (Freo to locals), is one of the country's original craft breweries, Little Creatures. Founded by a group of mates, including long-time Aussie beer-preneur Phil Sexton, in 2000, it's now part of a corporation but retains its place in the hearts and minds of Australians ever since the team used to do keg deliveries in a VW Combi. The fantastic location, in a laid-back town just south of state capital Perth, also helps.

They produce a number of brews these days, including Roger's, a very drinkable English-style amber ale but watching a persimmon sun set over the Pacific with a Little Creatures Pale Ale, one of the country's original craft beers, is a quintessential Australian experience.

THINGS TO DO NEARBY

WA Shipwrecks Museum
Located within an 1852 commissariat store, the Shipwreck Galleries are considered the finest display of maritime archaeology in the southern hemisphere. *museum.wa.gov.au*

Beaches
Stretching south of Fremantle is a series of stunning beaches. Many are suitable for bathing or swimming, such as South Beach and Coogee Beach, which also has a shark net. Bus services link them.

FERAL BREWING COMPANY

152 Haddrill Rd, Swan Valley, Western Australia;
www.feralbrewing.com.au; +61 8 9296 4657

◆ Food ◆ Tour ◆ Takeout
◆ Family ◆ Bar

Artisan chocolate, cheese-making classes and vineyard dining are valid reasons to venture 20km (12½ miles) from downtown Perth to the Swan Valley, but for travelling beer fans a visit to Feral Brewing trumps all of those. The Western Australian brewery is known across Australia for its Hop Hog American IPA – Feral's signature brew regularly tops Best Of lists and is now easily found on tap in Sydney and Melbourne – but a relaxed session at its rustic and rural base demonstrates there's more to Feral than one assertive pale ale.

Head brewer Brendan Varis was one of the first Australian brewers to produce a Berliner Weisse beer – the sour, super-refreshing Watermelon Warhead is infused with watermelons from the Swan Valley – and Feral's Brewpub

THINGS TO DO NEARBY

Fremantle
Heritage Victorian architecture, excellent museums and great pubs combine at this raffish port town that was the birthplace of Australian craft beer three decades ago. *www.visit fremantle.com.au*

Petition Beer Corner
Petition Beer Corner's ever-changing selection of 18 taps showcases interesting brews from around Australia and the world. The selection of bottled beers is equally stellar. *www.petitionperth.com*

Long Chim
Expect authentically robust Thai street food at this hip eatery in Perth's State Treasury Building. Asian-inspired cocktails provide a soothing respite from the massive flavours. *www. longchimperth.com*

Food Loose Tours
Explore tapas restaurants, gelato stands, and specialist whisky and bourbon bars on an after-dark walking tour through Perth's emerging Northbridge neighbourhood. *www. foodloosetours.com.au*

Series regularly offers seasonal and one-off brews. Secure a table on Feral's shaded deck and order up a tasting paddle of the core range – other standout beers include Karma Citra, a hoppy and malty Black IPA – and browse the menu for such hearty dishes as trussed pork belly, braised lamb or barbecued salmon. Ask if the B.F.H. (Barrel Fermented Hog) is available, a special version of Feral's most famous beer that is fermented in French oak barrels.

4 PINES BREWING COMPANY

29/43-45 E Esplanade, Manly, Sydney, New South
Wales; www.4pinesbeer.com.au; +61 2 9976 2300

◆ Food ◆ Tour ◆ Takeout
◆ Family ◆ Bar ◆ Transport

THINGS TO DO NEARBY

Manly Beach

One of the country's most
famous beaches, Manly
beach is not only naturally
very beautiful but is a real
hub of entertainment on
the weekends.

Manly Surf School

It's much harder than it
looks, but fun trying: learn
how to surf the waves
along with the tribe of
Aussie surfers on Manly
Beach. *www.manlysurf-
school.com*

Shelly Beach

With over 500 species
of sea life in the harbour,
Shelly Beach (a short
10-minute stroll from
Manly) is an ideal spot for
snorkeling or scuba diving.
*www.manlyaustralia.
com.au/info/thingstodo/
snorkelling*

**Ghost Tour of Quarantine
Station**

A spooky night-time tour of
an old quarantine station
where the sick and infirm
were kept for over 150
years (many never left...).
*www.quarantinestation.
com.au*

The original Northern Beaches craft brewery, 4
Pines has definitely established itself as one of
Australia's best. Its multi-award winning flagship range of
beer is impressively diverse; not only can you can expect
to try some of the finest Kölsch, pale ale, hefeweizen,
stout and Extra Special Bitter in the country, but you
can also look forward to regular 'Keller Door' seasonal
releases. Keller Door is 4 Pine's beefed-up seasonal range,
where the brewers get to really let their hair down – think
Imperial IPAs, double Cascadian dark ales, West Coast red
rye IPAs and oaked Baltic porters. Basically, there's something for all levels of beer geekery at 4 Pines.

Conveniently located across the water from the Manly

Wharf, this is a great spot to sit back and people-watch, as
tourists arriving on the ferry from Sydney's Circular Quay
hit the beach for the day, then settle in to watch the sunset
with a frosty brew in hand. Even better, have a tasting
paddle close by, where you can try them all. But if you
do try just one, make it the 4 Pines stout: with its smooth
chocolate, coffee and bitter cocoa notes, this is a great
example of a well-made dry, Irish-style stout.

MODUS OPERANDI

14 Harkeith St, Mona Vale, Sydney, New South Wales;
www.mobrewing.com.au; +61 2 8407 9864

◆ Food   ◆ Tour   ◆ Takeout
◆ Family ◆ Bar   ◆ Transport

During a six-month craft beer-soaked tour of the US in an old motorhome, Modus Operandi creators Grant and Jaz didn't just collect photographs and souvenirs, but also packed a few very talented American brewers in their suitcase for the ride back Down Under. The result was immediate success.

Adding themselves to the growing list of great Northern Beaches craft breweries, they set up shop in the Sydney surfside suburb of Mona Vale and instantly started to pile on the awards. Beers such as the Zoo Feeder IPA and the Simmy Minion Pale Ale (now known as Modus Pale Ale) saw craft beer lovers flocking to the brewery. There is something special about sipping fresh beer overshadowed by the very

tanks it was brewed in, and here at Modus you are drinking inside the brewery itself. But the best perk is the vintage canning machine, which allows you to pick your beer of choice (after some serious research, of course...) and have it poured straight from the tank into a huge 1L can, which is then sealed for you to take home. The must-try beer is the Former Tenant Red IPA: big, aromatic and aggressively hopped, with a solid toffee-caramel malt backbone.

THINGS TO DO NEARBY

Mona Vale Beach
Not far from the brewery is beautiful Mona Vale Beach and the well-protected Bongin Bongin Bay, an ideal spot to surf, swim or just laze on the sand.

Newport Arms Hotel
One of Sydney's most iconic pubs, Newport Arms, with its mammoth beer garden brimming with bronzed Aussies, is famed for its magnificent views across Pittwater. *www.merivale.com.au/thenewport*

Barrenjoey Headland
Hike to the top of Barrenjoey headland (you might recognise the lighthouse from Home & Away) and to a breathtaking view across the entire Northern Beaches peninsula.

Pittwater Kayak Tours
Bordered by huge tracts of unspoilt national park, Pittwater offers secluded beaches, waterfalls, islands and beautiful estuaries that can only be explored by water. *www.pittwaterkayaktours.com.au*

YOUNG HENRYS

76 Wilford St, Newtown, Sydney, New South Wales;
www.younghenrys.com; +61 2 9519 0048

◆ Food ◆ Tour ◆ Takeout
◆ Family ◆ Bar ◆ Transport

The cool kids of the Sydney craft beer scene, Young Henrys has developed quite a name for itself. There isn't a bar in Newtown – a lively, student-friendly quarter of Sydney's inner west – that doesn't stock its beer, and it attracts a variety of food trucks on weekends. The brewery itself is adorned with funky artwork, graffiti and a huge collection of beer paraphernalia, with a backdrop of huge metallic beer tanks being fussed over by a small army of bearded brewers.

It's a perfect spot for an afternoon session (it closes at 7pm), so get in early and kick back with the likes of a Newtowner, an 'Aussie Pale Ale' with English and Australian malts. Don't leave without trying the Real Ale, a British-style bitter with an Aussie hop kick.

THINGS TO DO NEARBY

King Street
Newtown is Sydney's capital for all things alternative and King St has it all: retro op shops, unique cafes, street art and piles of bars.

Enmore Theatre
Sydney's longest running live theatre, where you can catch a variety of local and international performances, including comedy, musical theatre, ballet and live music. *www.enmoretheatre.com.au*

HOLGATE BREWHOUSE

79 High St, Woodend, Victoria;
www.holgatebrewhouse.com; +61 3 5427 2510

◆ Food   ◆ Bar   ◆ Takeout
◆ Family   ◆ Transport

The family-owned Holgate Brewhouse harks back to the days when every country town in Australia had a small brewery or brewpub. It has occupied the handsome red-brick hotel at the heart of Woodend since 1999, combining good Aussie pub food (burgers, parmigiana, fish and chips), guest accommodation and a taproom serving beers straight from the tanks out back.

There's one exceptionally good reason to make the trip north out of Melbourne: Holgate's Temptress, a seductive chocolate porter that you will remember for the rest of your days. It's infused with cocoa and whole vanilla beans, adding a luxurious layer to the blend of seven dark and toasty malts. Holgate's other beers are very good but the Temptress is a brew to make you swoon.

THINGS TO DO NEARBY

Wine tasting in the Macedon Ranges
There are lots of wineries close to the country towns of the Macedon Ranges, many excelling at cool-climate wines. Check out Hanging Rock Winery's sparkling Chardonnay.

Hanging Rock
A small reserve protects this six million-year-old geological formation that inspired a famous book and film. The hilltop can be explored on foot. Occasionally rock concerts are staged here too.

NEW ZEALAND

How to ask for a beer?
I'd like a beer, please
How to say cheers? Chur! (an abbreviation of cheers, bro!)
Signature beer style? Pale ale
Local bar snack? Kenny's Kumara chips
Do: Keep your beers cold in a 'chilly bin'
(pronounced 'chully bun' by Kiwis)

Motueka, Rakau and Riwaka are just some of the New Zealand names that are changing the world of beer. These are hop varieties developed by New Zealand's high-tech agri-scientists and their uniquely fruity tropical flavours are the magic ingredient that are setting the country's creative New World craft beers apart.

This is truly a nation on the edge of the world. Just 4.5 million people live on these two volcanic islands in the Pacific Ocean. Most of them live in the largest city, Auckland, on the North Island. Yet today, collectively, they're able to support around 100 craft breweries the length of the islands, from Hallertau in Auckland to Emerson's in Dunedin at the foot of the South Island. That's a remarkable feat but then this is a nation that frequently punches above its weight, in gender equality, environmentalism and rugby.

Wind the clock back a decade or two and Kiwi drinkers were confined to a few mass-market beers (such as Speights). During the 1990s craft brewers came and went but it wasn't until the turn of the millennium that inventive, independent breweries began to be established more securely. Some of the most successful names in NZ brewing, such as Renaissance and Tuatara date from this period. They've inspired and developed talented brewers who have gone on to start their own breweries, such as 8 Wired.

But back to the hops. New Zealand's extremely high standard of ingredients has also fuelled the boom in craft beer here. Few countries have cleaner water or more disease-free crops. Agri-business is taken very seriously and the new generation of hybrid hops will have been carefully created in a laboratory. Nelson in Marlborough is the nation's hop-growing capital. Long known for its Sauvignon Blanc grapes, it's a similarly-named locally grown hop that's making waves: Nelson Sauvin. It adds flavours of peach, gooseberry and tangerine to beers. Such is its appeal that it has crossed the Pacific to be used in several outstanding Californian IPAs, together with lime-and-lemon Motueka.

While the country's hops do travel, New Zealand's range of 200-300 craft brews doesn't leave its shores so readily. If you want to experience the full, fresh fruitiness of Kiwi ales, you'll need to jump on a plane. Most international flights arrive in Auckland, which has a good number of breweries to get your tour started. The Beer Tourist website (www.

BAR TALK - JOSH SCOTT

New Zealand has some of the most interesting hops in the world, with tropical and herbaceous characters

TOP 5 BEERS

- **HopWired IPA** 8 Wired
- **Elemental Porter** Renaissance
- **Death From Above** Garage Project
- **Hop Zombie** Epic
- **Tu-Rye-Ay Midnight Rye IPA** Tuatara Brewing

beertourist.co.nz) is an invaluable companion in planning your itinerary. From Auckland, it's worth stopping in Hawkes Bay on your way down to the nation's windswept capital Wellington. The capital – think San Francisco but with more reasonable property prices – is home to Tuatara Brewing, Fork and Brewer, and Garage Project (see p267). Many breweries have taprooms but even if they don't most towns and cities have at least a couple of good bars or pubs serving local beers on tap.

Crossing the Cook Strait (Captain James Cook, so the story goes, brewed the first beer in New Zealand in 1773, using local leaves) leads beer tourists to Marlborough and the plethora of breweries around Nelson and Blenheim. On the east coast, Christchurch has several excellent venues, such as Eagle Brewing, and committed beer tourists can continue all the way to Dunedin and Queenstown.

HALLERTAU BREWERY

1171 Coatesville Riverhead Hwy, Riverhead, Auckland;
www.hallertau.co.nz; +64 9 412 5555

◆ Food   ◆ Tour   ◆ Takeout
◆ Family   ◆ Bar

THINGS TO DO NEARBY

The Tasting Shed
Robust flavours travel from southeast Asia via the Middle East to Spain at this eatery combining big city sophistication with a vineyard's rural vibe. *www. thetastingshed.co.nz*

Muriwai Beach
Walk high above this rugged black-sand surf beach to see the avian courtship rituals – and subsequent fluffy chicks – of the Takapu Refuge gannet colony.

Kumeu River
Sample some of NZ's finest Chardonnays at Kumeu River's Tuscany-style cellar door. Head winemaker Michael Brajkovich became NZ's first Master of Wine (MW) in 1989. *www. kumeuriver.co.nz*

Waiheke Island
Around 45 minutes by ferry from downtown Auckland, Waiheke's subtropical microclimate combines vineyard restaurants, rocky and remote bays, and even a couple of craft breweries.

Despite being named after an area of Germany renowned for growing hops, Hallertau is a very New Zealand affair. Surrounded by the vineyards of rural West Auckland and a short drive from surf beaches, the brewery was first established in 2005 and its *biergarten* is hugely popular on weekends. Beer fans crowd in for seasonal brews and guest beers from around the country, while parents kick back as their children take on the playground with Kiwi confidence. An open kitchen turns out wood-fired goodness, including great pizza, and regular live gigs include some of the country's most popular musicians. Hallertau founder Steve Plowman is a big music fan, and brewing collaborations with musicians include beers made with a heavy metal band, the robust Beastwars IPA, and a brown ale crafted with Hopetoun Brown, a horn-heavy soul and funk duo from Auckland. Beyond Hallertau's core range of four beers – dubbed simply 1 to 4 – the brewery is an NZ pioneer in crafting barrel-aged and sour beers. Look out for special bottled brews, including Funkonnay, aged in Chardonnay barrels for a year, and back on the taps, the hoppy Maximus IPA is the one brew you've got to try.

MOA BREWING

258 Jacksons Rd, Blenheim, Marlborough;
www.moabeer.com; +64 3 572 5146

◆ Food   ◆ Takeout
◆ Family

Marlborough, at the top of the South Island, is the heartland of New Zealand's Sauvignon Blanc wine making. But its grape credentials are being challenged by a growing number of breweries in the region, including this one, named after a gigantic flightless bird that roamed this fantastical land.

Moa was founded by winemaker Josh Scott and Dave Nicholls, who nurtured their fledgling into one of New Zealand's largest independent breweries. The cellar door, surrounded by vineyards just outside the local hub of

Blenheim, offers tastings of much of Moa's brews, from the session-drinking Classic range to the Reserves, which tops out with a tripel and an Imperial stout. All use some of the purest water in the world and often amazing Kiwi hops.

THINGS TO DO NEARBY

The Mussel Inn
One of New Zealand's most beloved brewpubs lies halfway between Takaka and Collingwood, on the other side of Marlborough, a three and a half hour drive from Blenheim.
www.musselinn.co.nz

Abel Tasman National Park
On your way to the Mussel Inn you'll pass this beautiful national park – make a long weekend of it and take a hike or kayak along the coast.
www.doc.govt.nz

© Moa Beer

RENAISSANCE

1 Dodson St, Blenheim, Marlborough; www.
renaissancebrewing.co.nz; +64 3 579 3400

◆ Food   ◆ Transport
◆ Tour

This craft brewery occupies the oldest commercial building in central Blenheim, which housed a couple of wineries before Californians Andy Deuchars and Brian Thiel arrived to kickstart Renaissance in 2005.

Their project now produces a wide range of beers that are widely available in good bottle shops across New Zealand and Australia. Each beer is thoughtfully designed: the Voyager IPA, for example, references the original strong, sea-faring English ales by adding Fuggles hops to the mix. And the Odyssey Belgian-style witbier has orange peel and coriander added the boil as was traditional.

Renaissance doesn't have a tap room but it does have the atmospheric Dodson Street Beer Garden next door, which serves food and the freshest brews.

THINGS TO DO NEARBY

Omaka Heritage Aviation Centre
As collections go, Peter Jackson's assortment of WWI aircraft in Blenheim is enviable. Planes are displayed in dramatic dioramas designed by Jackson's film company.

Saint Clair Estate
Marlborough has a multitude of cellar doors to chose from and this one, in Blenheim, makes some of New Zealand's most more-ish sauvignon blanc. There's an onsite café too.
www.saintclair.co.nz

EMERSON'S BREWERY

70 Anzac Ave, Dunedin, Otago;
www.emersons.co.nz; +64 3 477 1812

◆ Food　　◆ Tour　　◆ Takeout
◆ Family　◆ Bar　　◆ Transport

THINGS TO DO NEARBY

Otago Farmers Market
Held outside Dunedin's railway station – built in bluestone from 1903 to 1906 – this Saturday market is packed with street eats and local produce. *www.otagofarmersmarket.org.nz*

Taieri Gorge Railway
Departing from Dunedin, scenic day excursions through the Taieri Gorge take in a landscape, incorporating tunnels, canyons and soaring viaducts. *www.dunedinrailways.co.nz*

Natures Wonders Naturally
Visit this spectacular coastal sheep farm on the Otago Peninsula – around 40km (25 miles) from Dunedin – to spy seals and yellow-eyed penguins on private beaches. *www.natureswonders.co.nz*

Toitū Otago Settlers Museum
One of NZ's best regional museums includes a fascinating section on Māori culture and a room dedicated to Dunedin's legendary Flying Nun Records. *www.toituosm.com*

The booming craft beer scene in New Zealand now features more than 100 breweries, but when Richard Emerson established his brewery in the southern university city of Dunedin in 1993, the beer market was dominated by two companies selling mainstream brews. More flavourful beers, such as Emerson's citrusy pilsner or the sessionable Bookbinder bitter, inspired many current players in the New Zealand craft beer industry; and more than two decades on, Emerson's is one of the country's biggest craft brands. The brewery was purchased by brewing giant Lion in 2012, and in mid-2016, a new NZ$25 million brewery, tasting room and brick-lined restaurant opened near Dunedin's raffish waterfront. Iconic brews first developed two decades ago are still tasting as good as ever in Emerson's five-beer tasting paddle, especially the well-balanced 1812 pale ale, and the taps are also kept busy dispensing seasonal beers. Adjourn for a cosy session in the restaurant's leather couches from early March to try Taieri George, an annual spiced winter beer made with honey that's a tribute to Richard Emerson's late father George, who was one of the founders of the Taieri Gorge Railway, a spectacular train journey.

GOOD GEORGE BREWING

32a Somerset St, Frankton, Hamilton, Waikato;
www.goodgeorge.co.nz; +64 7 847 3223

◆ Food   ◆ Bar
◆ Tour   ◆ Takeout

Miracles do happen. The former Church of St George is now one of New Zealand's most enjoyable brew-pubs. Hamilton beer fans frequent this high-ceilinged space throughout the week, and weekends on the outdoor deck sees the addition of local musos doing songs you'll probably know all the words to.

The Good George team are also playfully inventive, and recent brews have included a white stout with chocolate, vanilla and raspberry. Dessert anyone? Good George's very solid reputation is also built on excellent ciders and fruit beers. Try Doris Plum Cider at Little George, its cosy bar in central Hamilton, and don't leave town without sipping on a pint of Drop Hop Cider, a deliciously tart mash-up of apples and hops.

THINGS TO DO NEARBY

Waitomo Adventures
Build up a thirst by abseiling, rock climbing and negotiating an underground river in the Waitomo Caves, a one-hour drive from Hamilton through rolling pastures. **www.waitomo.co.nz**

Classics Museum
It's retro petrolhead heaven at this museum featuring big-finned American convertibles and Euro sports cars. Don't miss the Amphicar, an amphibious automobile. **www. classicsmuseum.co.nz**

FORK & BREWER

14 Bond St, Wellington;
www.forkandbrewer.co.nz; +64 4 472 0033

◆ Food ◆ Takeout
◆ Bar ◆ Transport

With a brewing CV encompassing at least nine breweries around the planet, the Fork & Brewer's Kelly Ryan is one of New Zealand's most respected beer makers, harnessing strange yeast strains and experimental hops for a continuous stream of new brews. Core brews on the 40 taps at this central Wellington location usually include Big Tahuna, a citrus-packed West Coast IPA, but it's on the brewery's smaller pilot system that Ryan's technical skill really comes to the fore. His beers have included briny seawater from Cook Strait, which separates NZ's North and South Islands, and also native forest herbs, such as peppery *horopito*. Look for the poster advertising Farmhouse du Fru Ju, an award-winning beer made with a beer-loving Lonely Planet writer.

THINGS TO DO NEARBY

Ortega Fish Shack
Quite possibly Wellington's best restaurant craft beer list combines with a brilliant seafood-influenced menu and a relaxed but sophisticated New Zealand approach to service. *www.ortega.co.nz*

Wellington Cable Car
Jump on this red cable car (built 1902) and emerge to explore the Wellington Botanic Gardens. On the way, experience views of Wellington's compact harbour. *www. wellingtoncablecar.co.nz*

GARAGE PROJECT

68 Aro St, Aro Valley, Wellington;
www.garageproject.co.nz; +64 4 802 5234

◆ Food   ◆ Takeout
◆ Bar   ◆ Transport

THINGS TO DO NEARBY

Zest Food Tours
Sample artisan chocolate, batch-roasted coffee and specialty cheeses on a walking tour of NZ's capital. The itinerary includes lunch at Wellington's Logan Brown restaurant. *www.zestfoodtours.co.nz*

Weta Cave Workshop Tour
Go behind the scenes and learn about the Academy Award-winning special effects movie-making wizardry in *The Hobbit* and the *Lord of the Rings* trilogy. *www.wetaworkshop.com*

Museum of New Zealand Te Papa Tongarewa
New Zealand's national museum includes the superb *Gallipoli· The Scale of Our War* exhibition about NZ's involvement in an important WWI campaign. *www.tepapa.govt.nz*

Zealandia
More than 30 bird species native to NZ live in this eco-sanctuary. Around 30km (18½ miles) of walking tracks can be explored independently or on guided tours. *www.visitzealandia.com*

Visit a beer festival in New Zealand or Australia, and it's easy to find the Garage Project stand. Just look for the biggest crowd taking in the inventiveness and sheer theatre the Wellington-based brewers always display. Previous festival brews have included Two Tap Mochachocca Chino, an imperial stout blended on-site with a cream ale, and restless ingenuity also shines through at its Tap Room in the heritage suburb of Te Aro.

Twenty beers are always available – usually including Garagista, one of NZ's best pale ales – but there's also plenty of scope for the experimentation of the brewers: Jos Ruffell, and brothers Pete and Ian Gillespie. La Calavera Catrina is a lager with smoked habanero chillies, rosewater and watermelon, and Death from Above is a big 7.5% pale ale with mango and Vietnamese mint.

Garage Project's ongoing invention doesn't only include unique ingredients, and its Wild Workshop fermentation facility in downtown Wellington is dedicated to producing bold beers by harnessing wild yeasts adrift in the natural environment of the NZ capital. Garage Project makes a huge number of beers, but Hāpi Daze – Hāpi is the Māori word for hops – is an essential showcase of fragrant and zesty NZ hops.

INDEX

A
Addis Ababa 13, 15
Akureyri 183
Alaska 72
Albuquerque 54-5
Ambleside 212
Amhara 15
Amsterdam 201
Argentina 38-9
Ashdale 43
Asheville 37, 56-9
Auckland 260-1
Aufsess 235
Austin 60-1
Australia 235, 238-57

B
Bamberg 135, 168-9
Bangkok 128
Banská Štiavnica 209
Bath 212
Batroun 19
Beechworth 240-1
Běijīng 99, 102-3
Belgium 136-45, 234
Bend 62-3
Bergamo 190-1
Berkeley 64-5
Berlin 170-1
Berriedale 242
Bishops Castle 213
Blenheim 262-3
Bobs Farm 243
Bodegraven 202-3
Borgorose 192
Boulder 66-7
Bratislava 209
Brazil 40-1

breweries
3 Floyds Brewing Co 82-3
3 Fonteinen 142-3
4 Pines Brewing Co 254
Afro Caribbean Brewing Co 31
Alexander Brewery 17
Allagash Brewing Co 85
Anvil Ale House 29
Archea Brewery 193
Asahi 113
Avery Brewery 66-7
Baird Beer 115
Baladin 196-7
Ballast Point 89
Bandido Brewing 51
BapBap 159
Barngates Brewery 212
Bath Ales 212
Bayerischer Bahnhof Gosebrauerei 176
Beavertown 221
Beeranek 149
Beer Komachi 108
Big Sky Brewing Co 80
Birra del Borgo 192
Birreria Zahre 194-5
Birrificio Artigianale Follina 193
Birrificio Indipendente Elav 190-1
Bissell Brothers Brewing Co 86
Black Sheep Brewery 229
Black Shirt Brewing Co 70
Bootleg Brewery 247
Borg Brugghús 183
Boxing Cat 105
Brasserie Cantillon 138
Brasserie de Chanaz 156
Brasserie des sources de Vanoise 165
Brasserie la Goutte d'Or 161

Brassneck Brewery 46
Bratislavský Meštiansky Pivovar 209
Brauerei im Eiswerk 177
Brauhaus zum Schlüssel 173
Brauhaus zur Malzmühle 172
Breakside Brewery 87
Brew by Numbers 222
Bridge Road Brewers 240-1
Bright Brewery 244
Bristol Beer Factory 214
Brouwerij De Molen 202-3
Brussels Beer Project 139
Burial Beer Co 57
Burren Brewery 187
Callister Brewing Co 47
Cape Brewing Company 32
Cascade Brewery 246
Cerveja Letra 207
Cervejaria Bohemia 41
Chit Beer 127
Clocktower Brewpub 44
Colonel Brewery 19
Commons Brewery 87
Coppertail 95
Craftworks 125
Dancing Camel Brewery 17
Dashen House 15
Deck & Donohue 161
Deschutes Brewery 62-3
Devil's Peak Brewing Co 27
Dogfish Head Brewery 80
Dois Corvos Cervejaria 205
Double Mountain Brewery 76
Duque Brewpub 206
Eagle Bay Brewing Co 245
Ecliptic Brewing 88
Einstök Beer Company 183
Élesztő 179

INDEX

Emerson's Brewery 264
En Stoemelings 138
Fabbrica della Birra Perugia 195
Feral Brewing Company 253
Fieldwork Brewing Co 64-5
Fork & Brewer 266
Fourpure Brewing Co 223
Franciscan Well 185
Galmegi Brewing Company 123
Galway Bay Brewery 185
Garage Project 267
Garden Bräu 15
Gässl Brau 194
Good George Brewing 265
Goodieson 248
Great Leap Brewing 102-3
Green Man Brewery 57
Gruut Brewery 140
Hallertau Brewery 260-1
Hawkshead Brewery 232
Hilden Brewing Co 220
Hitachino Nest 110-11
Holgate Brewhouse 257
Hoodoo Brewing Co 72
Hook Norton Brewery 217
Howling Hops Tank Bar 224-5
Hyouko Yashiki No Mori 112
Jack Black's Brewing Co 25
Jerusalem Tavern 226-7
Jester King 60-1
Jónás Craft Beer House 180
Kirkstile Inn 229
Kyoto Brewing Company 109
Lagunitas Brewing Company 84
Lanikai 78
La Uribeña 39
Les 3 Brasseurs 157
LeVel33 121

Little Creatures 252
Mahr's Bräu 168
Marble Brewery 55
Master Gao Beer House 105
Maui Brewing Company 79
Meander River Brewery 43
Meantime Brewing 228
Mikkeller 153
Mill Street Brewery 44
Moa Brewing 262
Modern Times 90
Modus Operandi 255
Moo Brew 242
Moon Dog 249
Moonzen Brewery 104
Mountain Goat 250-1
Murrays Brewing Company 243
Namibia Breweries Limited 21
National Brewery Centre 215
New Belgium Brewery 73
Newlands Brewery 26
Ninkasi 158
Northern Monk 218-9
Novosad & Son 149
Odell Brewing Co 74
Oedipus Brewing 201
Off The Rail Brewing 48
Ölgerðin Brewery 183
On Tap 39
Paname Brewing Co 162-3
Pasteur Street Brewing Co 130-1
Pfefferlechner 195
Pfriem 77
Pike Pub & Brewery 94
Pilsner Urquell 150-1
Pivovar Erb 209
Pongdang Craft Beer 125
Populuxe Brewing 95

Powell Street Craft Brewery 49
Rakwon Paradise 119
Rebel Brewing 230
Red Dot Microbrewery 121
Renaissance 263
Renegade Brewing Co 71
Rizmajer Beerhouse 180
Russian River Brewing Co 92-3
S43 – That Brewing Co 29
Saltaire Brewery 230
Schlenkerla 169
Sherpa Brewery 117
Sierra Nevada Brewing Co 68-9
Spezial Keller 168
Staatsbrauerei
Weihenstephan 174-5
St Austell Brewery 231
Steam Whistle Brewing 45
St Ives Brewery 233
Stone Brewing 91
Stone Brewing World 170-1
Stumptown Brewery 75
Sulwath Brewery 216
Surly Brewing Co 81
Swakopmund Brewing Co 21
Tawandang German Brewery 128
Ter Dolen 141
Three Tuns Brewery 213
Triangle 165
Two Birds Brewing 252
TY Harbor Brewery 115
Ubuntu Kraal Brewery 33
Westvleteren 144-5
Wicked Weed Brewing 58-9
Young Henrys 256
Zarza Brewing Company 51
Zoigl 177
Bright 244

INDEX

Bristol 214
Brussels 135, 138-9
Budapest 179-80
Buenos Aires 39
Burton upon Trent 215
Busan 123

C
California 64-5, 68-9, 75, 84, 89-93
Canada 42-9
Cape Town 13, 24-7, 31
Castle Douglas 216
České Budějovice 149
Chanaz 156
Chico 68-9
China 100-5
Chitwan 117
Cologne 172
Colorado 66-7, 70-1, 73-4
Copenhagen 153
Cork 205
Czech Republic 146-51

D
Delaware 80
Denmark 152-3
Denver 37, 70-1
Detroit 235
Dullstroom 29
Dunedin 264
Durban 29
Düsseldorf 173

E
Ecuador 50-1
Emek Hefer 17
Ethiopia 14-15

F
Fairbanks 72

festivals
  Beer Day, Iceland 181
  Beerfest Asia, Singapore 120
  Blumenau Oktoberfest 40
  Cape Town Festival of Beer 13
  Dark Lord Day, Munster, Indiana 83
  Főzdefeszt, Budapest 178
  Great American Beer Festival,
  Denver 37
  Kerstbierfestival, Belgium 137
  Munich Oktoberfest 175
  Pyongyang Oktoberfest 118
  Streekbierenfestival, Belgium 137
  Uribelarrea, Buenos Aires 39
  Zythos, Belgium 137
Florence 197
Florida 95
Follina 189
Fort Collins 73-4
France 154-65
Freising 174-5
Friuli 194

G
Galway 187
Germany 166-77, 235
Ghent 140
Guerneville 75

H
Hamilton 265
Harrachov 149
Hawaii 78-9
Ho Chi Minh City 99, 130-1
Hobart 246
Hong Kong 104

Hood River 76-7
Hook Norton 217
Houthalen-Helchteren 141
Hungary 178-80

I
Iceland 181-3
Indiana 82-3
Ireland 184-7
Israel and the Palestinian
  Territories 16-17
Italy 188-99

J
Japan 106-15
Johannesburg 31

K
Kailua 78
Kenilworth 31
Kihei 79
Klausen 194
Kyoto 108-9

L
Lana 195
Lebanon 18-19
Leeds 218-19
Leipzig 176
Lille 157
Lisbon 205-6
Lisburn 220
Lisdoonvarna 187
Loja 51
London 135, 221-8
Lot 142-3
Loweswater 229
Lyon 158

INDEX

M
Maine 85-6
Margaret River 245, 247
Masham 229
McLaren Vale 248
Melbourne 237, 249-52
Michigan 235
Milton 80
Minneapolis 81
Minnesota 81
Missoula 80
Montana 80
Munich 177
Munster 82-3

museums
  Cervejaria Bohemia 41
  Fränkisches Brauereimuseum 169
  National Brewery Centre 215
  National Hop Museum 145
  National Jenever Museum 141
  Pike Pub & Brewery 94
  Wine & The Grape 193
  World Of Beer 31

N
Naka-shi 110-11
Namibia 20-1
Nanjing 105
Nelson 234
Nepal 116-17
Netherlands 200-13
New Mexico 54-5
New South Wales 243, 254-6
New Zealand 234, 258-67
Niigata Prefecture 112
Nonthaburi 127
North Carolina 56-9
North Korea 118-19

O
Oregon 62-3, 76-7, 87-8
Ottawa 44

P
Paarl 32
Paris 159-65
Penryn 230
Perth 237, 252
Perugia 195
Petaluma 84
Petrópolis 41
Piozzo 196-7
Plzeň 150-1
Portland, Maine 37, 85-6
Portland, Oregon 37, 87-8
Portugal 204-7
Pyongyang 119

Q
Quito 51

R
Reykjavík 135, 183
Rome 135

S
San Diego 37, 89-91
Santa Rosa 92-3
Seattle 94-5
Seoul 124-5
Shànghai 105
Shipley 230
Singapore 120-1
Slovakia 208-9
South Africa 22-33
South Australia 248
South Korea 122-5
Soweto 33

St Austell 231
Staveley 232
St Ives 233
Swakopmund 21
Swan Valley 253
Sydney 254-6

T
Tampa 95
Tasmania 242, 246
Tel Aviv 13, 17
Texas 60-1
Thailand 126-8
Tokyo 99, 113-15
Toronto 44-5

U
United Kingdom 210-33
USA 52-95, 234

V
Vancouver 46-9
Victoria 240-1, 244, 249-52, 257
Vietnam 129-31
Vila Verde 207
Villarodin-Bourget 165

W
Washington 94-5
Wellington 237, 266-7
Western Australia 245, 247, 252-3
Westvleteren 144-5
Windhoek 21
Windischeschenbach 177
Woodend 257

Y
Yarra Valley 235

ACKNOWLEDGEMENTS

Published in May 2017
by Lonely Planet Global Limited
CRN 554153
www.lonelyplanet.com
ISBN 978 1786 57795 5
© Lonely Planet 2016
Printed in China
10 9 8 7 6 5 4 3 2 1

Managing Director, Publishing Piers Pickard
Associate Publisher and Commissioning Editor Robin Barton
Editors Karyn Noble, Nick Mee
Art Direction Daniel Di Paolo
Layout Ben Brannan, Hayley Warnham
Illustrations Jacob Rhoades
Image Research Ceri James
Print Production Larissa Frost, Nigel Longuet

Contributors: Isabel Albiston, Brett Atkinson, Carolyn Bain, Amy Balfour, Robin Barton, Oliver Berry, Joe Bindloss, John Brunton, Lucy Burningham, Tim Charody, Lucy Corne, Candace Driskell, Megan Eaves, Janine Eberle, Ben Handicott, John Lee, Shawn Low, Lorna Parkes, Christopher Pitts, Liza Prado, Evan Rail, Kevin Raub, Brendan Sainsbury, Dan Savery Raz, Tom Spurling, Steve Waters, Luke Waterson, Karla Zimmerman

STAY IN TOUCH lonelyplanet.com/contact

AUSTRALIA
The Malt Store, Level 3, 551 Swanston St,
Carlton, Victoria 3053 T: 03 8379 8000

USA
124 Linden St, Oakland, CA 94607
T: 510 250 6400

IRELAND
Unit E, Digital Court, The Digital Hub,
Rainsford St, Dublin 8

UNITED KINGDOM
240 Blackfriars Rd, London SE1 8NW
T: 020 3771 5100

Paper in this book is certified against the Forest Stewardship Council™ standards. FSC™ promotes environmentally responsible, socially beneficial and economically viable management of the world's forests.